Clark   S F Bennet (Cadillac)   S W Slater (Hotchkiss)   A Brown   T Pullinger

Sir A L Mays-Smith   Lt. Col C Jarrott   J M Starley   Capt M Campbell (Itala)

Col A Cole   A McCormack (Wolseley)   E Manville

The
MOTOR MEN

The first motor show was held in the Agricultural Hall, Islington, London in 1897/8.

The MOTOR MEN

Pioneers of the British Car Industry

Peter King

Quiller Press
London

Published by Quiller Press Ltd.,
46, Lillie Road, London, SW6 1TN

First published 1989

ISBN 1 870948 23 8

Design and production in association with
Book Production Consultants, 47 Norfolk Street,
Cambridge.

Designed by Peter Dolton

Typeset by Witwell Limited, Southport

Printed in Portugal by Printer Portuguesa SpA

End papers: This picture, origin unknown, a
copy of which hangs in the Royal Auto-
mobile Club, is clearly a composite. The
characters are leading members of 'the
trade' and include STANDING BACK ROW: W R
Morris, Hamilton Hobson, S F Edge, S
Shorland, Col Seely Clark, S F Bennet
(Cadillac) S W Slater (Hotchkiss), A Brown,
T Pullinger.
STANDING MIDDLE ROW: D'Arcy Baker (Fiat),
Sir W M Letts, H T Vane, Sir A L Mays-
Smith, Lt-Col C Jarrott, J M Starley, Capt
Malcolm Campbell (Itala). SEATED: S M Lan-
chester, Sir H Austin, C Johnson, Col R A
Cole, A McCormack (Wolseley), E Manville.

Photographic acknowledgements

National Motor Museum
2, 8, 8/9, 9, 12, 20 (both), 20/21, 22/23, 33,
34, 46/47, 51, 70/71, 94/95, 97 (both), 111
(bottom), 124, 133, 134, 151

The Patrick Collection
12 (bottom), 69, 164/165, 165

Coventry City Council
36, 38, 39

BL Heritage Limited
48/49, 53, 60, 62/63, 67, 79, 84, 111, 126,
154/155

Austin Rover
54/55, 56, 75, 81, 83 (both)

Autocar
68

Rolls-Royce Motor Cars Limited
88, 91, 99, 101

John Frost Library
107

Jaguar Cars Limited
130, 130/131, 132

Ford Motor Company
135, 136, 137

Lucas Industries
159, 160

Quadrant Picture Library
41, 93

Vauxhall Motors
137, 138

Colour photographs

The Patrick Collection
pp 1, 5, 8 (top), 9 (bottom), 10–11, 13, 16,
18–19, 22–23

National Motor Museum
pp 2–3, 4 (bottom), 6–7, 9 (top), 12, 14–15,
17, 20, 21, 24

Coy's of Kensington
pp 4 (top)

Contents

This book is sponsored by
The Patrick Trust and The Patrick
Collection in aid of the NSPCC
Birmingham Centenary Appeal

Acknowledgements

For the basic information about the industry in the introduction, I have drawn from three historical studies, and these have also been valuable sources of material for the careers of the pioneers. They are: *Wheels of Misfortune*, Jonathan Wood; *The British Motor Industry 1896-1939*, Kenneth Richardson; and *The Motor Industry* George Maxcy and Aubrey Silberson. Other useful general histories are listed in the selected bibliography.

A full list of car firms is to be found in G. N. Georgano's *Complete Encyclopaedia of Motor Cars*. Two detailed books about the giant figures of the industry, *William Morris, Viscount Nuffield* by R. J. Overy and *Herbert Austin, The British Motor Car Industry to 1941* by Roy Church, have provided invaluable material not various other biographies. A further useful source has been the *Dictionary of Business Biography*. Material on industry figures has also been found in the Royal Automobile Club, in the Modern Records Centre of Warwick University (including material supplied by the British Motor Industry Heritage Trust) and in the Coventry City Record Office where the archives contain tapes as well as company records. Other sources, books and directories are listed in the bibliography. The library at the National Motor Museum, Beaulieu has also been a valuable source and I am much obliged to the librarians at all these centres for their considerable help. They include Richard Storey at Warwick University, David Rimmer at Coventry, Chris Leftley at the RAC and Linda Springate at Beaulieu. I am grateful to the authors and publishers of many other books about the motor car firms for their permission to quote from them, and a list of these is given in the bibliography.

I should also mention the advice given by the motor historian Jonathan Wood, although he is not responsible for my selection of motor men nor for any judgements upon them, except where I have quoted from his own recent history. My thanks are also due to the help given by Alexander Patrick and the Patrick Collection, Birmingham.

For dealing with the problem of manuscript, typescript and editing I am deeply indebted to Sandra den Hertog, Angie Hipkin and to my publishers Jeremy Greenwood and Hugo Frost.

Finally I should like to thank Bill Husselby who originally conceived the idea for this book and without whose help and encouragement it would not have been published; and my wife Cherry for her support throughout its preparation.

Author's Note

The Motor Men are grouped mainly in clusters around the firms which they developed or in which they starred.

Since many of them moved from firm to firm, the biography of a man who starred in one firm may have appeared earlier in the book as part of the story of the firm which he founded or helped found.

The book is not chronological, except in the most general sense. To help readers find their way, the motor men who qualify for detailed biographies are always noted in the text by the abbreviation (qv). Their names can also be found in alphabetical order in the index on page 166.

Readers who wish to follow the story of the firms in more detail may find the books list on page 168 useful.

I have felt it desirable to include a small amount of repetition and overlapping in order that each biographical entry will be more or less complete in itself, without the need for extensive reference to other entries. Some entries are incomplete and this does not mean that certain facts are unobtainable, but simply that I have not been able to find them.

Car enthusiasts will be certain to find ommissions amongst the hundred motor men described here. I can only crave their indulgence and remind them that I have tried to cover the industry at large which has inevitably meant that some of the favourites, particularly the racing and rally men, have had to be excluded.

P. K.

Introduction

A Brief History of the Industry

The year 1896, when the Locomotives on Highways Act was passed through Parliament, gave the British motor industry an effective signal to come into existence. Before that, restrictive legislation had blocked its progress. Pioneers like Frederick Lanchester made headway, but it was French cars which set the standard everywhere. Although the Daimler Motor Company began selling cars in Coventry in 1896, its first products were based on French, not German practice. For a time Daimler seemed to have a monopoly, through the operations of the British Motor Syndicate, but the courts ended any such illusion in 1901. General engineering firms like Vickers, and cycle manufacturers like Rover and Humber, were well-fitted to take on motor car manufacture, and they now did so.

The famous London to Brighton run of 1896, in which Herr Daimler took part, celebrated the emancipation of the car, but it was some years before popular prejudice was overcome. Lord Montagu believes this was because 'the car didn't have four legs. It was felt that anything which threatened the horse was to be distrusted. The railways provided a good enough way to get about ... In addition motorcars were dangerous.' Montagu suggests that his father's *coup* in arranging for Prince Edward, the future king, to sample driving, first in the New Forest and later at his London residence, Marlborough House, turned the tables, and 'society started to accept' the motor.

At first, the motor men, mostly ex-members of the cycle industry, produced cars in small numbers at high prices. Many of the early firms failed. Before 1913, nearly 200 different makes of car had been launched on the market, but only

half of them survived. By 1911, total UK output of cars and commercial vehicles reached 19,000 units. This was the year that Henry Ford set up his factory in Manchester; by 1913 he was building 7310 'British' models a year, followed by Wolseley (started by Herbert Austin) with a further 3000 cars, followed by Humber (2500), Rover (1800) and Sunbeam (1700). These six firms accounted for about half the output of the industry in total. France was building twice as many cars, many of which were imported to Britain. The USA were producing ten times as many as France. The British were held back in part by the absence of a components industry; to keep prices down the pioneer William Morris turned to the USA for supplies.

In these early days, the car bodies were built of wood. 'You had the saw mill, machining wood to exact specifications. There were wood shavings everywhere, because the pieces never fitted exactly. It was more of a fitting job than an assembly job.'

The 1914-18 war was a mixed blessing for the industry. Production almost came to an end, but the demands of the war machine taught the early pioneers something about mass production techniques. The 1921 slump came as a shock to their hopes of expansion and a large number of firms did not survive beyond 1925. The balance of the industry recovered well, and production increased rapidly. The bigger firms were the more likely to survive and by 1929 three firms – Morris, Austin and Singer – accounted for 75 per cent of the industry's total output of cars, with the first two firms responsible for 60 per cent. The number of firms fell from 88 in 1922 to only 31 in 1929. By 1939 there was a further consolidation, with only about 20 independent car-producing firms making up the industry.

While America's industry was devastated by the depression of 1930/1, the British motor industry suffered only a temporary setback. By 1932, Britain surpassed France as Europe's largest car maker, a position it occupied until 1955. The industry's record years were 1929, 1933 and 1937 – nearly 380,000 cars were built in 1937. 'The concentration of interests in the hands of the Big Six (Morris, Austin, Ford, Standard, Rootes and Vauxhall – some of which brands embraced the names of earlier leaders) made it difficult for individual manufacturers of new cars to enter the industry, and particularly for anyone who wanted to make a cheap-priced car.' Cars became one of the growth industries of the 1930's for these established firms, although Morris and Austin saw their market shares decline as the other four firms took over. While total output rose (27 per cent over the decade), Morris Motors' share fell by nearly half. By 1938, the six firms were responsible for 90 per cent of the output of British cars.

The changeover in market share which had taken place at the top of the industry is indicated by the following table.

	1929	1939
Morris	51%	27%
Austin	37%	24%
Ford	6%	15%
Standard	5%	13%
Rootes	—	11%
Vauxhall	1%	10%

The outbreak of war in 1939 meant that the production of cars was again reduced to a very low level, but there was a great expansion of capacity to enable the motor industry to aid the aircraft and aero-engine industry to meet national commitments, as well as to build a variety of tanks, armoured vehicles and armaments of all kinds.

From 1945 onwards exports achieved great prominence. Before the war they were of less significance; even in 1937, the best pre-war year for exports, only 14 per cent of the industry's production of cars was sold outside the home market.

About 78,000 cars were exported. By 1950, the position was more or less reversed, with only 25 per cent of output sold on the home market.

Today, cars are manufactured by teams of people working with robots. When the car industry began in Britain, less than a hundred years ago, a man like Herbert Austin could build a car single-handed. Another change from the past is that a significant part of the British motor industry is today under foreign control – very different

Saturday, November 14th, 1896.

MENU

THE MOTOR CAR CLUB
DINNER
IN CELEBRATION OF THE PASSING OF THE
LOCOMOTIVES ON HIGHWAYS ACT, 1896,
THE "MAGNA CHARTA" OF MOTOR CARS.

FIRST MOTOR CAR TOUR LONDON TO BRIGHTON,
BY INVITATION OF MR. HARRY J. LAWSON,
PRESIDENT OF THE MOTOR CAR CLUB,

The two smaller pictures feature the famous Emancipation Run from London to Brighton in 1896. Harry Lawson, a man of ambiguous motives, was a prominant figure and, according to the menu, organiser of a dinner to celebrate the event. The larger picture was taken at the Lord Mayor's Show in London the same year and the German-built Daimler is being driven by its inventor (front, right). The Daimler car was briefly part of Lawson's manufacturing empire and he arranged this publicity stunt.

at a university, like Charles Rolls, were very much the exception. Indeed while there were only 1500 engineering students of any kind at British universities in 1901, Germany could claim 7130. For the British, an apprenticeship was the usual type of education – even for boys from well-off families – and the most popular entry was into the traditional atmosphere of the railway workshop. The shortcomings of British engineering in the latter part of the 19th century and the early years of the 20th have a good deal to do with the popularity of a railway workshop education. One could generalise by saying that British design kept on the rails but rarely took off.

Progress with car design was held back by ineffective engines (British aeroplanes suffered from the same problem) and this, too, could be put down to lack of education. One of the few car pioneers with an academic education, Harry Ricardo, explained how, with a few exceptions, design had 'been in the hands of cycle makers, superb mechanics well-versed in the art of light mechanical design, but abysmally ignorant of thermo-dynamics, or of the many other factors upon which the performance of their engines depended.'

This story of the pioneers concentrates on the men in the Midlands who built the industry prior to 1945. In that year, with the war's end, the industry was about to enter a new phase in which many of the conventional motor men would find it hard to operate. Some of them had already separated, or been separated, from their creations. It is perhaps too early to judge the extent of the contribution they made to the growth of the British manufacturing industry in the first half of the 20th century, but is certainly not too early to begin to collect together the facts which will enable later historians to make that judgement. This is a first attempt to collect in one book the cast of characters who dominated the automobile stage in the first 50 years of its existence.

As a footnote, there is a remarkable irony in the takeover, in 1988, of the rump of the British car industry by what remains of the aircraft industry, British Aerospace. The pioneers of the motor industry would have been amazed had they lived to learn of this extraordinary transaction. A number of early motor car designers played a greater or lesser part in the development

from the 1930's when Herbert Austin and his wife owned about half the shares of one of the biggest car firms in the country. One similarity between the industry of today and its earlier years is that the greater concentration of employment remains in the Midlands where about half of the labour force is employed.

This book tells the story of the individual motor men who created the car industry in Britain. Some of them succeeded, others failed. Few of them achieved worldwide fame as designers and the 'innate conservatism of British car design, typified by the products of Austin and Morris, was already discernable by the 1920's.' In 1927, the head of the Foreign Office diagnosed the car firms as wishing to 'go on building not what is wanted but what they think ought to be wanted; i.e. what they have always made.' This could be blamed on the motor men, but it is probably more accurate to put the responsibility on the Great British Motorist who has never had a dedicated taste for advanced design.

Another important factor was the lack of any formal engineering training for most of the pioneers. Those who took an engineering degree of aeroplanes and, in particular, of aero-engines. Messrs Royce, Bentley, Siddeley, Fedden and Ricardo made well-known contributions to aviation design although the work of Coatalen and others is less adequately documented. But the motor industry more or less to a man turned itself inside out during the two World Wars to help the aircraft industry meet its manufacturing obligations. As an example, the Rolls-Royce aero-engine firm would never have produced enough Merlins had it not been for the magnificent effort made by Ford. The motor industry

men believed that their knowledge of production techniques far outplaced that of the aviation concerns which an eminent historian has described as being in the mid 1930's little better than a cottage industry. Forty-odd years after the end of the second World War, therefore, the takeover of Austin Rover by the aircraft men is one of the most remarkable changes in the structure of British manufacturing, and its implications whatever these may be, will be a fruitful study for future historians.

The Royal Automobile Club developed rapidly to play an important part in the organisation of motoring in Britain. Here its headquarters in Pall Mall are shown dressed for the coronation of King George V in 1911. Horses were still a prominant feature of road transport.

Chapter One

Early Years

The motor car did not have its origins in England but primarily in France and Germany, both of which produced cars in 1886 although it was the French who were the first to fully exploit their inventions. It was natural therefore that British businessmen should first turn to French cars and French designs in the expectation that by copying them they could dominate the UK market. The story of the motor car industry begins with these men of business and their associates, who were sometimes motor enthusiasts. This early period also includes one odd man out, the only truly original British motor engineer – Frederick Lanchester.

| F R Simms |
| W Harvey and Arthur du Cros |
| H J Lawson |
| H O Duncan |
| John Boyd Dunlop |
| E J Pennington |
| S F Edge |
| Montague Napier |
| Percy Martin |
| Charles Jarrott |
| Dudley Docker |
| Geoffrey Burton |
| J S Critchley |
| Ernest Instone |
| Bernard Caillard |
| Major Walter J Wilson |
| F W Lanchester |
| Harry Ricardo |

Frederick Richard Simms
1863–1944

F R. Simms is a seminal name in the British motor industry for several reasons, most notably because he secured the rights to make the Daimler car in Britain. Yet he never built a Daimler himself and instead sold the licence to the infamous H. J. Lawson – of whom more later. British by descent, Simms was born in 1863 in Hamburg where his Birmingham-born grandfather had established a shipping equipment firm some 40 years earlier. He studied patent law and became a skilled draughtsman and something of an inventor. When he was 28, Simms saw a little tramway in Bremen worked by a Daimler petrol engine and he immediately made friends with the inventor. Simms became a director of Daimler's firm until 1892 and the following year secured the patent rights for Great Britain and the Colonies. In company with his cousin and another friend he then formed the Daimler Motor Syndicate with a capital of £6000, but the firm built no cars and a few years later, when Lawson (qv) bought it from him, Simms gave shareholders back their original investment plus 200 per cent. He himself was appointed consulting engineer to Daimler in the UK. Two years later he also negotiated the sale of de Dion-Bouton's British patent rights to Lawson's syndicate.

Simms was a considerable publicist and formed the first British Motor Car Club; indeed it is said he invented the term motor car for what was then the horseless carriage in 1896 in a letter to the *Autocar*, which ended, 'I feel certain that the popular name will be either the autocar or motorcar, for the latter of which I humbly flatter myself to be responsible.' He also invented the name petrol. In June 1897 he prepared rules for the Automobile Club, but found a set already existed. He is however credited as 'founder' by the club, as well as of the Aero Club, which he formed with two friends. Later he founded, in 1902, the Society of Motor Manufacturers and Traders. Perhaps he did too much and designed too much, but for all that he was described by a contemporary as 'a straight-dealing and loveable man', and by Edge (qv) as 'well-read and cultured'. It is said that he produced the first draw-

Simms imported a number of Daimler cars to England and he is shown here with the first, demonstrated at Crystal Palace in 1895. Below he is at the controls of his rail gun, one of his many inventions, about 1901.

ings for the gear-driven motor cars of Daimler and that he produced many of the first modern features such as the one-half-speed cam shaft, the safety bumper and magneto ignition (in conjunction with Bosch, to whom Simms was introduced by the president of the Berlin Automobile Club). He also pioneered armour-plated vehicles for Vickers, Son and Maxim. He set up his own firm of consultants in 1900 where he designed the first lawn mower for Ransome, Sims and Jeffries and one of the first motor tractors for ploughing. He established a works in London in 1902 but in 1907 decided to give up the manufacture of cars in favour of the Simms Magneto, based on Bosch's invention.

There are accounts of an uneasy relationship with Bosch, and Simms's financial and business practices in this connection have been called into question. Nevertheless, he ensured an important supply of magneto production when the 1914 war came, not only by setting up in the UK but by the foundation of the Magneto Company of New Jersey, originally just a sales company.

'Simms's importance to the motor industry may in the long term be due not so much to his business activities as such, but to the catalytic effect of his determined personality on the development of the industry and the representation of the motoring and motor industry interests.' So writes a modern commentator. Technically, his greatest invention was his development, in association with Bosch, of the high-tension magneto.

His company, Simms Motor Units, established in 1913, specialised in the production of horns, petrol gauges and lighting sets, as well as magnetos. 'FRS', as he was known, remained at its head until 1935, when he retired at the age of 72.

Simms married twice and from the second marriage in 1910 there were two daughters.

Harry John Lawson
1852–1925

An inventor, promotor and manufacturer, 'unique in the annals of the industry' according to Duncan (qv), Lawson was born in 1852, son of a famous Puritan preacher who exercised his talents, curiously, at the Royal Pavilion, Brighton. The father was also a clever model-maker, who provided models of Stephenson's inventions. The young Lawson became a student at one of the mechanical institutions founded by Stephenson for engineering. He also helped his father make models of Stephenson's equipment including his miners' safety lamp. He later adopted the name 'safety'

for bicycles. He seems to have become involved in the bicycle trade in Brighton and in 1876 he patented a low bicycle, having, two years earlier, designed a safety bicycle which is described as the first with a chain to the rear wheel. By the late 1870s he was manager of the Tangent and Coventry Tricycle Company, and was continuing to design bicycles, although making no attempt to manufacture them.

In 1884 he approached BSA, who made two prototypes for him but declined to manufacture his design. In the same year he took out a patent for a ladies' safety bicycle. At this time Lawson turned to cycle company finance, transforming Haynes and Jeffries of Coventry, who had made some of his early bicycles, into the Rudge Cycle Co. He was also with the Humber and Pneumatic Tyre Co. Lawson had taken out a patent for the so-called 'first British Motor Car' on 27 June 1880, and he gradually began to conceive that, just as he was taking advantage of the bicycle boom to launch companies, so he could 'create a motor car industry in the country and control it himself'. In the 1894–5 period, he converted cycle and tyre companies into public companies to the considerable financial advantage of himself and his colleagues.

In 1895, with two others, Lawson registered the British Motor Syndicate Ltd with a plan to 'corner the British side of the motor industry by buying up all past, present and future patents in the expectation of running across some 'master' patents. They figured that the fees secured from royalties and manufacturing and selling licences would cause a continual flow of dividends and eventually raise the price of shares beyond the imagination of the most sanguine holder.' These are Duncan's words, who assisted in the enterprise from 1896 to 1898.

Edge says that, at the time Lawson formed the BMS, he would pay anything for the 'so-called patent rights' to some motoring invention. 'He paid away £10,000 as the ordinary man would a £5 note; like many men whose previous ventures have met with marked success, it did not occur to him that he could make one or two false moves which would mean his fortune slipping between his fingers.' Money had little or no meaning for him; he was extremely generous and was quick to spot ability in others. 'Lawson was undoubtedly a clever man; his weakness was in his failure to foresee the type of motor vehicle which would eventually become popular.'

Called 'the little man' by his intimates because he was only five foot tall, Lawson, having formed the British Motor Syndicate Ltd with a capital of £150,000, obtained an option on the old Coventry Cotton Mills, covering 12½ acres, on which a factory had been built at a cost of £30,000. He then bought up Simms's (qv) Daimler Motor Co., with a capital of £100,000 which was oversubscribed by 10 per cent. He personally received £40,000 for giving Daimler a licence to build cars, and indicated that manufacture would proceed in the Old Mills - or Motor Mills as he called them. Simms and Lawson now set about purchasing the patents of de Dion-Bouton, for which they paid about £10,000 in cash and £10,000 in shares in BMS - these latter proving to be worthless. Then Lawson paid £100,000 in cash for some American patents owned by E. J. Pennington of Indiana (qv). His idea was to licence out manufacture of the 70 or 80 patents he now owned.

At their first company meeting in 1896 Lawson announced a dividend, 'the first in the horseless carriage industry, of 10 per cent, at the rate of 30 per cent per annum - an interim dividend which I hope before the end of the year will be considerably more.' He added, 'The public has begun, however slowly, to wake up to the fact that a horseless carriage is a necessity.' He talked of all the other ramifications of the expansion of motor cars - including the need for chauffeurs for 'it would be quite out of character for a lady (say, attending an evening party) to drive her own motor car; that cannot be expected. She must, of course, have her motorman.' He was greeted with rapturous applause.

Later, he formed the Motor Car Club which was installed on the second floor of 40 Holborn Viaduct in a very elegant suite of apartments. The members all wore blue serge suits with brass buttons, 'more like the full dress of a navy admiral than anything else'. Duncan brought the French designer Bollée over from Paris and Lawson paid £20,000 for the rights in the Frenchman's motor tandem which he immediately took to Coventry for demonstrations.

After arranging a great exhibition at the Imperial Institute, South Kensington (his rival, Salomons, put on a competitive show, the same

week, at Olympia), Lawson floated the Great Horseless Carriage Co. with a capital of £750,000. About half was subscribed of which two-thirds went to Lawson's BMS. The Horseless Carriage Company also moved into the Mills. Humber itself also moved to the Coventry Mills and various other Lawson companies were installed on upper floors. Unfortunately for Law-

Harry Lawson and his wife at the start of the Emancipation Run of 1896. The same year this energetic man organised an exhibition in London under the auspices of his Motor Car Club, which was soon superseded by the Royal Automobile Club. The picture bottom left shows a group of Daimler shareholders after a meeting held the following year at Lawson's Coventry factory. His eloquence kept their investments flowing for a time.

son, the mills burnt down and everything was lost including Bollée's machine and all his drawings. After a difficult negotiation with Bollée, substitutes were provided.

Lawson entered a German car in the Lord Mayor's procession in November 1896, but his greatest publicity stunt was five days later when he organised a 'procession to Brighton'. This celebrated the passing of the 'Locomotives on Highways Act'. The public enthusiasm which followed this first Brighton run was so considerable that £1 shares in his company were changing hands at £3 following the success of the Brighton run. Lawson unsuccessfully tried to refloat the company for £1 million. In fact, credit for repealing the Locomotive Act should go to Sir David Salomons, although Lawson led the public to believe it was his effort.

One of Lawson's companies, the Horseless Carriage, was converted after two years into the Motor Manufacturing Co. Ltd., but Lawson filled the board with his cronies and it was soon in

trouble. George Iden, who had controlled the factory since 1898, resigned in December 1903 and six months later the company was in the hands of the receiver.

Of all his various projects, the Daimler name was the only one to survive to this day. At one of its company meetings he forecast that, 'We are celebrating the birthday of the most wonderful industries that God has ever blessed mankind with ... since the world began.... Each large town will have its own manufactories, and Nottingham carriages will vie with Birmingham carriages for lightness, elegance and speed.' Alas, nothing of the kind happened, at least as far as Lawson was concerned. Already he was distrusted. The Stock Exchange Gazette wrote, 'The fact that Harry J. Lawson is the controlling spirit is a very bad omen for the company and augurs a speedy acquaintance with the bankruptcy court.'

The reason for Lawson's failure has charitably been ascribed to the fact that, no technician himself, he was unfortunate in his choice of directors and engineers. Although he brought the best cars from France 'the English engineers would not concede technical superiority to any other nation and failed to take advantage of their experience. Too proud to copy, they must needs improve and experiment according to their own preconceived ideas. As a result, thousands of pounds were squandered.' This is L.C.T. Rolt's explanation: 'Lawson's master patents became increasingly difficult to uphold until finally they were sold to the Napier company for the proverbial song in 1907.' The shareholders who lost their money by responding to his inflated promises blamed only Lawson.

Lawson had failed in lawsuits in 1900 and 1901 to uphold his claim for payments to his companies for infringement of patents. By 1903 a receiver was appointed. In 1904 he was indicted for conspiring to defraud, and charged with making false statements to induce persons to buy shares or lend money. He was vilified in the press. He conducted his own case and was sentenced to one year's hard labour.

Distrusted by his industry colleagues, all Lawson's schemes turned to dust. He faded from the scene, apart from occasional letters to the motoring press. He died in 1925 leaving only £99 gross.

Herbert Osbaldeston Duncan
1862–1945

H O. Duncan was born in London in 1862 of Scottish parents, and was the grandson of a man he described as 'Squire' Osbaldeston, owner of the best stable of racehorses in England, Master of the Quorn Hounds and renowned in Leicestershire hunting circles. Duncan said that according to the English custom, the Squire 'gave his grandson his name and part of his fortune'. [What giving Duncan 'his name' means is not clear.] Duncan went to Taplow College where he acquired his taste for sport, particularly cycling. In 1878 he became a member of

Duncan's memoirs give one of the liveliest accounts of the early days of the industry and its leading personalities.

the Belgrave Bicycle Club and thenceforward set out to make a career in cycling. He claimed to have been 'the first bicycle racer to be presented to a sovereign – King Humbert of Italy'. He also became a famous journalist of cycling and later founded the *Motor Review*. He did a good deal of work in France, including representing the Cov-

entry cycle firm of Rudge, and took over Humber's interests there.

H. J. Lawson (qv) of the British Motor Syndicate took him on as commercial manager after noting what Duncan did not mind seeing described as his 'sterling qualities'. Amongst other jobs this included managing the first Motor Exhibition of 1896 at the Imperial Institute, South Kensington. He took part in the Brighton ride in 1896 wearing the naval uniform favoured by members of the Lawson Motor Club. When Lawson's scheme foundered, Duncan took over the management of de Dion-Bouton in France, where he remained from 1898–1916, later becoming their 'British Empire' representative based in London.

He was a great observer of the motor industry scene and in 1926 published his memoirs *The World on Wheels* in which he gave a good deal of credit to himself. He died in France, where it seemed he had lived for some years.

William Harvey du Cros
1846–1918

H arvey du Cros (pronounced du Crow) seems to have been one of the most remarkable businessmen of his age, although he started from modest beginnings. The family is believed to be of French stock which settled in Ireland after the revocation of the Edict of Nantes. He was not interested in school work and had left home at the age of 14 where, according to his son, he was unhappy because of 'unappeasable differences between his parents, in which his sympathies were on the side of his mother'. He joined a firm in Dublin as a 'clerk' where he rapidly became one of its key bookkeeping managers, although quite unqualified. At the age of 30, he was advised by his doctors that he was overworking and should concentrate on developing athletic interests. In this, as in everything else he did, his progress was astonishing. He became fencing champion and light- and middle-weight boxing champion of Ireland – as well as founding a club which won the Irish rugby championship. He was a swimmer, a runner and a good yachtsman, and he then

This Wolseley 12 of 1904 was one of the last cars built by Herbert Austin before he fell out with the Vickers management who controlled the Wolseley Tool and Motor Car Company which was trading unprofitably. The following year he formed the Austin Motor Company.

Before the outbreak of war in 1914, Austin's own firm had grown to medium size, was firmly in the black and was building hundreds of cars a year, like this 10hp *Coquette* of 1913. His cars were well-built if slightly old-fashioned.

The Napier was a rival to the Rolls-Royce but after 1914, when this model was built, the founder of the firm, Montague Napier, turned his interest increasingly to aero-engines.

The Silver Ghost has been described as Henry Royce's masterpiece and was claimed by the firm to be the 'Best Six Cylinder Car in the World.' It was unveiled in 1906 and later acquired the name 'ghost' in recognition of its quietness. This is a 1914 model, chassis number 27LB. The car in the window of the present-day London firm Coy's is a model from about a decade later.

decided to fill in his spare time by becoming a cyclist. He supervised the training of his six sons, and together they formed a racing team. By the time he was 40 he had made enough money to retire from business.

Cycling became the foundation of a second business career for du Cros because of his development of the invention of the Scottish vet, John Boyd Dunlop (qv). The latter had disposed of his rights verbally to a Dublin cycle agent, William Boden, who went into partnership with the manager of a leading Dublin newspaper. Both were friends of Harvey du Cros, now President of the Irish Cyclists Association. They asked him to join their tyre venture and he agreed, provided that he assumed complete control. They wanted

Du Cros, who from small beginnings founded a worldwide industry, must have had tough characteristics of which posterity is unaware.

to raise £15,000 but succeeded only in obtaining £10,000 from the public. Harvey du Cros despatched his sons round the world in the early 1890s to preach the gospel of Dunlop – Arthur (qv) to England, William and Fred to Belgium and France, and Harvey Junior, Alfred and George to the United States and Canada. From

this little Irish company developed the vast tyre industry of the world. Harvey du Cros later visited France, Germany and the United States, arriving in New York on Christmas Day 1890, carrying with him the first tyres seen in America. Unfortunately just at this time, Dunlop discovered that his patent had been anticipated 53 years earlier by Thomson. They were thus a company with 'no patent, little capital, no factories, no technical knowledge of or facilities for tyre-making' and a tyre which, good as it was, Dunlop himself described as 'a crude beginning'. Fortunately, they acquired the patents of Charles Welch, an Englishman who invented detachable tyres. It is clear that Harvey du Cros was a major influence on the firm in the early 1900s 'although his exact role is difficult to distinguish from that of his sons, particularly Arthur'.

Duncan (qv) describes how du Cros worked with H. J. Lawson (qv) and with S. F. Edge (qv) who 'guided him to a number of motor deals, agencies and patent rights'. Despite his success with Dunlop and with cars, du Cros told Duncan: 'I do not understand the workings of mechanical contrivances ... the carburettor is a great puzzle.' According to a 1907 Directory he held the distribution rights for Panhard and Levassor cars (one of the most successful in their world) for Britain and the Empire.

Harvey du Cros became Member of Parliament for Hastings in 1906 – a Conservative win at a time when Balfour's party was losing everywhere – and was followed into Parliament by two of his sons. Married twice, du Cros died in 1918.

Arthur du Cros
1871-1955

Although du Cros's father, Harvey, must have been reasonably well off by the time his sons were growing up in Dublin, Arthur, as a boy of 15, was earning 12/6d a week on a civil service office stool. He 'did not long remain a clerk, for during these years he had been steadily building up for himself a reputation of pre-eminence upon the cycle track, and in this field he was to become, before he reached the age of 20, one of Ireland's cycling champions, a holder of world records and a popular figure not only on the cycle tracks of Ireland but also of England and France.' These are his son's words.

Arthur du Cros, like his father Harvey, was somewhat small in stature, despite his athletic prowess, and his son says, 'I have little doubt that his [athletic] success was due to the intense *mental* concentration which he brought ... to bear upon anything which he undertakes.' When Harvey became engrossed in the launching of the Pneumatic Tyre Company, he handed over his paper business to Arthur 'to terminate or continue as he thought best'. Not finding his trade a congenial one 'he successfully disposed of the family interests in it, and was on the point of embarking for Australia to seek fame and fortune ... when he was transferred to Coventry by the Pneumatic Tyre Company (at his own request without any salary) upon a year's trial. At the end of that year he had made such good use of this unique opportunity to prove his merits that he was ... voted a salary of £600 a year with a bonus of £200.' He repaid his father the living expenses for the previous year and then 'proceeded to build up a fortune with an ease and assurance that has never deserted him. He also spent it with equal ease.' By 1892 Arthur was general manager of the Tyre Company.

Du Cros was a fervent patriot, and became a volunteer and later a territorial in 1895 and concerned himself with military innovations such as flying. He entered local politics in Coventry in 1895 and tried to follow his father into politics. He was unsuccessful at that election but later won a further four and was an MP for a total of 15 years. In the first world war he initiated the Motor Ambulance Movement. He was a keen collector of paintings and antiques and remained a fervent sportsman. At one period he took time off to sail round the world on his yacht, an outstanding enterprise in those days.

He retired as chairman of the Tyre Company in 1930. He was married three times and had two sons and two daughters by his first wife. Arthur's brother Harvey (named after his father) sometimes known as Harvey Junior, was managing-director of the Swift Motor Co, which had a good reputation pre-1914, and in 1900 he became a director of Austin, forming a technical collaboration between Austin and Swift. Another brother Alfred (1868–1946) was, like his father

and Arthur, a Member of Parliament. The du Cros family as a whole can be said to have provided business acumen and stability to the car industry at a time when its respectability was somewhat suspect due to the machinations of Lawson.

John Boyd Dunlop
1840–1921

Dunlop was born in Ayrshire in south-west Scotland, the son of a tenant farmer, in 1840. He studied in Edinburgh and completed his training as a vet at the Royal Dick Veterinary College there. In his early 20s he migrated to Northern Ireland, setting up first in Kirkpatrick and then in Belfast. He had a big practice, employing twelve horseshoers, who worked in a covered yard big enough to experiment with cycle wheels. These experiments arose because, when his son Johnnie was ten, he asked his father to find some device to make his solid-tyred tricycle run more smoothly on the granite setts of the city's streets. Dunlop built a pneumatic tyre of rubbered canvas, enclosing a rubber tube. The tricycle, fitted with his tyre, was tried out secretly in 1888 and, following successful tests, Dunlop patented his invention. Dunlop was a vigorous, somewhat irascible man who pushed his new tyres, which, principally through their success in racing, quickly became famous.

Now enters Harvey du Cros (qv). He set up, in 1889, a company to develop the tyre, paying £500 cash and £3000 in fully-paid-up shares for the rights, which Dunlop had disposed of to friends of du Cros. In fact, Dunlop's ideas, although he did not know it at the time, had been anticipated many years before. Thus the patent protection was flimsy. Dunlop's patent was only 44 words covering three lines of type, and ending with the words '...to be attached to the wheel or wheels in such a method as may be found most suitable.' The complete specification covered a mere page.

It was thus something of a triumph that du Cros and his sons succeeded in building up the huge Dunlop business, but it was triumph in which Dunlop himself had little share. A biographer writes, 'His career was a classic example of an inventor largely devoid of entrepreneurial skills ... his role in the foundation of the large British rubber manufacturing company which now bears his name was a limited one.' Although there is no suggestion that du Cros acted badly in taking over the development of the invention,

Dunlop benefitted little from the invention of the tyre, although his name survives through the firm developed by du Cros.

it is clear that 'Dunlop was dissatisfied with his own share of the financial rewards his invention had generated, but he seems to have underestimated the efforts needed to adapt his idea to commercial use.'

When he resigned from the tyre company, Dunlop became chairman of a large draper's shop in Dublin. He had married the daughter of a farmer from Ballymena who became a saleswoman, but not a sufficiently expert one to help launch her husband's invention. He died in 1921 leaving only £9687 gross.

Edward J. Pennington
1858–1911

Edward Pennington has been described as the 'company promoter and charlatan *par excellence* of the horseless carriage era'. An American from Indiana, Pennington was forced to leave his native country after a series of near-frauds on banks and financiers across the USA. He was delayed in starting as his prototypes were not ready so he wired in explanation, 'Residence burned to the ground.' He finally reached London in time for a demonstration early in 1896. Rucker, the managing-director of Humber, was the first to see his so-called inventions but Pennington's price was too high. However, Rucker introduced Pennington to Lawson who paid £100,000 'in hard cash' for the patents. The machines were built by Humber in their Coventry works and then at Lawson's mills.

Pennington was always well dressed with diamond studs, cuff-links and a diamond-studded watch. He paid great attention to appearances and surrounded his works at the Coventry Mills with red and 'salmon' geraniums. He fitted up luxurious offices and an elaborate drawing office to dupe British investors as he had done those in America. When the Great Horseless Carriage Co. was transmogrified into the Motor Manufacturing Co. this firm only lasted two years 'because of the management's fixation with producing Pennington's motorcycles, fire engines and other unconventional vehicles.' In 1896 alone, Pennington registered 28 patent applications.

Duncan describes how Pennington made a 'motor gun car' in 1896 which 'created more or less a sensation in military circles'. He says he drove it round the country near Coventry, Kenilworth and Warwick, and up many steep inclines including Stoneleigh Hill. With two persons in the machine he went from Leamington to Coventry (10½ miles) in 24 minutes, covering the muddy roads satisfactorily because the car was fitted with large balloon pneumatic tyres and, it was said, could be lifted over a hedge or ditch by two men.

Humber had been building Pennington's cars but production even in its heyday probably amounted to no more than 15 vehicles, of which not one went to a private buyer. He next appeared at the Crystal Palace Show in 1898 and had offices in London, but he was involved in considerable litigation with dissatisfied customers and returned to the United States.

For a time, Pennington continued to operate companies both in Britain and America. By 1900 he was being sued by Lawson for the use of patents which he had already sold to his British Motor Syndicate, and the following year his London-based company went into receivership. In America times were equally hard and he even

The American, Pennington, was one of the few men to 'con' Lawson. Here he is shown on his 1896 tricycle with his wife (right) and sister, during a visit to London. His self promotion included publishing illustrations such as that below, which aimed at convincing investors of the suitability of his bicycle for cross-country work. The patent drawings show (above) his igniter for explosive engines and (below) his airship of 1895 to which he returned later in life.

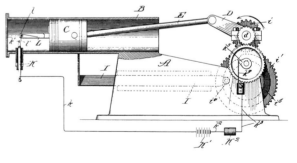

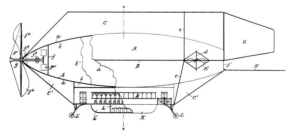

had to resort to selling those essential tools of his trade – his wardrobe of fine clothes.

It is increasingly difficult to trace his movements from 1904, although it is known that he abandoned automobiles and attempted to take up 'aerial craft'. Pennington died suddenly in 1911. An American account of his life concludes that 'he now lies in a 12-dollar grave' in Springfield, Massachusetts, with no headstone to mark the spot. 'Even in death Edward Joel Pennington has his trail well covered.'

Selwyn Francis Edge
1868–1940

S. F. Edge was born in Sydney, New South Wales, in 1868 and came to England to go to school at Belvedere House College, Upper Norwood. His family were well-off and employed private tutors for him. He began to ride bicycles – first, the original boneshaker – and it was said he could ride and race anything on wheels. He started racing seriously when he was nineteen. He was usually accompanied by his dog, a bull terrier called 'Bully'. In 1891, Edge became traveller for a cycle firm whose products were made for them by Rudge of Coventry, and he continued to break long distance cycling records. In 1895 he had his first ride in a motor car, in Paris, and the following year took over the management of Dunlop's tyres business, working from their Regent Street office. He was a protégé of Harvey du Cros (qv) who often invited him to weekends at his country house at Corney, Oxfordshire. 'The young du Croses, however, were not very partial to Edge's commercial activities in the Dunlop company' and he was moved to a cycle company in Dublin, which failed in 1899, whereupon his relations with du Cros fell under a cloud for a time.

While he was the London manager of the Dunlop Rubber Company, Edge had written to Charron, the famous French racing cyclist, who had resigned from Humber and returned to Paris, asking if he would 'give me a run in his car'. Duncan, who lived in Paris at the time, met Edge for dinner on arrival and said 'although he had not driven one himself, he had tried several cars and was most enthusiastic about them.' At this point, Edge had not even seen a motor car. His first drive, with Charron, was in a Panhard-Levassor. He notes that, 'When for any reason it was necessary to halt while the engine was running, the whole car shook as if it were stricken with the palsy.' Nevertheless, after his one-hour run, Edge was convinced that 'the death-knell of the horse as a means of locomotion had been sounded'. Edge now started motoring 'in earnest' making what for those days were comparatively long journeys of 100 miles or so. He and Jarrott (qv) became close friends, and they both adopted an idea of Edge's which was to wear a specially-made costume of leather with a fur lining – a form of dress later universally adopted by both motorists and airmen.

Edge says that du Cros formed the John Griffiths Cycle Corporation in 1893 for the purpose of controlling the retail cycle trade in the interests of the Dunlop tyre. Edge had no faith in this 'ill-starred venture' which folded, when the cycle boom faded, in 1898, and Humber without any warning cancelled their agency. Edge tried, without success, to interest du Cros in motor vehicles. Then living in Bloomsbury, he approached Lawson (qv) who, as well as his Holborn Viaduct showrooms, had a large depot in the Euston Road. He and Jarrott worked on the cars Lawson bought, testing them in the Euston Road.

Despite his enthusiasm and ability in these early days, S. F. Edge said later, 'I admit frankly that in my most optimistic moment I never visualised the motor industry of this country developing into what it is today.... All this has been rendered possible by a few men who saw in the design of cars a means of producing them by the tens of thousands. In the early days, every part of a car or motor cycle had to be manufactured by hand ... If a new part were required, it often meant waiting several weeks for it to come from abroad. Service as we understand it today was unknown.... No manufacturer in the Midlands, for example, had a service depot in London.... If one bought a car, it was always delivered minus lamps, horn, windscreen, hood, spare wheel, luggage grid and the thousand and one refinements which are found on the cheapest cars today.... These usually involved a further expenditure of the best part of £100.'

In 1899, Duncan, Edge and Jarrott formed the de Dion-Bouton British & Colonial Syndicate with a capital of £10,000. Edge was managing-director and Jarrott was manager, and they operated from offices in the Dunlop building in Regent Street. Duncan describes these as 'the golden days'. Edge was also involved with Lawson who was trying to monopolise the motor industry by suing every manufacturer who infringed the patents he held. An Automobile Mutual Protection Association was formed to fight these alleged infringements. Lawson won one case but a second case in 1901 was lost to Friswell (qv) and although Lawson threatened to appeal, he did not do so. If a small royalty had been sought it might have been paid, but both Lawson and Edge were too greedy, asking for 5 per cent of the value of a car fitted with such items as a Maybach-type carburettor.

Edge now met Montague Napier (qv) and persuaded him to build a car based on his Panhard. At the same time he persuaded du Cros to form a private partnership to sell Napier-made cars and imported Panhards. This became the foundation of the Napier business, Edge being the test driver and Napier the engineer. In 1902 Edge drove a Napier to victory in that year's Gordon Bennett race, so giving Britain its first major victory in an international motor race. Later, he suggested that Napier produce a six-cylinder car and, in 1903, held a press launch at the Trocadero to announce that it was going into production. This 30hp model effectively intro-

Edge had seen de Dion-Bouton motorised tricycles in Paris and when he worked for Lawson in Holborn he found one had been imported. His first long drive was from London to Canterbury and back. Eventually he collected a small fleet of tricycles including (bottom picture) a 6hp version which he described as one of the most diabolical ever manufactured. Motor tricycle racing quickly captured the public imagination at a time when motor racing was unknown – the late 1890's. Later, in 1907, when Brooklands opened, it attracted motorists like (left to right) Cyril Edge, Lord Montagu, Monty Napier and Stanley Edge.

duced the configuration to the industry and was soon copied by Napier's and by British and Continental contemporaries. In 1903 alone Napier built 250 of these 'gentleman's carriages' which cost £1300 each (something like £40,000 in today's money) and had discretely but luxuriously furnished interiors. This car led the field until Rolls-Royce came out with the Silver Ghost. By 1907, Napier was financing Edge in obtaining de Dion and Mercedes patents and the two were working closely together.

There was litigation from dissatisfied shareholders after Edge's floating of de Dion-Bouton Ltd. in 1907 and, despite the fact that they won, Edge received £50,000, some of which he passed on to Napier who had supported Edge with £10,000. A financial paper of the time called the whole transaction 'S. F. Edge's benefit'. According to Duncan, 'Edge must have made a total of nearly a quarter of a million out of the de Dion-Bouton and Napier concerns.' Even Harvey du Cros senior fell out with Edge, and they settled out of court. Duncan remarks that if the facts

had been given a public airing, 'it would have proved, if not sensational, at least extremely entertaining'.

Edge and Napier had by this time become inseparable names in the motoring world. A contemporary says Edge's manner was 'most amiable, intermixed with a little sarcasm. It left one wondering whether he had taken the subject under discussion in a serious manner'. Despite this lightness of touch, he was said to be a demon for work, not bothering to stop for lunch, except to eat 'a sandwich and a few grapes'. In fact, it is thought that few men understood Edge, and in the end he even fell out with Napier, with whom he severed connections in 1912. There was a financial settlement which prevented Edge from engaging in the motor business for the next seven years, during which time he occupied himself by farming and was Controller of the Agricultural Machinery Dept. of the Ministry of Munitions from 1917-18. He claimed that 'with Dan Albone of Biggleswade [I] introduced the farm tractor in this country'.

Montague Napier
1870-1931

Napier was born in London into a family of engineers originally descended from a Scottish blacksmith. His grandfather, a pupil of Henry Maudslay, great grandfather of Reginald (qv) had in 1836 founded in Lambeth a firm specialising in printing machinery. His son, Napier's father, 'a competent, even brilliant, engineer-*cum*-inventor, was an opinionated eccentric who cared little for commercial success.' He built precision weighing machines for arsenals, banks and mints but by the time he died in 1895 the family business had faded almost to extinction.

Napier was very secretive by nature and not much is known about his early life, but according to his obituary he was 'introduced into the practical side of the business at an early age' and on his father's death he bought the firm from the executors. About 1899 he was introduced to S. F. Edge (qv) who describes him as 'a man of striking appearance; standing nearly six feet in height and with a face not unlike an apostle.' (He had a beard like those favoured by artists painting religious pictures.)

His biographer says that 'Napier's engineering ability seemed to Edge exactly what he needed as a complement to his own marketing flair, and with financial backing from Harvey du Cros (qv) Edge set up the Motor Vehicle Co. which contracted to buy from Napier all the cars he could make. In 1902/3 Napier moved his works from Lambeth to roomier premises in Acton. In 1904 he launched the first commercially-successful six-cylinder engine, and thereafter Napier's interests were focused on engine design. The car business, promoted by Edge, prospered and the firm brought out taxis, 'business vehicles' and small cars, building in all more than 1000 vehicles in 1909 and 1910. Indeed in his *Who's Who* entry Edge claimed that he had founded the Napier car business. However, his partnership with Napier broke up in acrimony in 1912 over a row about whether commercial vehicles were included in his commission arrangements. Another factor was undoubtedly the strong competition from Rolls-Royce which meant that Edge could not take all the vehicles made by Napier. It was rumoured that Napier paid Edge to sever the contract.

According to Edge, the main object of Napier's life was to have a factory which was 'the perfect organisation'. But shortly after Edge resigned, he claimed that he noticed Napier's interest in the factory and its cars were 'beginning to wane.... His thoughts wandered towards the financial side of his business to too great an extent.'

Certainly Napier was cautious financially, investing a considerable part of the firm's profits in stocks, the interest from which kept the firm going in difficult times. In the years up to the war, the firm as developed by the two men had its strength in 'large, powerful, hand-built cars in which the personal quirks of the buyer were given the freest possible rein at an appropriate price'. Napier felt that business at this level would never continue although Rolls-Royce, his main competitor, believed the opposite, so just before the war he created a new public company with a share capital of £650,000 plus a £100,000 mortgage stock, to build cars of a more popular type, unlike those for which the firm was famous.

Edge and Napier were a splendid partnership with Edge master-minding the racing programme. Below they are seated in the 4-cylinder car which won the Gordon-Bennett race of 1902 – the only occasion on which this famous trophy was brought to England. The picture on the right is taken from Edge's book and features 'my fleet of 6-cylinder Napier racing cars' which proved so successful at Brooklands' race track.

Brooklands was an extensive estate near Weybridge owned by a keen motorist H F Locke King. He saw the potential of Brooklands as a racing track which he opened in 1907.

When war broke out in 1914, cars continued to be made in some numbers, but Napier's own interest turned increasingly to aero-engines, of which there was a national shortage. At first he built engines designed at the Royal Aircraft Factory, but later undertook to design one himself at his own expense, on the understanding that the company would pay him back, and pay royalties, if it were successful. His famous Lion engine, for which design began in 1916, was the result. By 1924 about half the British aircraft flying were of a type fitted with Lions, and he was far more successful than Rolls-Royce, whose main effort was still in cars.

In 1915, Napier's health had broken down (he probably developed cancer) and, like Royce, he moved to the south of France. He set up a design office in Cannes, with moves to Le Touquet when the Riviera was too hot. Napier had an aversion to carrying any luggage when travelling and on arrival at a hotel he would send the page out to buy him a pair of pyjamas and anything else he needed. These would be left at the hotel until his next visit. At intervals, new shirts and underclothes would be purchased and the old ones discarded.

He remained a large Napier shareholder, but in effect became design consultant to the firm on a very lucrative basis for himself. His success in aero-engines continued for the life of the Lion, but he was unable to design a satisfactory successor and both the Bristol and Rolls firms overtook Napier's. He died aged sixty in 1931, having had little to do with cars for nearly 20 years. Their production had ceased in 1924.

In his will he left the income of over £1 million largely to his nurse and reputed mistress, Norah Fryer. He made no mention in his will of his wife, although there were bequests to children, hedged about with the threat that any child who challenged its provisions should forfeit all interest thereunder. The residue of the estate, after Mrs Fryer's death, was to go to cancer research.

Percy Martin
1871–1958

One of the rare Americans to have anything to do with the British car industry, Martin was born in Columbus, Ohio, in 1871, and graduated as a mechanical engineer in electrical engineering in 1892. He was a prominent member of his university, Ohio State. He joined General Electric from college and worked for them in Milan and Berlin. His involvement with the British car industry was virtually an accident. On his way back to the USA from Europe he stopped in London where he met H. F. L. Orcutt who had been asked by Sir Edward Jenkinson, chairman of Daimlers, to find a works manager following the departure of J. S. Critchley (qv) for Brush. Martin joined the firm in 1901 and stayed with it until his retirement in 1934, becoming a naturalised British citizen. In 1902 he married an American girl he met in Berlin.

At Daimler, he designed new 12 and 22 hp cars and, within a year of his arrival, had turned round the company with a more rational model policy. Hitherto, Daimler had relied largely for their promotion on royal patronage – the Prince of Wales having bought a Daimler in March 1900, saying, 'I shall make the motor car a necessity for every Englishman.' Though an American, Martin did more to make Daimlers available to Englishman than ever the Prince succeeded in doing.

In 1906 Martin was made managing-director, and in the same year he recruited Edward Manville, a pioneer electrical engineer. He also teamed up with Charles Y. Knight of Wisconsin, a fellow countryman, whose sliding or sleeve valve engine was taken up by Daimler and developed by F. W. Lanchester (qv), then a consultant. This 'Silent Knight' engine was first put on the market in 1909. Although Daimler had 2-3000 workers turning out 60 cars a week, it is doubtful if the firm was a financially secure operation. So, when BSA bought out Daimler in 1910 for over £600,000, the biographer of Docker (qv) claims the arrangement, which involved Daimler paying BSA £100,000 year, brought the company 'to its knees'. Another historian writes of the BSA purchase as a 'rescue operation' for

Daimler. It may have been the other way about as Percy Martin became managing-director of the reconstituted Daimler concern and one of the three Daimler directors on the BSA board. Daimler's performance as a manufacturer continued to be rather feeble – for example in 1913, when they built 1000 cars, in America, Cadillac turned out over 17,000.

When war broke out in 1914, the group's factories turned over to military production, including aero-engines and aeroplanes. The great bottleneck was aero-engines. Sir James Weir was brought in by the government to reverse the inadequate supply of aviation material and he chose Martin as Deputy Controller of Petrol Engine Supply at the Ministry of Munitions and gave him a seat on the Air Board. The Weir/Martin team slowly improved the position, although engine supply remained precarious until 1917/18, with the main reliance being on French designs. Somewhat surprisingly, Martin was not honoured for his services, perhaps because he was an American.

Martin returned to Daimler after the war, where one of the employees remembers him as 'a

very large man who smoked big cigars and ... everybody sort of went in fear of'. Work was Martin's life and he was proud of the fact that, in 1929, he was instrumental in the acquisition by Daimler/BSA of the fluid flywheel and the adoption of the epicyclic gearbox.

Otherwise it cannot be said that the Daimler operation was a great success. In 1927, for example, the firm produced no less than 23 models, 5 engine types and 12 different chassis. The following year, Daimler's chairman became chairman of BSA, yet the firm remained in deficit. A year later the distinguished engineer, Lanchester, lost his job. By the mid-thirties sales were up to £176,000 but there was still a trading loss of £25,000. A former director warned Martin that 'the unfortunate business of appointing directors having no knowledge of business has been toler-

ated too long in this country'. This was apparently a reference to the BSA nominees at Daimler. In 1931, Daimler paid £26,000 for the Lanchester company, with a view to building a small car aimed at the middle-class market. They brought the Lanchester manufacturing operation to Coventry and for a time ceased production of their own models. It was not until 1933, when Martin retired, that BSA were back in the black and Daimler improved.

Martin retired to his farm at Kenilworth, near Coventry, where he devoted himself to his pedigree Guernsey cattle.

Charles Jarrott
1877–1944

I have raced because I loved it. I raced at the very beginning of the sport because I loved it, and I would race today because of my love for it, but a race of the present day would offer none of the charm which a race of five years ago afforded. It would have none of the sporting feeling or good comradeship between the fellow-competitors. It would be instead of a play, a tragedy – a tragedy of commercialism – a fight to the death in the arena, with each hired man striving for the death of his rival, showing no mercy and expecting no quarter.' So wrote Jarrott in 1906. In fact, he gave up racing after an accident in the Gordon Bennett race but, in 1904, Herbert Austin, then with Wolseley, asked him if he would take one of the new 96hp Wolseley racing cars to the Isle of Man trials. The car was then entered in the Gordon Bennett race in Germany, and this became Jarrott's last great race when, after a succession of misfortunes, he was placed 12th. He wrote:

> The memory of those long white roads with their never-ending fringe of lofty trees flashing by with dazzling rapidity; the roar and stress of the wind intermingled with the hiss and spit of the engine; the flying kilometre stones and the rapidly approaching goal – I long even now for the possibilities ... of living again all I went through. It is all gone and finished; but I would not exchange my memories with any man.

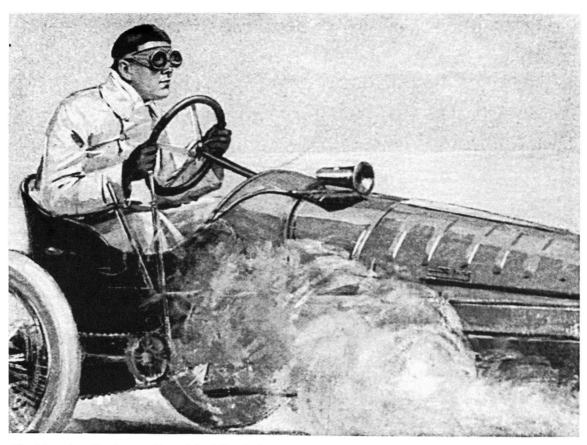

Although Jarrott began life as Secretary of Lawson's British Motor Syndicate he later took to racing and the illustration at top is the frontispiece he chose for his book on the subject. Certainly racing and manufacture were always closely connected.

In 1897, Jarrott, 'a bright young man' who knew nothing about cars, had made an impact on Lawson (qv) who appointed him secretary of his syndicate, whose offices were at Holborn Viaduct. Later, he left it to run a sales agency with Edge (qv), then working from the Dunlop Tyre office in Regent Street. Together with Duncan, they set up the de Dion-Bouton British and Colonial Syndicate, which for a short time had the Hon. John Scott-Montagu (later Lord Montagu) on the board.

Jarrott's principal fame was as a racing driver, and he wrote a book of reminiscence which gives a colourful picture of the early days of motoring. However, Edge says, 'It cannot be said that he took any very active part in making the British motor industry what it is today [1934].... He was a brilliant racing driver ... but as a Britisher, one would have liked to see Jarrott at the wheel of a British car rather than racing

on, and holding agencies for, foreign cars.'

After his 1904 retirement, he concentrated his efforts on selling De Ditrich and Crossley cars, having established a distributing firm with William Letts in 1902. It was acquired by Crossley in 1910 and Jarrott continued to trade under his own name for some years afterwards.

Dudley Docker
1862–1944

The surname of Docker, insofar as it is remembered at all today, is associated with the adventures in the 1950s of Sir Bernard Docker and his wife, Norah. For a generation of newspaper readers, they epitomised capitalism at its most irresponsible, riches at their most tasteless and publicity-seeking at its most avid. Their 863-ton yacht *Shemara* and their gold-plated Daimler were outstanding pieces of conspicuous consumption.' So writes the biographer of the man to whom Sir Bernard owed his eminence – his father Dudley Docker.

Dudley Docker was born in 1862 at Smethwick, the son of a solicitor who was one of the best-known men in Birmingham and district, and was called 'Lord High Everything' because he collected so many offices. Dudley went into his father's firm, but hated the law and abandoned it for the varnish business, which he and a brother conducted from under a couple of GWR railway arches.

Meanwhile, the brothers played cricket for the county, and this helped Dudley's business as he could gain entry to most offices by his fame as a sportsman. In 1895 he married into a prominent Birmingham legal family, the Herberts, and his wife inherited almost half her father's estate after having brought a considerable dowry. In 1902 Docker merged five large rolling stock companies and acquired a reputation as a great industrialist. His biographer claims that his scheme was a 'historic moment' which 'transformed Britain's industrial structure'. He was also a skilled self-publicist. In 1906 he was invited to join the board of BSA and may have been a major shareholder.

BSA was formed in 1861 to build arms. In 1893 it began producing components for the bicycle trade. In 1906 it bought a factory next to the Lanchester works and by 1907 it was producing undistinguished cars, copies of the Italian Itala. This motor car division was not a success. The cars were designed by a Colonel E. E. Baguley, of whom a report commissioned by Docker said 'Baguley has proved incapable of organisation, his only solution for bottlenecks being to employ more staff; he has presided over anarchy not only in design, production and after-sales service, but in essential matters like … the supply of cars.' In 1909, for example, Daimler was working on four different models but produced only 65 vehicles. Docker had been made deputy chairman of BSA in that year and he set about rectifying matters by arranging a merger with Daimler. He 'seems to have felt the need to repeat in the motor-car industry a merger that would set Midlands businessmen talking as the rolling-stock merger had done a few years before'.

At the time, Daimler was one of the largest employers, with 2000 to 3000 workers turning out 60 cars a week – mostly rather expensive models. Docker had himself owned a Daimler since 1906 and he also knew the Daimler management, Percy Martin (qv), Edward Manville and George Flett. BSA paid over £600,000 for Daimler and in the *Financial Times* the deal was called 'one of the most important ever affected [sic] in the motor industry'. Docker's biographer however says that while 'this complimentary tone about the merger has prevailed ever since … the truth was less favourable'. Docker had arranged that Daimler should pay BSA £100,000 a year, even if they had to overdraw at the bank in order to do so, and this brought the company to its knees. A description of him, a little later, shows something of his business behaviour:

> Dudley Docker, shrewd and ruthless to a degree, looked like an amiable owl. Behind small, thick glasses his bright eyes stared at you. His small head seemed to be held immobile by an old-fashioned stick-up collar. He rarely turned his head, keeping his unblinking glare straight in front of him. His approval came with a short 'yes', more often with a grunt and a kind of hiccough. It was enough. Another three or four millions had gone through.

Dudley Docker's son Bernard was the most famous member of the family, and his wife Norah was even more notorious. Here Sir Bernard (left) is showing the 1951 gold Daimler to Princess Margaret at the Motor Show of which it was the star exhibit.

Docker retired as deputy-chairman of BSA in 1912, probably because he felt overworked. In that year, he had arranged to 'loaf for a year' on a Scottish estate, shooting, fishing and playing golf, but the scheme collapsed and thereafter he seems to have suffered a kind of claustrophobia saying, 'I have been so overcrowded and feel so unwell.' His merger had not done much for BSA cars which continued producing undistinguished models of their own fitted with Daimler engines. By 1913 Daimler employed 5000 workers but produced only 1000 cars.

Later, in the war, Docker revived his merger skills, and managed to work with Vickers to form Metropolitan-Vickers, an organisation which included British Westinghouse. Docker made an immense fortune from all these transactions, much of which his son inherited. He was authorised by Vickers to investigate the sale of Wolseley Motors to Austin, to improve Vickers' profitability and, seized once more by his passion for mergers, he proposed that Wolseley, Austin and Morris should all amalgamate. But here he ran up against the implacability of Morris and his proposal failed. Docker played no further part in the motor industry although his flamboyant son, Bernard, was always regarded as a motor industry 'figure' during his period as chairman of BSA.

Geoffrey Burton
1893–1954

Son of a Canon in the Church, and trained in engineering at Cambridge, Burton served in the Royal Engineers during World War I and then entered works management in the West Midlands. From 1930–34 he was managing-director of a steel works at Brierly Hill, Staffordshire, and then moved to BSA as managing-director. It was a natural transition to Daimler as chairman where he was expected to sort out the company's problems. Mistakenly, he believed that Pomeroy's (qv) attempt to increase production of small cars was an error and he influenced the departure of Pomeroy, and several colleagues. In 1937 Edward H. W. Cooke was appointed managing-director and he reversed the Burton policy, planning to break into the popular market with a 10hp Lanchester. Although he was defeated in this ambition by the outbreak of World War II, Burton continued as a director of BSA until 1944. He was knighted in 1942, probably for his war service at the Ministry of Supply where he was Director-General of Mechanical Equipment. Later he became chairman of Dennis Bros and Blaw Knox Ltd.

James Sidney Critchley
1872–

Born near Birmingham and educated at King Edward's Grammar School there, Critchley probably had some kind of formal engineering training but the only thing known about his early days is that he was a considerable athlete, noted for rugby, cricket, high-jumping, running and boxing. He is next heard of in 1896 when Simms interviewed him for the job of works manager at the newly-acquired Coventry Motor Mills. He was the first manager there and he and Simms are said to have been largely responsible for getting production of 3½hp phaetons under way once the cotton machinery had been removed. The young Critchley went on to become 'one of the few men in England with a practical knowledge of motor engineering' in the period up to about 1910 when most of those in the business were either ex-cycle manufacturers or racing enthusiasts.

Critchley himself was a racing supporter who had been present at the 'never-to-beforgotten' Brighton run and who prepared Daimler cars for the climb to the top of Worcestershire Beacon in 1897 and, in the same year, for the run from John O'Groats to Land's End. The driver on the latter occasion was J. J. Henry Sturmey (qv). The prize that is said to have

given him the greatest personal pleasure was the Gottlieb Daimler £500 plate on the opening day at Brooklands in 1907. (Brooklands was started by Hugh Locke-King, a country gentleman who owned the estate at Weybridge, Surrey on which it was constructed. The idea for a race track seems to have been his own with no input from the motor industry as such.)

After the major rows in the Daimler boardroom and at shareholders' meetings in 1898/9, Critchley attempted to improve the company's

Critchley is the figure standing on the right in this picture of the Daimler car which he prepared for the climb to the top of Malvern Beacon in 1897. The car was owned by another director of the company the Hon. Evelyn Ellis who is seated at the controls. Considerable publicity use was made of this photograph, taken at the summit. The more conventional advertisement is dated a year earlier.

fortunes by introducing a light car design using an imported Daimler engine of 4hp. He was also promoted to be general manager so that he could give more time to the administrative as well as the technical side of affairs. He entered a number of Daimler cars for the Thousand Miles Trial, initiated by Alfred Harmsworth (later Lord Northcliffe) and himself won the event but soon afterwards resigned to join Brush Electric. He had probably recognised that Daimler, despite its early start in the motoring industry, was too troubled a ship ever to sail into calm waters. Percy Martin replaced him at Daimler.

Brush and British Electric Traction began to manufacture cars in 1902 but Critchley moved on to higher things. He had been active in forming the Automobile Club and was three times vice-president of the SMMT. He was anxious to enter politics and, after a strenuous campaign as a Conservative and Unionist, won a seat in 1911. He was also on the Coventry City Council.

In 1921 he joined with Ernest Instone (qv) and others to found the distributors Stratton-Instone Limited which took over the former Daimler showrooms at 27 Pall Mall.

Ernest Instone
1872–1932

Educated at King Edward's Grammar School, Birmingham, where James Critchley (qv) was an exact contemporary, Instone was the son of Thomas Instone, a director of the Daimler Motor Syndicate founded by Simms in 1894/5 before he sold out to Lawson. Instone joined the firm, in which his father had been involved, about 1896, and along with a number of other managers resigned three years later in the eruptions which followed the setting up of a Committee to investigate the firm's affairs. Instone went off to Paris and later joined Simms-Bosch. However when Daimler was reorganised under the chairmanship of Sir Edward Jenkinson, he agreed to return as commercial manager and stayed until 1921. In that year he resigned to join several other ex-Daimler managers in forming the distributorship Stratton-Instone. These included Undecimus Stratton, formerly Daimler's London manager, Joseph Mackle, who also had been with the firm since 1908, and J. S. Critchley. Operating from the old Daimler showrooms in Pall Mall, they handled Daimler, BSA and Lanchester cars in the London area. After the deaths of Stratton and Instone, Mackle formed Stratstone in 1932. This moved to Berkeley Street in 1940 and still prospers as a distributor.

Bernard Caillard
1882–1966

Albert and Douglas Vickers, of Vickers the giant armament firm, took an interest in cars largely because they believed there was a potential for armoured fighting vehicles. Herbert Austin had been in correspondence with Sir Hiram Maxim of Vickers about aeroplanes and he persuaded them to take an interest in Wolseley cars. Early on, the board of the Wolseley Tool and Motor Car Co., included as chairman Vicker's financial director Sir Vincent Caillard. He presided over a car manufacturing organisation which was the biggest – if the most unprofitable – in the industry. The Caillards were well connected (related to Disraeli) and after 1914, Sir Vincent devoted himself to politics, and worked with Dudley Docker (qv) to form the Federation of British Industries, although he remained on the Wolseley board. This contained three ineffectual members of the Vickers family (including Colonel Stuart Pleydell-Bouverie).

Bernard Caillard, Vincent's son, was in charge of the running of Wolseley at Vickers House. Not only did Sir Vincent put him on the board of Wolseley but also engineered his appointment to the Vickers board. According to a contemporary, he was 'quite incapable of running any business'. Douglas Vickers described the decline of the company as follows: 'When the manufacturer's costs are high he cannot quote low prices; when he cannot quote low prices he cannot fill his works; and when he cannot fill his works, his costs are higher; and so it goes on.' And so it went on until Wolseley was sold to Morris in 1927. Caillard meanwhile had been removed from both boards in 1925.

Major Walter J Wilson

Sometime about 1900 the huge armaments concern Armstrong, Whitworth & Co. put its mind to the question of building cars, just as the Vickers brothers (its rivals) were doing. One director, Sir Andrew Noble, argued that there was more money to be made out of building one river gun-boat a year than 6000 cars, and Lord Rendel, another prominent director, agreed. But in 1902, when the Boer War ended, and gun business tailed off, the firm nevertheless entered the car industry by buying an interest in Wilson, Pilcher & Co of London – without, however, disclosing the fact to most of the directors. This passion for secrecy was one of the reasons for the gradual decline of the firm and its eventual take-over by Vickers.

Wilson-designed cars were put on sale in 1904, without success, and he left Armstrongs in 1907, just as one of his cars was being shown at Olympia and arousing considerable interest. Armstrong, Whitworth then went back into car manufacture and had three models in their range

by 1910 and four by 1911. By 1914, the range was reduced to one model and the war brought their whole car enterprise to an end.

Wilson's claim to fame is that he invented the epicyclic constant–gear gearbox which first appeared on the Wilson-Pilcher car in 1901. It was later used in tank design during the first world war, and reappeared as the pre-selector gearbox in 1927 when it was fitted to a wide range of cars, of which Armstrong-Siddeley was the first.

Frederick William Lanchester
1868–1946

Lanchester has been described as 'one of the most accomplished gentlemen ever to be wasted on the motor industry'. He was certainly one of the most distinguished engineers and inventors of his time. The son of an architect and surveyor, Lanchester was born in Lewisham, now a London suburb but then a village outside the city. His grandfather had been the owner-captain of a merchant vessel. Lanchester had four brothers, three of whom became connected with cars. In 1885, aged 17, he went to the Normal School of Sciences (later the Royal College of Sciences) leaving after three years without actually qualifying. This included a period at the Royal School of Mines at South Kensington. He was a national (that is, state-supported) student at this period, living in digs in London and he rapidly developed an independence of spirit which, coupled with an intensely enquiring mind, made him a formidable young man.

In 1887, without any qualification from his college, he took a humdrum job as a draughtsman in Birmingham and soon became assistant works manager at Forward's gas engine works. He had a small legacy of 20 shillings a week from a godfather and was able to lead something of an independent life – for example travelling to Paris in 1989 where he saw cars on show at the exhibition. On return he talked to his two brothers, George and Frank, about his views on car design. He was then living a simple life in villages outside Birmingham but as he progressed in the gas engine firm he spent more and more

The Alvis company was set up after World War I and it was not until well into the 1920's that their cars began to attract a market. This is a 1931 12/50 wide-bay two-seater with the fashionable dicky.

Vauxhall, a small London company which moved to Luton, Bedfordshire in 1905, employed the distinguished engineer Laurence Pomeroy. In 1912, when his *Prince Henry* car won the Swedish Winter Trophy (driven by Percy Kidner) Pomeroy was made chief engineer at the age of twenty-nine. Later the firm was bought by General Motors of America. A painting by Michael Turner.

Above The 1924 Sunbeam 350hp driven by Malcolm Campbell at Pendine Sands when he broke the Land Speed Record at 146.16 mph – and again in 1925 at 150.87 mph.

Left The Armstrong-Siddeley company was developed by John Siddeley out of the original Siddeley-Deasy and the remains of Armstrong, Whitworths car concern. He was a boss in the Victorian mould who built these somewhat conventional cars and over-ruled any of his engineers who had more advanced ideas.

About the time Lanchester was working on his first car, he had begun experiments with model self-propelled aeroplanes, like this one he holds in his garden, sometime in 1894 when he was aged only 26. His basic ideas on the theory of flight were highly original.

time in the city. He rented a workshop from his employers so that he could develop his inventions; the 25 years from 1890 was Lanchester's great creative period when he not only developed cars but also made fundamental observations about aviation. He and his brothers also experimented with an engine-driven boat.

In 1892 Lanchester went to the United States on behalf of his friend Sir Dugald Clerk to try to sell some of his patents, but without success. He had about this time begun his aeronautical studies using small gliders. With his brother George he acquired premises in Ladywood Road, Birmingham and began work on motor cars. As Duncan (qv) pointed out, when Lanchester started on his first car, there was nothing to copy, so his designs were original, and it was originality for its own sake. By 1895 he was making trial runs and developing innovative features – it is said that of the 36 primary features in the modern car, Lanchester was responsible for 18. His was also the first car to be designed specifically for pneumatic tyres. Lanchester was still working for the Forward Engine firm, where he

was now chief designer, as well as developing his own car, which was Britain's first full-sized automobile.

In 1897, he set up a bachelor home in two rooms at 53 Hagley Road, where he was to remain for the next 20 years. He was a convivial, artistic man and it is said that his rooms resounded to the songs of Hugo Wolf, Brahms and Schubert, sung with gusto in his powerful high baritone voice (ten years later he actually took voice training lessons). While busy with the car he was also now developing his theories of aeronautics. As early as 1894 he had read an historical paper to the Birmingham Natural History and Philosophical Society on *The Soaring of Birds and the possibilities of Mechanical Flight* and although this paper was not printed, and Lanchester did not keep a copy, it formed the basis of a revised version, worked on over the next two years, which Lanchester offered to the Physical Society in 1897. This paper contained one of the most vital discoveries in technological history – the circulation theory of sustenation – but the paper was rejected by the Society.

Lanchester's first car was built in 1896 and ten years later he had developed a chassis like this incorporating many of the primary features of the modern car. Alas he died a disappointed old man, unable to reap the financial rewards of his inventions.

Ridicule had been poured on them as a result but an aviation historian says this is unfair as 'Lanchester's language was almost incomprehensible'.

To return to the cars, Lanchester had set up a syndicate in 1895 to build motor cars to his design and patents. The first car had reached 12 mph and was run on the roads, in defiance of the Red Flag Act, early in 1896. This was followed in 1897/8 by a two-seat phaeton which was awarded a gold medal at the Richmond motor trials in 1899. In 1899, Lanchester left the Forward Engine Company and was working full-time for the syndicate. There he was joined by his youngest brother whose social and commercial skills spread news of the pleasures of the 'sport' of motoring to a large circle of people. Lanchester's car became widely known and in the following year he entered it for the Automobile Club 1000 mile trial and succeeded in running at 20–25 mph throughout. With this success behind it, the syndicate decided to go into large-scale production and acquired a works at Liverpool Street, Birmingham. It also enlarged its original Montgomery Street premises and eventually merged the whole works at the latter.

The operation was never on a sound financial footing and it is clear Lanchester was no businessman. By 1904/5 the company was in the

hands of a receiver. The business itself was rescued by Charles Pugh (qv) although Lanchester, when the company was reconstructed, had to give up his post of general manager and become designer and consultant at a reduced salary of £250p.a. He also had to surrender all his shares. 'These events increased Lanchester's distrust and dislike of financial gentry' amongst whom he classed Pugh, with whom his relations quickly deteriorated.

From 1905 onwards, Lanchester continued his fundamental work on motor vehicle technology and became something of a national figure. He was a considerable character, full of humour, and his biographer tells many amusing stories of how he and his brothers dealt with the police in the days before public motoring was legal or respectable. A description of him at this time says:

> He was certainly not the academic type – heavily and strongly built, with a large head, yet he was quick of movement and also had something of boyish ungainliness in his appearance. There was a boyish freshness and vigour in his attitude to everything.... He used a humourous manner of speech, often accompanied by paradoxical remarks and flashes of wit.

Under its new control, the Lanchester firm, building cars to his design, became increasingly more profitable, but despite this there was continual friction between Lanchester and the directors. Meanwhile he was continuing with his aeronautical work and if his reputation in the car business was national, his aviation studies brought him an international recognition. 'One of the most important events of 1907' was the publication of his erudite book *Aerodynamics* followed by another book the following year. Lanchester is described as 'one of the great figures of aeronautical history' but 'his books were very difficult to understand, even by specialists; consequently his theory was not applied by anybody and his books made no impact on practical aviation.'

In 1909 he was appointed consultant to the Daimler firm although he struggled on at Lanchester as well, finally resigning in 1914. The more conventional Lanchester cars of later years were the work of his brother George. Lanchester found Daimler much more congenial and he earned a good living there. 'In all my life,' he said, 'I have never been associated with such a harmonious group of men.' It was a splendid period in his life – as a national personality he was writing, speaking and lecturing with all his accustomed energy and 'his large physical presence and formidable opinions began to be seen and heard at the meetings of the professional bodies.' In 1910 he was elected President of the Institution of Automobile Engineers, founded about ten years earlier.

While at Daimler, Lanchester invented the tortional vibration damper which prevented vibration and crankcase failures which were, in Ricardo's (qv) words, 'ghosts that haunted the six-cylinder engine'. Lanchester patented this in 1910 and received substantial royalties as well as £4000 for the US rights. The invention 'still used throughout the world, was Britain's first major contribution to the car engine technology'. While at Daimler, he also built an aeroplane and later served in the Advisory Committee on Aeronautics during World War I.

His wartime activities necessitated his moving for a time to London and then, in 1919, when he was just over 50 years old, he married Dorothea Cooper. She was a great help to him in his somewhat disorganised life and later, when he became blind, she would write up his notes from his dictation. In 1924 they returned to Dyott End, Oxford Road, Birmingham, and here he now turned to inventions concerned with radios. Five years later he set up a business to develop his ideas on musical reproduction and radios.

Cars continued to be his major concern and in the mid-twenties, as well as consulting for Daimler, he also worked for Wolseley. Apparently he felt a little ignored by Daimler – for example he complained when he was not consulted by BSA/Daimler about their takeover of the Holt Thomas aviation group after the war. However, in 1926 he signed a contract with Daimler under which, in return for not working for any other car firm, he received £3000 a year. Unfortunately this coincided with a period when Daimler's financial problems meant that their main interest was production, in contrast to Lanchester's which were experimental. Lanchester, like the other directors, took a cut of £1000 in salary and spent his time developing a subsidiary – Lanchester Laboratories. By 1929 the rift between him and Daimler was such that he left, buying out the Laboratory organisation. He continued to make a living with consultancy work and by taking out patents on gramophones and radios, but lived increasingly in strained financial circumstances. In early 1934 he had a serious illness which involved two operations and he also contracted Parkinson's disease.

The following year he published two books,

one a study of Relativity and the other a long verse poem, but shortly thereafter his poverty was such that not only could he not afford to buy the books which, as a voracious reader, were part of his life, but also, although in some senses the founder of the motor car, he could no longer afford to run one. He worked for a time as an external examiner in university engineering, not a completely successful experience, and, although he continued to turn out papers on cars, he found to his chagrin that he was not as well-known in the motor car industry as his brothers George and Frank (the latter became President of the SMMT). He said, somewhat bitterly, 'It is an amazing experience to find that, without any loss of my faculties, the world has no use for me.'

In his later years, the trustees of the SMMT took over his house mortgage and allowed him £200 p.a., but a collection in the industry mounted later brought in only £1450. In 1946 Lanchester died, blind, childless and, for a time, forgotten.

Harry Ralph Ricardo
1885–1974

Ricardo was born into a family of engineers and set up an independent consultancy which played a prominent part in engine development for both motor and aeronautical applications.

The son of a distinguished London architect, Ricardo read mechanical engineering at Cambridge and was expected to enter his grandfather's firm of consulting engineers. However he had become involved with the University Professor of Mechanics, Bertram Hopkinson, in developing a light petrol-driven internal combustion engine for aircraft. Early in 1907, enthusiastic about designing engines for aeroplanes and cars, Ricardo bought an old shipyard at Shoreham, Sussex and established the Two Stroke Engine Company. Their Dolphin car was exhibited at Olympia, but, short of capital, they built only eight cars. 'His relations, who had plenty of money but were not willing to risk it, advised them to regard it all as valuable experience and the company was virtually out of business by 1910.' Ricardo went on to become a distinguished consulting engineer specialising in power units. Curiously, his abortive attempt to enter the car business in 1907–10 is not included in his entry in *Who's Who*, which describes him at this time as a mechanical engineer with the family firm of consulting engineers – so perhaps he worked at both occupations simultaneously.

Ricardo went on to make considerable technical and research contributions to engine development and he and Lanchester are the two 'originals' of the British car industry's early days. Ricardo's work, particularly on the universally-popular side-valve engine, had a world-wide influence and represents one of the few British contributions to automotive engine design between the wars. His work was, in fact, widely pirated, according to Jonathan Wood. After a test case against Rootes, car companies were more inclined to pay royalties to Ricardo, whose Shoreham-by-Sea company is still very much in business.

Ricardo became a Fellow of the Royal Society in 1929 and was knighted in 1948.

Chapter Two

Cycling and the Midlands

The motor industry and the Midlands became more or less synonymous by 1910, and this was because many of its pioneers were members of the cycle industry, or were keen cyclists. This section of the book features some of the Midlands cycling men who were founders of famous firms such as Wolseley, Humber, Singer and Triumph. Many other motor industry pioneers could be featured here, specifically Herbert Austin and William Morris, but these two giants have chapters to themselves. J. K. Starley was another bicycle man but he is featured more fully in the section on Rover.

Thomas Humber
William Hillman
Richard Henry Lea and Graham Francis
John Siddeley
Henry Deasy
Charles Pugh
Henry Sturmey

Thomas Humber
1850?–1920?

Typical of the cycling men whose thoughts turned to motor cars, Humber is of significance because of his early association with Lawson (qv) and because his name remained a prominent *marque* of family car long after his death. (The exact year of his birth and death have not been identified.)

Humber's own story of his start in life, as told to *Cycling* magazine about 1910, was that during a week's holiday from the Nottingham firm for which he worked in 1868 he overhauled an engine owned by another firm. He did the job so well that his expertise was talked about. When his employers heard, they told him they would discipline him for working for another firm, at which Humber left them. The man for whom he had done the holiday job provided him with tools and work for three days a week. Humber set up in a little shed at the back of his house – he was then 26 years old. In 1877 he moved to a larger premises. He then went into partnership to design racing bicycles of the 'high' type. Cooper, a famous racer, later joined the firm which moved to Beeston and, in a few years, the partners left Humber to set up on their own. Thomas Humber managed to raise enough money to continue.

In 1893 Thomas Humber was one of those who formed the Beeston Tyre Company Ltd. which, using Humber's patents, attracted over £1 million of capital within a year or two. Humber also built an internal combustion engine which was successfully manufactured for several years. H. J. Lawson bought into the company but, by 1897, it had began to run into difficulties due to the import of cheap American bicycles which affected the whole industry. With a loan from the bank, Humber now decided to go into motor car production which it did from 1898.

Walter Phillips, a manager with Rudge cycles, joined Humber and was instrumental in getting them into the motor business. He set up a new works at Coventry, which was to become the centre of production. Duncan tells how Phillips used to stand at the works gate, watch in hand, and tell late arrivals, 'The next time you are late, you can go and get your *screw* and clear away

from here.' Without apparent irony, Duncan says Phillips was often thanked for his kindness by staff or men cured of their poor timekeeping by his strong language.

By 1900, Beeston decided to 'distance itself' from Lawson, and the firm was reconstructed as Humber Ltd. About this time, Coatalen (qv) was working for Humber as designer and manager, and the firm was producing Britain's first successful effort at a popular light car, the 5 hp Humberette. This output was so successful that 'we were almost driven to assembling the vehi-

A rare picture of Humber taken at the height of his success as a bicycle manufacturer.

cles in the street, so great did the demand outstrip our supply'. In 1908 a new big factory was opened in Folly Lane, Coventry, renamed Humber Road. Despite this, the firm lost money, a total of £23,500 in the year, and Coatalen left to join William Hillman (qv) who had a factory nearby. In 1909 a shareholder, Lord Russell, led a scheme of capital reconstruction, and by 1913 the firm was second only to Wolseley in output.

Frederick Burgess, Humber's designer in 1914, created a team of sophisticated racing cars, but none succeeded in completing the Tourist

Trophy course. After the war, Humber continued to build rather large, conservative cars which were well behind the rest of the industry in design. This was in part due to the influence of the managing-director, Colonel John Albert Cole 'a dear old boy who had a wonderful knack of making a sonorous speech that was both impressive and carried extremely well'. Cole had first made his mark as an articulate speaker at a shareholder's meeting during the pre-war troubles. He regarded innovations such as separate gear-boxes as 'costly and possibly dangerous mechanisms'. Cole, whose guiding principles seemed 'too respectable for the cut-and-thrust of the motor industry' presided over a decline in the firms financial performance in, and 1928, when no dividend was paid, the Rootes brothers stepped in and took a controlling interest. Cole continued as chairman until 1943 when he retired at the age of 75.

William Hillman
1847/8–1926

It is not certain what Hillman's father did, but he was probably a shoemaker from Stratford, Essex. Nothing is known of his early life. Like his friend, James Starley (qv), he was trained at the engineering works of John Penn at Greenwich, and Hillman followed Starley to the Coventry Sewing Machine Company, where both men became involved in the pioneering production of French 'boneshaker' bicycles. Starley's Ariel, the first practical penny farthing, patented in 1875, was built with Hillman's assistance. The same year, Hillman left to set up his own company making cycles and also roller skates and sewing machines. He had plenty of engineering and business skills but, inevitably, no financial resources, and he therefore entered into partnership with W. H. Herbert who had inherited capital from his father, a builder and farmer (Herbert's brother Arthur founded the UK's largest machine tool company). Hillman's efforts were so successful that he soon had four factories in Coventry and, by 1896, one in Germany. George Cooper joined in 1896 and with his help cycles were set up as a separate enterprise from the

other activities. It had 600 employees building 33,000 cycles a year and Hillman was soon a millionaire with an impressive home, Abingdon House in Stoke Aldermoor, Coventry.

Early in the century, Hillman became bored with the success of his established business and in 1905 decided to start up car manufacturing, with plans for a factory in the garden of his house. He enticed the young French designer Louis Coatalen (qv) from the Humber factory which was one field away and, in 1907, formed the Hillman-Coatalen Company. The French-

Hillman, here seen in his bicycle manufacturing days, later turned to cars with considerable success.

man married one of Hillman's six daughters but, in 1909, was persuaded to leave his father-in-law and join Sunbeam. He had left Hillman with a series of moderately successful cars, mainly small in size. These continued in production after the war, output being about 1500 cars a year. Hillman died in 1926 and in 1928 his firm, then under the joint-managing-directorship of Black (qv) and Wilks (qv) was bought up by Humber, by then part of the Rootes brothers' empire.

Both Black and Wilks had married Hillman daughters, but both left to join other firms.

Richard Henry Lea and Graham Francis

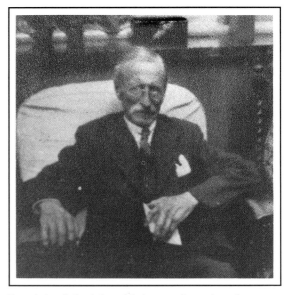

Francis had worked with three of the largest machine tool manufacturers in the world, two in America, one in Berlin, before forming his partnership with Lea to build 'high grade cycles'.

Richard H Lea and Graham Francis had both been closely involved with the Coventry cycle industry, Lea as works manager of Singer and Francis in a similar position with a business controlled by the Hillman family called Auto Machinery Co. Both men had travelled abroad extensively selling cycles. Together the two set up a high-class cycle manufacturing firm in 1895, in a small works in Days Lane, selling under the name Lea. It was successful and they formed a company in 1896 and moved to bigger premises in Lower Ford Street.

In 1902 Lea commissioned a friend, Alexander Craig, who later became head of Maudslays, to design a 15/20 hp car. However Craig's car was not a success and only three were built. After the war, during which munitions were produced, Lea engaged Arthur Anderson, previously a designer with Singer and Calcutt, to design a 12 hp car, but only 30 were built between 1920–3. After Charles van Eugen was appointed chief designer in December 1922, the Coventry Simplex resulted and the firm's sales position improved. Lea-Francis agreed that the Vulcan company could build cars under the Lea-Francis marque, but these were unsuccessful, 'an acute embarrassment to the firm and resulted in further financial trouble' which, aggravated by the 1929 slump, took the firm into receivership in 1931. Hugh Rose and George Leek, both formerly employed by Riley Motors, bought the assets of Lea-Francis and formed a new company under that name. Leek had been one of Riley's managers for 21 years before being appointed general manager in 1932. When he began to disagree with Victor Riley on policy two years later, he decided to leave and take over Lea-Francis. He engaged Hugh Rose to design new models for him. Their new car was unveiled in 1937 but of course its design had nothing to do with Lea or Francis. Francis appears to have had little to do with the firm since the 1920's and resigned in 1924 to concentrate on Skepco.

A conventional studio picture of Richard Lea, taken in 1890, about five years before he went into partnership with Francis.

John Davenport Siddeley
1866–1953

Like so many other motor men, Siddeley's interest started with cycling. He was born near Altrincham, Manchester, of a reasonably prosperous family (his father was a hosier) and educated at Altrincham, becoming a member of the well-known local Anfield Bicycle Club. He designed his own bicycle, and was the first person to ride from Land's End to John O'Groats, using the machine he had built. After a period in the Humber works as a draughtsman, he moved to Coventry in 1895 as manager of the Rover Cycles' racing team. Next he was recruited by Dunlop, where he became interested in the use of pneumatic tyres for motor cars. By 1900 he was managing-director of the Clipper Tyre Company. The next year he was British agent for the French Peugeot car and shortly afterwards he formed the Siddeley Autocar Company which did little more than add his design of radiator to the Peugeot chassis.

In 1893 he married the daughter of a silk manufacturer of Macclesfield, and they had two sons and two(?) daughters. He always remained very fond of his wife and died broken-hearted less than a month after her death in 1953 in Jersey, where they had moved in retirement.

To return to the beginning of the century, Siddeley is described as quiet, meticulous and old-fashioned in manner, but 'he could in practice be fierce and ruthless'. He showed this in his negotiations with Vickers Ltd. who owned the Wolseley company. Siddeley approached Albert Vickers through the offices of the banker Lionel de Rothschild. It was agreed that the Siddeley car would be built at the Vickers factory at Crayford, and these were first exhibited at the Crystal Palace show in 1903. Two years later, Wolseley were instructed by Vickers to approach Siddeley with a view to a takeover, and to ask Siddeley to become manager of Wolseley. Siddeley was commited to the modern vertical engine in the Panhard manner, while Wolseley was building the more conventional horizontal engine designed by Herbert Austin (qv). Wolseley offered to buy Siddeley's company and this led to the departure of Austin. On Austin's resignation in the summer of 1905, Siddeley became general manager, and in 1906, Siddeley's friend, Rothschild, was elected to the Wolseley board. However, profitability continued to elude the company, and by 1908 the Vickers directors were miffed that 'the time-honoured name of Wolseley was slowly but surely taking second place to that of the company's general manager.' Both the car and its engine were more often than not called 'Siddeley'. Vickers were also miffed that Wolseley had lost over £200,000 under Siddeley's stewardship. There was a row in the early part of

Siddeley was a tough commercial manager in the Victorian mould who lived on in to the 1950's and became Lord Kenilworth.

1909 and Siddeley handed in his notice. Rothschild left soon after.

Siddeley was then taken on to run the Deasy Motor Co started by Major H. P. P. Deasy (qv) and used his undoubted entrepreneurial talents to rescue the firm from oblivion. During the 1914–18 war, Siddeley turned the car works at Parkside, Coventry, over to the manufacture of aeroplanes designed at the Royal Aircraft Establishment, as well as aero-engines, and the firm rapidly become an industrial enterprise of considerable size. When the RAE was reduced in status halfway through the war, its staff were encouraged to join industrial firms, and two of its leading aero-engine designers joined Siddeley. He was such a difficult man in his dealings with engineers that one of them, S. D. Heron, soon left in dudgeon to go to the USA, where he helped one of the major aero-engine companies to succeed – an early example of the brain drain. The other, Major Green, kow-towed to Siddeley and remained to head up the postwar engine division. In 1919, the Siddeley-Deasy works, now covering 25 acres, were sold to Armstrong, Whitworth, the armament firm, for over £400,000. The new owners were run at the time by Sir Glynn West who, it was said, 'behaved like a maniac' and was so jealous that he stopped Siddeley from joining the Armstrong board. Siddeley retained control of the management and, under his firm leadership, profits rose from £88,218 in 1920/1 to £226,527 in 1924/5.

The mismanagement of Sir Glynn West led to the financial collapse of Armstrong in 1926 and in the reconstruction that followed, although many of Armstrong's interests were taken over by Vickers, Siddeley persuaded the company to sell him their aircraft interests, the motor firm and various subdivisions and, in 1927, he renamed all these Armstrong-Siddeley. In 1928, he bought the A. V. Roe aircraft company for an estimated £250,000 from Crossley Motors.

'Apart from the abortive Stoneleigh light car of 1922, Armstrong-Siddeley's products were always solidly-built, family vehicles emphasising good workmanship, comfort and ease of driving rather than high performance.... Production was always on a modest scale, running at about 300 a year...' At this time the firm employed about 5000 workers and it was said Siddeley knew them all by sight if not by name. One of them described him as 'very patriarchal in appearance – quite a gentleman. Always courteous when he saw us out [of the factory], he always raised his hat and acknowledged one.'

Siddeley is also described, perhaps over-cautiously, as 'a man of strong personal preferences with a stubborn streak, who was not always receptive to engineering outside his experience'. In the Armstrong-Siddeley group, he gave priority to motor cars, with aero-engines second and aircraft third, which left his aviation managers and engineers frequently discontented. The company lost its pre-eminence in air-cooled

aero-engines and the chief aviation designer, John Lloyd, was dismissed for some months in 1933–34 for arguing that non-Siddeley aero-engines should be used in Siddeley aircraft. In 1935, Siddeley sold Sopwith the Armstrong-Siddeley group which joined with Hawker Aircraft and became Hawker-Siddeley group. Siddeley remained on the board for only one further year.

He was president of the SMMT in 1937/8 and 1938/9 and knighted in 1932. He used much of his money for good works. For example, in 1935 he offered £10,000 to Cambridge University for aeronautical research, which was initially refused by pacifist interests. He also bought Kenilworth Castle for the nation, becoming, himself, Lord Kenilworth in 1937.

Siddeley had three sons, all of whom he put in the business. One of them, Norman, was 'a bit of a rebel' and he went off to South Africa to set up a car distributorship, but Cyril and Ernest continued in their father's footsteps.

Although Siddeley was an autocratic and difficult man, his business success was remarkable. He turned the very small Deasy company into the nucleus of a large motor-producing concern, and built it up during the 1914–18 war into a substantial armaments business. He had come into contact with Armstrong, Whitworth during the war and his acumen in gaining control of a major part of their business after their failure in 1926 was a great coup. Quite why he sold out to Sopwith ten years later is not clear, but as he was by then seventy yers of age he may have felt he deserved a rest.

The Hawker-Siddeley group was were never as interested in cars as John Siddeley had been, and, although the business continued for some years, the cars of the postwar era were not of great distinction and survived only to 1960.

Captain Henry H. P. Deasy
1866–1947

Deasy was born in Dublin, the son of the Lord Justice of Appeal there. After serving in the 16th Lancers, he left the army to become an explorer and won the Royal Geographical Society gold medal for his work in

This picture of the unfortunate Captain Deasy was published in 1908, the time that his connection with the company he founded was becoming tenuous.

Western Tibet. He took an interest in cars early on and was keen on trials and competitions. Like other rich men of the time, he had cars built to his specification, and in 1903 created a world record with a 14 hp Martins by driving it up a gradient of 1 in 4.5 on the ballast of a Swiss cogwheel mountain railway.

In 1905/6 Deasy, by then an importer of Swiss Martins cars, got together a group of rich friends and formed the Deasy Motor Co., of which he became chairman. Other directors included Sir Richard Waldie-Griffiths and Sir Robert Buchanan-Jardine. E. W. Lewis was taken on as designer and a factory purchased from the moribund Iden Motor Factory at Coventry and Lewis put in as works manager. Sales premises were also acquired in the Brompton Road, London. E. W. Lewis had, for a time, been Daimler's chief designer and joined Deasy from Rover.

Things started to go wrong from an early date. One of the earliest cars broke down in the Isle of Man Tourist Trophy Race and Deasy had to complain that this was highly prejudicial to sales. Nonetheless orders for eleven cars were obtained at the Olympia show. Deasy continued to complain about Lewis's design and workmanship but it seems that he did not carry the other

directors with him because before long they had taken on a Mr George Ruddick who was soon in joint control of the business with Deasy.

In the spring of 1907 Deasy set off on a continental demonstration tour but he had not gone far when a wheel came off the car. At the next board meeting there was a row, presumably arising from Deasy's criticisms of Lewis, and the upshot was that Deasy resigned as chairman and managing-director, although still remaining on the board. By this time money was short and the directors and the bank were pumping in cash to keep the company afloat. By April 1908, Lewis was ejected as works manager, H. E. Smith being appointed in his place. Lewis continued for a time as consulting engineer. It seems that Deasy went on driving the cars, as he set up a long-distance record between France and Switzerland at this time, but he played little part in the business and no longer attended board-meetings.

Drastic measures were now needed if the company were to survive and these took the shape of John Siddeley who had just parted company with the Vickers-Wolseley organisation. He was appointed joint managing-director with Ruddick in June 1909 but Ruddick did not last long – his resignation was accepted on 1st October that year. By the following March, Lewis had also left, and Siddeley was in effective control. He seems to have got on well with Sir Richard Waldie-Griffiths Bt, the then chairman, who remained chairman of Deasy and Siddeley-Deasy for some years, and who also continued to put money into the firm. Another financial prop was Lord Leigh who probably kept the firm going until war contracts began in 1914.

Nothing further is heard of Major Deasy after 1908.

Charles V. Pugh
1869–1921

Pugh, born in Rotherham, the son of a jeweller and ironmonger, was brought up in Birmingham, where he was a scholar at King Edward VI School. After leaving school, he joined his father's firm and was a keen cyclist and racer. In 1891 he founded a cycle manufacturing business, the Whitworth Cycle Co. Later, it amalgamated with the ailing Rudge Cycle Company, Coventry. Despite the slump in the cycle industry in 1897, which drove others into cars, Pugh was successful in his traditional business. However, in 1899 he became chairman of the Lanchester Engine Co. Ltd., although his interest was purely financial — engineering being handled by F. W. Lanchester (qv). The company was chronically undercapitalised and went into the hands of a receiver in 1904, although Lanchester and key associates remained. It became the Lanchester Motor Company, but Lanchester's distrust of financiers caused his relations with Pugh to deteriorate, and the connection was severed in 1914 when Lancaster left the company. Pugh was also chairman of the Atco motor mowers concern, which his family continued to control for many years.

Henry Sturmey
1857–1930

Formerly a private school teacher, and later inventor of the Sturmey-Archer three-speed gear, Sturmey met the influential Midlands publisher, William I. Iliffe, when the latter was a printer. Sturmey asked Iliffe to print his *Indispensible Cyclists Handbook* and when Iliffe graduated from publishing cycle magazines to the *Autocar*, the first motoring periodical, he made Sturmey its editor in 1895. Unfortunately Sturmey thought 'his commercial interests would be advanced by entering the motor industry itself while still acting as editor' and he bought nearly £14,000-worth of shares in H. J. Lawson's (qv) Great Horseless Carriage Co. Indeed, Sturmey became a director of Daimler Motor Company of which Lawson was officially chairman at this time, and deputised for him at most company meetings. Although Daimler's historian says 'he was [then] regarded as the live wire of the concern' it was admitted that he had very little knowledge of motor engineering although some flair for mechanical things.

At a board meeting in July 1898, Sturmey was severely criticised by some of the other directors, as a result of which he sent out two circulars to shareholders defending himself. The board then called an extraordinary meeting to deal with Sturmey, but this erupted into a committee of investigation which produced a damning report on the whole company. There was a further shareholders meeting the following year and in due course Sturmey, Ellis and others resigned to be replaced by E. H. Beyley and Sir Edward Jenkinson. Sturmey's connection with Iliffe also came to an end when it was apparent to the publisher that the long reports he published in the *Autocar*, defending Lawson, were to some extent inspired by the editor's business arrangements. Sturmey's involvement with Daimler appears to have ended in 1899.

Chapter Three

Austin and his Empire

Austin began as an employee of the Wolseley company when it was making sheep-shearing equipment. He fell out with it when its directors, egged on by Vickers, brought in John Siddeley (see the previous section). Some of the men who worked with Austin are featured here.

Herbert Austin
Stanley Edge
Charles Engelbach

Herbert Austin
1866–1941

Very little is known about the personal life of Herbert Austin, who was to be one of the key figures in the history of the first forty years of the British motor industry. The facts of his commercial career are available but exactly why he did what he did has to remain conjecture. His life began conventionally enough with a rural mid-Victorian childhood on a farm, not unlike that of that other pillar of the car industry, William Morris. Austin's father was appointed farm bailiff to Earl Fitzwilliam at Wentworth in Yorkshire in 1870 when his second son was four years old. Herbert went to the local school, and then to Rotherham Grammar School, five miles away, where his favourite occupation was to draw geometrical pictures and patterns. As his father's brother was an architect it seemed natural that an apprenticeship with his firm would occupy the boy's talents. For some reason it did not, and so his father followed the usual Victorian procedure of putting his son's name down for a railway engineering apprenticeship with the Great Northern Company.

Before he could take this up, something happened which changed the course of his life. This was a visit to the home of his mother's brother who, in 1883, had visited Australia and who now inspired his nephew with stories of the prospects there. In 1884, the two went off to Australia; the uncle became manager of a small engineering company and Herbert began working for him. For reasons unknown, he left his uncle after two years and moved on to other engineering companies, one of which was asked to manufacture components for the Wolseley Sheep Shearing Machine (WSSM) firm, just started up by Frederick Wolseley (qv). By this time, 1888, Austin was an engineer with something of a reputation. He had regularly attended night classes in Melbourne where he became a prize-winning student, and at the age of 21 he had submitted designs and estimates for a swing bridge which, although it did not win the contract, earned him a special commendation and, he later recalled, strengthened his self-confidence. In 1887 he married an Australian, Ellen Dron, and the following

The first automotive product made by the Wolseley sheep-shearing company under Austin's direction was a one-cylinder three wheeler of 1895, based on the de Dion design. Less than 10 years later, Herbert Austin was driving his family around in this fairly conventional-looking car, also a Wolseley, built before he set up his own firm.

year took up the post of manager of a small engineering firm.

When he met Wolseley, that Dublin immigrant had already been working on his sheep shearing inventions for over ten years. Great accuracy in machining the components was necessary, and Austin's work proved to be highly satisfactory, in addition to which he spotted numerous weaknesses in the Wolseley designs and took out patents for improvements. When Wolseley decided to transfer the manufacturing business to England, Austin was already a figure of significance in the enterprise, so Wolseley gave Austin shares in the new company and, in 1893, appointed him manager of the English concern.

Arriving in Birmingham, Austin found that not only had the machine components made by local small engineering firms for Wolseley been inadequately inspected, but the finished goods had been sold by the thousand in defective condition to overseas markets, thus damaging Wolseley's reputation. It was not easy to overcome the sales-resistance caused by this poor start and Austin began to look around for other products to boost turnover and profits. By 1895 the firm was

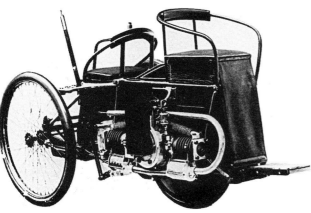

was probably in the following year that he built his 2hp car similar to the Bollée. In 1896 the Wolseley directors agreed to invest £2000 in plant for motor manufacture under his personal supervision and by the end of that year he was ready to display a second article, another three-wheeler, at the National Cycle Exhibition at the Crystal Palace. Austin's patents were taken out in conjunction with WSSMC and the firm produced various improvements to the design over the next year or two. The third Wolseley car, built in 1899/1900, was his first four-wheeler, the Voiturette, and this was highly successful when he entered it – with himself at the wheel – for the first large public trial of cars at the 1000-mile trial organised by the Auto-Club of Great Britain.

What motivated Austin in his dedication to motor car engineering? There is no evidence, and the answer must be guesswork. It is said that when he had lived in Australia he was impressed by the possibilities for motor transport offered by that vast, and then empty, country, but it is therefore curious that until 1921 he was preoccupied with nothing much except relatively-expensive, high-quality motor cars, 'which bore little resemblance to the serviceable, low-cost utility vehicles of the kind Henry Ford sold to American farmers'. Nor does he seem to have been driven by a desire to make a fortune. He appears to have held to the principle that there was a just reward for effort, and he expected the Wolseley company to provide him with that; again like Morris he was not a lavish spender and abhorred what he called 'super luxury'. He possessed the conventional Victorian virtues of hard work and thrift, plus, as will be seen, a flair for overcoming huge obstacles which appeared to be placed in his way by fate. He was a considerable inventor and perhaps this, combined with his skill as a manufacturing engineer, found its highest outlet in the motor car, which he enjoyed racing as well as designing. Drawing remained a passion – he once said, 'The long winter evenings (of my youth) would have been quite awful unless I had been able to indulge in my hobby – drawing.' Like Morris he was also moderately musical, spending some of his leisure hours playing the violin.

With the success of the Wolseley marque at the 1900 trials it was natural that Austin should

making machine tools and parts for bicycles for the cycle assembly firms of Birmingham and Coventry. Austin enterprisingly also became an agent for finished bicycles which he supplied to an Australian importer.

About this time he became one of the first British engineers to try to build a motor car. Already in the early 1890s he had taken out patents relating to steam engines and tyres. In 1894 he had seen his first 'horseless carriage' at a Paris exhibition and had been particularly impressed with the three-wheeled Bollée, and it now turn his mind to quantity production. Several major companies were developing similar plans, including the large armaments concern Vickers which in 1896 had decided to enter the motor trade. There had already been some correspondence between one of their directors, Sir Hiram Maxim, and Austin about aeroplane design, in which the former was interested, and after the Automobile Trials, Maxim approached Austin again about a collaboration on motor cars. Austin knew that the WSSMC directors did not have the finance available to expand production, or were unwilling to find it, and at this time he was forced to do his experimental car work in the evenings with road tests at the weekends. He was clearly irritated by the attitude of the Wolseley board, having already written formally to the directors in 1899 to complain. 'I think it would tend to make matters run more smoothly if I were taken a little more into the confidence of the Board,' he said, 'instead of being treated, as I have been lately, more like one of the mechanics.' It was therefore natural that Austin should look for outside finance, and he turned first to Captain Frank Kayser, a director of the Sheffield firm which supplied steel to Wolseley, and the son of a friend of Austin's who was on the board of Wolseley. He told Kayser that he had built up WSSMC, since he returned to England, largely by his own efforts. 'I have worked like a slave ever since I came here ... and yet today, despite having lived a very quiet retired life, I couldn't raise £200 outside my household goods.... Would you be pleased with my position? ... If I had been a drunken waster or an incompetent mechanic, then I should expect to be low down, but I have got energy still left to make a bid for something better.'

His contract with Wolseley was due to expire, and he did not hold out hopes that they could expand (even on the non-car side) sufficiently to take advantage of the patents they held. 'It will be necessary to give me a stake in the company that will be progressive,' he wrote to Kayser, putting forward the idea that he, Austin, should be involved in both the conventional sheep-shearing machine business and the new car concern which would be two separate organisations under a parent company. 'I could influence a good amount of capital if a new concern were started,' Austin wrote – by which he presumably

Austin at the wheel of his first car wearing the conventional bowler hat, a badge of office for the boss and his managers. The picture below is taken some 20 years later when he was embarking on the Austin Seven.

meant the Vickers money. He produced a prospectus for a public company to build cars, with a nominal capital of £30,000. It appears to have been at this time, late 1900, that Maxim put to Austin the proposal that Vickers should finance the development and production of Wolseley cars by taking over the machine-tool and motor manufacturing side of the existing Wolseley enterprise, retaining Austin as manager. This appealed both to Austin and also to the Wolseley directors, who received from Vickers £22,500, almost half in cash. Austin's contract, which ran from 1 March 1901, was at an annual salary of £500 plus 5 per cent of the new company's net profits. After an initial period of nine months, he was also to act as a director or consultant to the sheep-shearing company. The car manufacturing activities were to be located in a Birmingham factory, the Adderley Park Works, acquired by Vickers in 1899.

Austin's position seemed enviable, but in fact his relationship with the Vickers firm was not satisfactory and led to the first major obstacle in the development of his car business. This came about because Austin was committed to the design and use of horizontal engines, whereas

success appeared to be going to those who fitted vertical engines. Vickers supported Austin with cash, increasing the capital by £90,000 and a personal loan from Douglas Vickers of £40,000 in 1903, but they did not support his continued development of the horizontal engine – although Austin, for his part, appeared impervious to criticism. In 1905 John Siddeley (qv) approached Vickers direct about his own vertical engine and was invited to meet their board in May 1905 to discuss the purchase of his Autocar company. Following this, Douglas and Albert Vickers formed themselves into a Committee of Investigation into the Wolseley car business, and concluded that they must proceed with the manufacture of the Siddeley type of engine, which had now become the accepted trend in design for motor vehicles in Europe. To avoid a further clash with Austin, who was still adamant about the virtues of the horizontal engine, Siddeley was commissioned to produce his car at another Vickers factory at Crayford in Kent.

Albert Vickers continued to press Austin to change his design, which he stubbornly refused to do, and there was some kind of row after Siddeley's appointment, following which Austin left the Adderley Park factory in a huff. In the biography written partly by Austin's daughter, it is maintained that the disagreement about the engine was an excuse rather than the basis of Austin's leaving. Four months before his five years contract was due to expire, Austin, at Vickers' request, handed in his resignation, and Siddeley took over. Austin was then aged 38, and, like a good many other inventive men, he had fallen out with those who were putting his ideas into commercial practice. He was not, however, deeply committed to a narrow, technical specialisation, despite the row over engines, and it is said that his cars were 'unashamedly copied from other sources' and his 'ability as a stylist was his real *forte* as a motor man'. Austin could therefore live to fight another day, which is what he proceeded to do.

By now, he was convinced that his big mistake, both at WSSMC and at Vickers, had been to have managed a business without owning it. Before formally resigning from Wolseley he had chosen a disused printing works at Longbridge as the site of a new factory, and within a few months he had formed his own company, the

Austin Motor Co Ltd, registered in December 1905. The asking price for the land and buildings was £10,000 and Austin calculated that he needed between £15,000 and £20,000 capital. It seems probable that most, if not all, of the initial capital was provided by Austin himself with the balance coming from his friend Kayser. Two years later, more money was subscribed by Harvey du Cros junior who thus became a third director. Austin's reputation must have been substantial to have enabled him to get the support of Harvey du Cros junior, the managing-director of the Swift company, and son of the chairman of Dunlop.

The new company was able to get credit from suppliers, deposits from customers and money from the Midland Bank. Both sales and profits rose steadily. Turnover nearly doubled between 1908 and 1910 and more than doubled again in

the following three years. Unfortunately for Austin, who had been so determined to retain his independence, he was paying out considerable dividends to Kayser and du Cros. It thus became difficult for him to find the capital to finance expansion. In 1913 he mentioned to the main director of Krupps, one of his suppliers, that he was 'rather cramped for want of capital' and was immediately offered £100,000. It is not known if this was accepted, but further capital was certainly obtained in that year. The factory, situated then in a rural area, had been selected because it offered good communications and offered room for growth. The number of employees rose steadily, reaching nearly 300 by 1913.

Austin himself set up office in one of the rooms of the old printing works, where he remained from 1905 to shortly before he died in 1940. The first car was, however, designed in the study of the house he had bought in Erdington. It was called Berwood Grove and was a substantial Victorian mansion where he had his own study, which doubled as a drawing office. He was

helped by a young draughtsman A. J. W. Hancock, who became chief designer of the company and remained so until Austin's death. Also working at Berwood Grove in these early years was the young A. V. Davidge and another young man, W. A. Howitt, who acted as Austin's secretary. Hancock has described how 'we used to have our midday meal and tea at Berwood Grove, and after luncheon, Austin would give us a few minutes in the garden before we resumed our studies, for this is how they seemed to us at the time, although they had a very practical purpose. Davidge and I had a very interesting job getting out the drawings which, I remember, we made on thick tracing paper, so they could be blue-printed without further copying.' Finally the team loaded their drawing boards and T squares into Austin's 8 hp Wolseley car and he drove them the fifteen miles to the factory. When the first car was completed in the spring of 1906, Austin told the works manager, a Mr Carvell, to take the two boys on a celebration trip to Malvern.

The cars Austin produced were a success, although they were essentially derivative. It is said that the similarity of, say, a '1907 Austin to a contemporary Gladiator or Clément is marked'. Austin's skills lay in sound engineering and clever styling. The *Autocar* called his car 'an engineer's job in the best sense of the word'. The features of this 'touring carriage', as Austin himself described it, enabled 'a gentleman' to drive his own limousine, with good all-round visibility. In addition, 'it should be possible for a lady to raise or lower any portion from the inside while travelling, without undue exertion, so that if the weather changes, or the current of air is too strong for any quarter, the windows may be instantly raised or lowered.'

Austin was one of the first to switch from the open landaulet to the closed limousine body. He was also one of the first manufacturers to establish showrooms in major centres. By 1912 there was a West End showroom where Austin owners could obtain a repair service, hire a car, or use the club rooms. He also continued, for a time, as he had at Wolseley, to enter competition trials and in 1908 built a 100 hp sports car, which achieved publicity when one was purchased by Jack Johnson, the boxing champion. Between 1910 and 1913 he also took the water speed record,

The plant at Longbridge which Herbert Austin had started from a disused
printing works had by the 1920s become one of the biggest in the world,
outside the United States.

powering boats with V12 engines. Finally he
went into commercial vehicle manufacture. The
period up to World War I is therefore marked by
Austin's fertile designing capacity, with many
models emerging from the factory each year. He
claimed his intention was quantity production of
high quality cars, but this was clearly impossible
as long as he kept changing the models. Nor did
he show any inclination to produce small cars for
the mass market which he said he believed lay
over the horizon.

When the war came, Austin had prepared
himself with capital for expansion by going public in 1914, with a nominal capital of £650,000. He
personally did well, taking a tranche of shares
and agreeing to a five-year contract as chairman
and managing-director at a salary of £3500 plus
a share of the net profit. Afterwards he said,
'That was the biggest mistake I ever made. Had
it remained a private concern, its development
would have more personal and less spectacular.'
He had also developed a 'personal' style in his

relations with employees, although whether we
should today call it much more than paternalism
is debatable. The *Autocar* called the firm a
'democratic' body where Austin held weekly con-
ferences with departmental heads. It seems
likely, though, that a man of such strong character as Austin would have dominated such meetings rather than indulge in much discussion. He
also organised social occasions, such as an
annual subscription dinner for staff and manual
workers attended by about 20 per cent of the
workforce. Austin's speech at the dinner was
redolent of the Victorian virtues. To 'live on a
higher plane of civilisation,' he told his employees, 'we must be prepared to work harder and
scheme more.' He himself was an example to the
team, designing many of the machine tools in
the factory, as well as the constant flow of cars.

There seems little doubt that he was by now
an object of admiration to the employees, one of
the leading figures in the British motor industry,
the firm ranking fifth in output after Wolseley,

Humber, Sunbeam and Rover. Another five firms each produced a thousand or more vehicles in 1913. Compared with the American Ford company, Austin's was a small-scale operation before the war, but at least, unlike some of his British competitors including Wolseley, his was profitable.

Hancock wrote many years later, 'In the final assessment, it is the opinion and regard of the people who work with and for him that sets the seal on a man's career, and there was real affection between Herbert Austin and his staff and workpeople. While he was "on the job" he was completely engrossed in it. But his staff came first when they were in trouble or in need of his help. That was Lord Austin as I knew him.' The argument here may be fallacious, but Austin's ability to inspire loyalty was remarkable. He was described as arriving at work, usually shabbily dressed and wearing a square-crowned bowler hat, the effect of which was to accentuate the angularity of his features and the squareness of his build. The workers respected him as a man who, whatever job they performed, he could do himself. 'Equipped with pencils in both hands, which he manipulated simultaneously, he was a daily visitor to the workshops, and frequently was to be found in both the car and machine-tool design departments. Like most good works managers, he had an instinct for spotting poor workmanship or design. However, he rarely smiled and 'presented a somewhat dour public image. A reserved and reticent man, he confessed (to) difficulty in verbal expression, while the trade press found him elusive.'

In one sense, Austin had a remarkable war. From being a mere Midlands industrialist, he became one of the foremost in the nation. Between 1914 and 1918, the Longbridge plant produced over 8 million shells, 650 guns, over 2000 aeroplanes, nearly 500 armoured cars and huge quantities of aero-engines, ambulances and lorries. In recognition he was knighted in 1917 and given the order of Leopold by the Belgian monarch. He had become a figure of such stature that he was the only motor manufacturer to become a Member of Parliament, standing as a Conservative in the 'Coupon' election manipulated by Lloyd George in 1918. The assumption is that he accepted his candidature (for a Birmingham ward) in a spirit of naivety, the evidence being his total disillusion with the political system during his period in the House, which ran to 1925, and which was characterised by his failure to make even a maiden speech, never mind anything more memorable. In 1929 he told *The Times*, 'I am convinced that the businessmen of England, including myself, are best engaged in giving the whole of their attention to their own particular job and thus bringing about a solution of the country's difficulties by natural means – the thriving condition of the Longbridge factory today will do more for example, to minimize the evil of unemployment than could all my efforts on the floor of the House.'

To return to the 1914–18 war, Austin's great tragedy was the death of his only son, Vernon, in France. Reluctantly Vernon had served an apprenticeship with Austin, but had left with the intention of becoming a professional soldier. After a year's service, he left and returned to the firm but was recalled for active service after war broke out. His father had intended to pass on the direction of the firm to the young Vernon by retiring when he was fifty and while, as Hancock said, the effect of his son's death was 'to make him work even harder; there seemed to be no bitterness in him', this 'terrible blow' was one from which there was no recovery.

His feeling that fate had struck him a crippling blow was reinforced after the war, when, despite his earlier triumphs, it now appeared that fate was going to steal his business away. In the traumas of the post-war world, Austin made bad decisions, including an attempt to revive the company's fading fortunes by the injection of capital, which drove the firm into the hands of the official receiver. His principal creditors, notably the Midland Bank, Eagle Star and British Dominion Insurance, decided that the time had come to step in. Austin, believing in 1918 that the war had another two years to run, was planning to re-introduce his 1914 20 hp car in revised configuration. Introduced in 1919, Austin dropped all his other models and produced this large overstrong car, inspired by the Model T Ford. It proved to be a slow seller. Longbridge by now was, according to an expert of the time, 'a plant of an entirely useless character for its future needs, and with a geographical disposition of its buildings that was very difficult to work economically.'

The 100,000th Austin Seven leaving the factory at Longbridge in 1929
received hardly the blaze of publicity which would be mounted today.

The man who made this comment, Charles R. F. Engelbach (qv) was one of the two men introduced by the bank to rescue the business. The other was Ernest L. Payton. At first Austin was reluctant to hand over the reins and pushed Engelbach into a remote modest office. The new arrival promptly moved to an office similar in size and position to Austin's own. Austin is said to have referred to him at that time as 'that bloody interloper'. He ignored Engelbach and pressed ahead with plans to increase tractor production and build a small light aeroplane for the 'civil' market, but neither proposal met with approval from the new blood. Nor did his policy of concentrating on larger models which were uncompetitive with the American imports of Ford and in any case were designed for a falling market. In a boardroom reshuffle, Austin lost his old friend and financier, Colonel Frank Kayser.

His reaction, at first, was to turn abroad for help. He joined in negotiations to sell Austin to General Motors. When these went off the boil, he approached a large Birmingham concern for £1 million debenture, negotiating with one of the Chamberlain family, but Austin's board of directors persuaded him to withdraw from any further such ventures. Throughout 1920 and early 1921 the firm continued to be in serious financial difficulties, spurned by the banks, the City and the Government. Engelbach was put in sole charge of production and Austin had to relinquish the title of managing-director. Payton, a financier, bought much-needed financial expertise to the company.

It was at this point that Austin showed his remarkable power of recovery. He had lost the Wolseley car business in 1905, he had lost his only son in 1915, and now it seemed he was to lose his own business. By extraordinary effort, this man, whom Nuffield described as one of the best motor engineers in the world, turned his energy away from the owner-entrepreneurship which now had no attractions for him, towards a creative, inventive and novel design concept. He still owned (with his wife) one half of the voting shares, but his attention was now concentrating away from 'his' business and towards a new car. While he worked, the firm contracted. In 1922/3 the output fell to 2500 cars and the workforce to a similar size.

Meanwhile Austin once more retired to his private house. He and his family had moved to Lickey Grange, with two hundred acres of park, where he lived in some style for the rest of his life. With the help of an 18-year-old draughtsman in the Hancock-mould, Stanley Edge (qv), his aim was to build a small car. He borrowed a two-cylinder air cooled Rover from his chief cashier, Arthur Day, to use as the basis of the design but in fact his specification came from elsewhere. It says much for Edge's tenacity that he succeeded in weaning Austin away from a twin, with the result that the Austin Seven had a small *four* cylinder engine and was, effectually, a large car in miniature. The aim he set Edge was for a four-wheeler able to go through the same gateway and into the same-sized garage as the motor-bicycle/side-car combination which was all the financially hard-pressed lower-middle classes of the time could afford. Hancock says that when Austin first drove his Baby Seven on a trial run, he brought it over to his house, telling his wife, 'There, that's what we have got to come to!' The car had been built in secrecy in a corner of the Longbridge factory and was officially launched at Claridge's hotel in July 1922 where Austin described his market as 'the man who, at present, can only afford a motorcycle and side-car and yet has the ambition to become a motorist'. The car was exhibited for the first time at the Olympia show in November that year and Austin's daughter always believed that 'the commercial turning point occurred when a Cambridge undergraduate purchased one, conferring upon the Seven a degree of social acceptability' – rather like the Mini half a life-time later. As the Baby Seven sales rose, the number of motor-cycles/side-cars fell, but not at anything like the rate predicted by Austin, who failed to see that their prices would be reduced to meet competition from the baby car.

Austin had produced a winner, not only in the commercial sense, but in competitive racing in which the Seven established many international class records. Sales of the car rose from under 2500 in 1923 to over 26,000 in 1929, continuing at more or less this level until 1936/7. The success was complemented by healthy sales of the Austin Twelve and together these products of

Longbridge represented about 25 per cent of total British output of private cars from 1928 onwards. It was a remarkable recovery by a firm which had been facing bankruptcy a few years earlier.

The credit must go to Austin (and Edge), and also to Engelbach and Payton; Engelbach had persuaded his co-directors to spend over half a million pounds on reorganisation at Longbridge, and Payton had found the money. Austin provided not only the ideas but also the energy, Hancock says his 'chief characteristic was his almost superhuman energy'. Others describe how he was invariably at the office before other workers, and indeed he chose the young Stanley Edge, it is said, because he arrived at work an hour before Austin. The latter's presence could be sensed by 'doors swinging to and fro and a rush of air in the hallway'. He was like 'a tornado, who used to tear around the works and offices'. Austin made money out of the Seven – he was paid a personal royalty on every car sold – but the company itself remained in debt through the early part of the 1920s. In these circumstances (owning over half the ordinary share capital) 'it is under-

One of Austin's tragedies was that the son he had wanted to put in charge of the business was killed in World War I and he failed to find a suitable successor from his own colleagues. He finally chose Leonard Lord.

standable that he should have shown enthusiasm for a proposal advanced in 1924 by Dudley Docker (qv) of Vickers, that the Austin, Morris and Wolseley motor firms should merge'. This would, in Austin's suggested arrangement, have put William Morris 'virtually in command'. Letters were exchanged between the two men, but nothing came of the proposal due to Morris's declared 'firm aversion of being responsible for other people's money'.

Once again Austin turned to America and to General Motors, but a proposed offer of £1.3 million was opposed by influential fellow directors including Engelbach and Payton. Austin explained, at his agent's dinner at Olympia in October 1925, why Austin 'did not marry the lass'. 'Her dowry was quite substantial, but my relations didn't like her and therefore the engagement had to be broken off.' Despite this set-back, Austin continued to look for a wealthy connection, and when Wolseley was put up for sale in 1926 he tried to bid for his old company but was defeated by Morris. Undaunted, Austin then approached Henry Ford, to whom he wrote,

'I am afraid you might consider it an impertinance on my part if I were to suggest that we might collaborate in the British market and in the British Dominions and Colonies to our mutual advantage.' Ford's reply was non-committal.

By 1926, Austin was 60 years old. If he had by then failed in the business sense to build a firm as financially sound as that of his rival Morris, it would be difficult to prove that the success of the Austin firm had not been – and would not remain – due to his engineering genius motivated by a desire to 'motorize the common man' and to keep the quality of production at a reasonable level in an era of falling prices. By his skill, the firm had survived the post-war slump, and it was also to survive the falling demand of the depression of the 1930s. He had, with Edge's help, understood the new demand for the small car – although Austin never made the cheapest British motor. Certainly he never built a 'great' car that would satisfy the student of the automobile, but he did build cars that people wanted, not only in Britain, but overseas. From 1929, when the British share in the world car markets was only 7 per cent, Austin played a leading part in boosting export trade to over 25 per cent in 1932/3. Even Adolf Hitler claimed that he had used a 'Seven' in the early days of the Nazi movement. When the recovery in the home market restarted in 1932, Austin was ready with another popular car, the Light Twelve. Again it was conservative in design, but it had a deep-rooted appeal to the unadventurous British driver. Austin cars have been described as having 'bodywork suitable for the top-hatted brigade' and from the little known about Austin's character, it seems the car may well have been a reflection of the man—if a bowler hat is substituted for the top hat. Certainly he believed that comfort and convenience had for too long been subordinated to appearance and streamlining, and no-one could accuse him of paying too much attention to the latter. Indeed the venerable Twelve, dating back to 1921, continued into production into the 1930's achieving fame as the typical London taxi of the time. By 1934 Austin was, if briefly, the largest British manufacturer of motor cars.

Early in 1936, the government approached Austin for help in preparing the nation for a war which the Armed Services believed would be

Before World War II broke out, King George VI visited Austin's shadow factory which was building aeroplanes. Typically, Leonard Lord appears to have taken the lead (second from right). The ageing Austin (fourth from right) was dead two years later.

initiated by Germany in the next three or four years. Austin's contribution to the 'shadow' factory scheme has never been fully assessed, but it was probably very considerable. His rival, Morris, behaved curiously when asked for his assistance, and did not play a part until after 1939. Austin, in contrast, became chairman of the Shadow Aero Engine Committee. In brief, its job was to organize the production of a large number of Bristol aero-engines (Rolls-Royce declined to be part of the scheme) which would be the bottleneck in an expanded aircraft rearmament programme. From his experience in World War I, Austin was able to negotiate with the government a scheme by which the larger motor manufacturers (except Morris) would manage, in return for a fee, 'shadow' factories initially built by the government near their own Midland factories. Austin was also influential in arranging

that each factory should at first build engine components, rather than complete engines, for assembly in the two nominated assembly plants. Before long the scheme was extended to produce aeroplanes as well as engines. Austin was one of those who criticised the Chamberlain government for sending buying missions to America to buy aeroplanes, urging them instead to decide quickly and then 'frankly tell industry what they want and how they want it'. In 1936 he was made Baron Austin of Longbridge. According to his daughter, he accepted the title with reluctance, having few social pretensions. Despite his peerage, he continued to be courteous and benign in temperament, and there are few complaints from his colleagues about any 'side' or lack of tact in dealing with them.

Up to the outbreak of war, new car models were being introduced, all with the active participation of the now elderly founder of the firm. Morris's biographer quotes a Freddie Henry of Austin's as explaining that, right up until 1938, 'the Old Man took a leading part in the design of the cars and, in addition, he was a first-class engineer. In fact he could be described as chairman, managing-director, production manager, chief engineer and plant engineer, for he was involved in all these matters from 8am to 8pm, Sunday and weekday!' This may be unfair to Engelbach and Payton, but it colourfully describes Austin's continued dedication to all aspects of the business. He had given little thought, until he was well over 70 years old, to the succession, perhaps because he could not bear to think about the loss of his son, his natural successor. Payton was a candidate, now aged 61. Engelbach was about the same age, but his health was not as good and he was almost blind. Both men seemed to Austin too old to take over. One of his agents said 'one of his greatest failings was his anxiety to do everything himself and his unwillingness to allow his colleagues to undertake any responsibilities.'

The problem was resolved when Austin met Leonard Lord (qv). After his abrupt departure from Morris, Lord had stayed out of the motor industry until recruited by Austin to take over at Longbridge in February 1938, succumbing 'to the seductive smell of oil'. Lord himself described his job as 'Austin with the whole jackpot' and there was probably little place in his philosophy for a Lord Austin any more than, ultimately, there was for Engelbach or Payton. Within months of his appointment Lord had so gained the confidence of Lord Austin that he assumed a leading part in the introduction of two new cars. Quite quickly, Austin found himself agreeing with Lord to the premature departure of people like Hancock who had been with the company since its formation. At an ex-apprentice's dinner held in January 1939, Lord told Austin, 'You'll need a couple of coaches to take them away before I've finished.' Thus what has been described as the Longbridge gerontocracy (government by old men) came to an end. Austin's empire would eventually merge with Morris's and Leonard Lord would be the new emperor.

To return to the outbreak of war: within months Austin was exhausted and had to resign from the chairmanship of the Air Ministry's 'shadow' factory committee. In the winter of 1940 he had a bad bout of pneumonia and he died of a heart attack in May 1941. He was not as rich a man as Morris, but he left over £1 million, having, like Morris, but on a much smaller scale, helped finance hospitals and made other charitable donations. He was also a major patron of the Cavendish laboratories at Cambridge where Rutherford and his team developed atomic science, to which he gave a quarter of a million pounds.

Although the forces which drove Austin to such a pinnacle of success are hard to understand, one of these was certainly his 'almost superhuman energy' and Hancock's words seem an apt epitaph: 'It seemed incredible that so much energy should suddenly cease, and that we should not see him again.'

Stanley Howard Edge
born 1903

The young Edge gained his practical experience in the Austin aeroplane factory drawing office in 1918 – never having been apprenticed. He also attended the Austin Technical College which was attached to the works. After the war he continued in the car drawing office where Austin is said to have spotted him because he arrived at the works even earlier in the morning than his employer. When only 18 years old, Edge was taken by Austin to work in the billiard room of his private house on the design of what became the Austin Seven. Austin was determined to produce a small car and financed the project out of his own pocket.

Sir Herbert was initially intent on producing a conventional two cylinder car but, after a protracted debate, Edge showed him that a small four cylinder engine could be produced for about the same price as a two cylinder one. Edge's inspiration was the French Peugeot Quadrillette and for the bottom half of the diminutive 696cc (later enlarged to 748cc) power unit he drew on the Belgian F.N. four cylinder motor-cycle engine.

Despite the part he played in the creation of this car of such great significance in the future of

Austin's, the firm let Edge go in 1927, when he was wooed away by Triumph for the princely salary of £4 15s. a week. There he worked in the team led by A. A. Sykes which produced the Super Seven. He wrote about his experiences at Austin, as well as one of the best long magazine articles about Austin himself.

Charles Englebach
1876–1943

Born in Kensington, the son of a War Office clerk whose family had Huguenot connections, Englebach went to school in Southport. At the age of 16 he was given £1000 by his godfather and became an indentured apprentice with Armstrong, Whitworth in Newcastle-upon-Tyne, where eventually he specialised in building naval gun turrets. He was offered – but declined – a professional singing career with d'Oyly Carte Opera Company. In 1900, Armstrongs became involved in making the Rootes Venables paraffin-engined car and Englebach became works manager between 1904–6. He then built a special factory to produce the more advanced 30 hp Armstrong, Whitworth cars, but the directors turned down Englebach's proposal to mass produce motor cars at a rate of 6000 a year. In 1914 he was called up for RNVR service but returned to take over the Howitzer department of the Coventry Ordnance works. He was awarded the OBE for his war work. Afterwards, following a short spell as general manager of a component supplier in London, he was chosen as works director at Austins by the banks, who were disillusioned with Herbert Austin's abilities as an administrator.

He was regarded as one of the finest production engineers in Britain, and made astonishing improvements to the Austin factory, despite a lack of co-operation by Austin himself, who was initially displeased at Englebach's appointment. The wounds were healed and Englebach became an architect of the firm's success. More about this period is given in the biography of Austin. Englebach is described as 'intelligent, witty and understanding humanity just as much as he understood the problems of producing motor cars'. Later, when his eyesight deteriorated and he had to be guided round the factory, he was forced to retire by Leonard Lord (qv) but retained his seat on the board. In the 1930s, he also served on the Ministry committee responsible for shadow factory production, which Lord Austin chaired.

He was a freemason, patron of the Boy Scout Movement, and his recreations were golf and yachting. In 1902 he had married a lady who had been brought up in Spain and was a trained painter, some of whose work hung in major galleries like the Tate. He died leaving £110,733 gross.

Chapter Four

Morris — Another Giant

William Morris exhibited all the classical features of the motor men. Of humble origins, he began as a cyclist, graduated to cars, and set up in the Midlands. Yet he was quite different in character, not only from Austin, with whom he had many common traits, but with most of those with whom he worked.

He succeeded where many others like him failed. Before 1913, some 200 different makes of car had been launched on the market but only half of them survived. For contrast with Morris, the story is briefly told here of two such firms.

William Morris
Peter Poppe
Miles Thomas
Leonard Lord
Alec Issigonis
George Harriman
Frank Woollard
Harper Bean
Frank Smith

William Richard Morris
1877–1963

Morris was an accomplished cyclist and would undoubtedly have been awarded a blue had he attended Oxford University. Both pictures of him were taken in the same year, 1895, when he had been running his cycle shop for two years.

Myths die hard, and as late as 1988 the *Daily Telegraph* was still perpetuating the story that William Morris, later Viscount Nuffield, was 'the son of a farm labourer' who rose from rags to riches. Even when he was alive there were those who thought him 'simple' and a senior civil servant in 1935 called him 'gnarl-handed' as if all he was good for was repairing broken-down cars. It is true that he left school at 15, and did not enjoy it very much, but if his father had not fallen ill, he would probably have had a secure middle-class upbringing. Most of his forebears had been small farmers in Oxfordshire and his father became a farm manager to his blind father-in-law when he married into a farming family. His mother's father ran a largish farm near Oxford and she had been educated at a private girl's school in the city. Morris's father had attended a local grammar school. However Morris himself stayed at the village school outside Oxford until he was 15, when his father's asthma made it necessary for Morris to leave to get a job and help support the family – he was the eldest of seven children, five of whom had died. He would probably have left school anyway, because even an attempt to take night classes in engineering was given up after two attendances. Later in life, he is supposed to have said that experience had taught him 'it is not always the men who have an expensive education who do things'.

Despite his lack of interest in academic work, Morris always said that he had wanted to study medicine and become a surgeon. He was particularly good with his hands, and could make things work, and would probably have been an excellent surgeon, if he had ever been able to pass the medical exams. Instead he combined his elementary mechanical skills with his other facility – athletics. At the age of 14 he already owned a bicycle (by no means all boys had one in those days) and had begun bicycle racing in Oxford. It was therefore logical that he found a job in one of the city's many bicycle shops. Bicycles and bicycle racing are not a particularly fashionable activity today, but in the early 1890s, when cars were virtually non-existent, they were a rather respected, and respectable, mode of travel and sport. You could get a blue at Oxford for cycling (not so today) and while Morris was racing there, the Hon. Charles Rolls was acquiring his half-blue at Cambridge. Morris did not hold his first job for long, as his request for an extra shilling a week in wages was refused, and he left his employer to set up on his own.

He started in 1893 at the age of 16, with savings of only £4, in a brick building at the back of his father's house. There he repaired bicycles and built one for the vicar of St Giles who was much pleased with it, and gave Morris a small production order to encourage him. Over the next few years the business expanded and he acquired a considerable reputation amongst undergraduates and local businessmen. By 1901, in his early twenties, he had saved enough money to take premises in the High Street and two other small

locations nearby. He paid for these in part by giving the owner two bicycles. Already he was making his first move towards motor vehicles – and had built and fitted a 1¾hp engine to a motorcycle. In all this work he was completely self-taught, picking up information from trade journals and engineering handbooks. He was much encouraged by his mother; Miles Thomas, who knew him well, believes that 'it was the fact that Morris recognised that he had to be the main source of [financial] support for his mother that spurred him on to such dynamic physical and commercial efforts.' Morris himself referred to the financial motive when he wrote, 'When I decided to start for myself it was because I felt that no-one else would pay me as well as W. R. Morris.'

Morris made a name as cycle racer as well as builder; in the 1890s he was district champion for Oxford, Berkshire and Buckinghamshire and in 1900 he was the holder of seven local championships – including the 1 mile title for Oxford City and the 50 mile title of Oxford County. In other words he was a champion sprinter as well as a long distance man. In 1904 he won both cups outright. Morris, who always looked fit, must have been an exceptional athlete. Even twenty years later, he was able to join in on a Cowley Works' football team run, quite unrehearsed and untrained, and come in first.

A cycling friend, Joseph Cooper, joined him in 1904 in forming a partnership to build motorcycles, based round a 2¾hp de Dion engine, which Morris exhibited at the London Motorcycle Show. Cooper, though, was too cautious, and would not agree when Morris wanted to build three motorcycles in advance of orders. The partnership broke up eventually although much later Cooper came back to work for Morris at the Cowley motor factory and the two men remained friends. Morris had meanwhile strengthened his 'organisation', if his modest firm could justify such a description. His father was looking after 48 High Street and keeping the books. At another small premises there were two men repairing undergraduate's cycles, and at a third small workshop, Morris did the mechanical work helped by an apprentice. For the past year he had been garaging undergraduates' motor cars and was advertising 'Motor repairs a speciality'. Although he often pretended to scepticism about the merits of advertising he had used it from his earliest days. Indeed he rode his own bikes in races to promote their sales.

What sort of man was he in his mid-twenties? He was sure of himself, but had an underlying sensitiveness which people sometimes mistook for lack of confidence. On the whole he thought things out exhaustively before acting – 'without worry, you never get anywhere' he said. He had developed a tenacity to find things out for himself, and if he wanted information from other people he would question them carefully before accepting what they said. He was quick to learn from experience and rarely made the same mistake twice.

These qualities were matched by a desire to succeed and to be seen to be successful. So one of the lessons he learnt early on – not to depend on partners like Cooper – was motivated not by a desire for independence as such, but by a realisation that he was capable on his own of achieving success. He wrote, 'There are very few types of business which I would not be prepared to tackle with some hope of success, relying entirely on my experience in general.' His self-confidence was reinforced by his experience of failure when dragged down by the lack of it in others. He had a second dose of this soon after the breakup of the Cooper-Morris partnership. An undergraduate at Christ Church, who had inherited a good deal of money, decided to start a firm with an Oxford businessman to sell cars and cycles, and they wanted Morris as works manager. He joined the company – the Oxford Automobile & Cycle Agency – but it failed less than a year after its formation – it is said because the undergraduate, who was supposed to be a sleeping partner, spent far too much money seeking out new customers. 'Practically all its debts were paid off by the sale of its assets, but Morris salvaged only his personal kit of tools, many of which he had made himself.' Although Morris had no hard feelings towards the businessman, he blamed the undergraduate for the failure of the venture, and for many years hated the University, would not give it money nor employ its graduates.

Disappointed, Morris returned to his old business in the High Street once again, operating under his own name which was becoming quite well known in Oxford. He gave up the idea of manufacturing motorcycles because they were

Morris's bicycle shop was in a prominent position in Oxford and soon became well-known to undergraduates. Its owner's cycle-racing achievements were also well-publicised, as was his fight with the City over trams and buses, the subject of the contemporary cartoon.

unreliable and spent more and more of his time on cars. In 1905 he bought a car of his own which he hired out with drivers, some of whom provided driving tuition. Morris also started a taxi firm. Cars were by then fashionable and he began to look around for agencies. In the 1906 election, a prospective Scottish MP decided that he must have a car in which to campaign, and he commissioned Morris to find him a reliable machine. Morris found it quite impossible to obtain any

WAKING UP OLD OXFORD.

THE MODERN St. GEORGE AND THE DRAGON.

kind of satisfactory car in Britain and he therefore went over to France to make a purchase. The
delivery journey from Paris to Scotland was
marred by so many breakdown dramas that
Morris lost money on the sale, even though the
car was finally delivered to the parliamentary
candidate, and this, like the other failures,
merely spurred Morris on to achieve success by
independent effort – he would design and build
his own.

By 1910 he had built a garage in Oxford,
adjacent to his original premises, which he called
the Morris Garage. For its day it was on a grand
scale and the local newspapers nicknamed it the
Oxford Motor Palace. He had acquired the agencies for Arrol-Johnson. Belsize, Hubmobile, Singer, Standard, Wolseley and Humber, the last
firm being amongst the leading British firms. He
also had motorcycle agencies for Douglas,
Enfield, Sunbeam and Triumph. At the age of 33,
starting with his capital of only £4, Morris had
established himself as a 'notable' person in
Oxford. His cycle and car firm was well known –
its products advertised his name in the streets of
Oxford day and night.

As a personality, he was known for his cycle
racing achievements and he was a convivial if
not madly social companion – he could play any
musical instrument by ear, and enjoyed an evening's singing with the other cycling enthusiasts.
His happiest moments, however, were in the
workshops – he was an inspired mechanic –
where he spent most of his time until 1914. The
other people working there nicknamed him
'Uncle' and a new employee said afterwards that
when he joined, the atmosphere was so amicable,
he thought it was a family firm where all the
others were nephews of William Morris. 'He was
an inspiration. ... Enthusiasm radiated from
him.'

A story about this period of his life illus-
trates his tenacity of character. Horse trams
were the normal form of public transport in
Oxford before World War I, but they were not
popular with the townspeople who felt that they
should be replaced with the new motor bus. The
city fathers resisted a change. Morris therefore
applied for a licence to operate a motorbus service. He held a public meeting and obtained
12,000 signatures for a petition in support of his
application. The council prevaricated. After

three weeks, Morris had had no reply to his application, so he set up the service regardless. The public flocked to Morris's buses and the horse trams were empty. The council members were annoyed with Morris but did not know how to deal with him without making themselves more unpopular. Morris solved their dilemma by handing over the operation of the motor bus fleet to the horse tram company. His relations with the city fathers remained strained and when he became more famous he twice refused the Freedom of the City of Oxford, until all the councillors active over the horse-tram incident had gone and Nuffield felt he could accept.

Morris showed equal tenacity in the development of his motor car. He had begun work on it in earnest in 1910 and laid down some basic principles 'of first importance'. These were:

> The ability to start at any time
> at a moment's notice,
> Simplicity of control when driving,
> Absolute freedom from trouble.

Morris had also developed some basic business principles. One, which he had enunciated when he had set up on his own in his teens, was that 'to build a great business, one must be content to turn back 99 per cent of one's profits into expansion'. Another was that to succeed meant taking risks, and all the risk-taking decisions in his business were taken by Morris alone. 'To him all life was a challenge,' wrote Miles Thomas. 'He had a simple-minded determination to make his mark in the world.... With complete faith in what he wanted to do he has always had an unwavering faith in his own abilities and judgement,' said another contemporary. A third valuable conviction for business success was his belief in the values of what he called 'the backbone of the country, the middle-classes,' which included hard-work, thrift, honesty and patriotism. These were values to which Morris himself adhered throughout his life. He said his success was 'the result of taking my opportunity - and working "like a black"'. He worked extremely long hours and would often turn up at a supplier's works at seven in the morning or ten at night. 'Work is still the natural mission of every real man,' he said. Managers who were not on the job were, he believed, 'pernicious to sound business' and he

accused the steel industrialists of having 'big cigars and nothing to do'.

As for thrift, Morris kept a very strict personal check on the finances of his business. 'Only by the use of such close checks have I been able to finance this concern largely from within. Happily I have no expensive hobbies! Nor would I care to live anywhere save next door to the works.' Over the whole period of his life, even at his most successful, his office was unchanged - a narrow, plain room with ordinary wooden furniture. The only gesture towards ornament was a glass cabinet containing his cycling medals and badges. Thrift was basic to his approach to business - to pay more than he need for something was the first step to ruin and frugality the key to success.

His marriage to an Oxford school-teacher, daughter of a furrier, only reinforced Morris's desire to live the simple life. She kept well in the background and Miles Thomas, who knew the couple well, says, 'She saw to it that her husband did not follow the habit that was popular among other motor magnates in the late 1920's and early 30's of throwing great parties to attract custom and goodwill.' Even though he took very little money out of the firm as a salary until its reconstruction in 1926, Morris had built up a business that was worth a good deal of money (had he chosen to sell it); he spent little money on anything connected with his wife or himself personally. Indeed his marriage sounds rather joyless and his first biographer can only bring himself to describe it as 'tolerably happy'. The impression is that Morris was 'a solitary' even to his wife. Miles Thomas says that 'his character made it difficult for him to enjoy close friendships', although it is clear that he could make a wide range of acquaintances from all classes - he was no snob.

Morris was pleased with the success he had achieved, and it would be wrong to leave the impression that as he set about designing his first car he did so in a negative frame of mind, aiming at a cheap 'utility' model. At this time he employed some fifteen to twenty men and boys to run the garage business and he learnt a good deal about the motivation of people who bought cars for the first time. Most people - most middle-class people - did not of course own cars and by 1910-11 Morris was 'convinced that there was

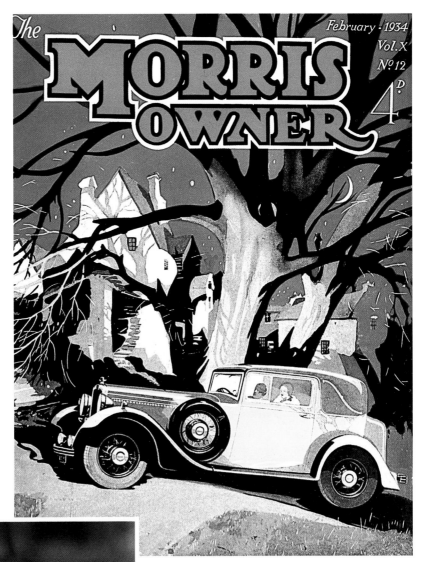

The February 1934 front cover showing a
Morris 25 Special Coupé with, below, a
badge from a 1938 Morris 8 Series E.

Special bodies were fitted to many popular makes of car like this Austin 10 of 1934, to meet the demand by customers who could not afford a luxury model but wanted something different. This car was built by Patrick Motors of Selly Oak, Birmingham, who also bought chassis from Triumph and Wolseley for conversion with special coachwork.

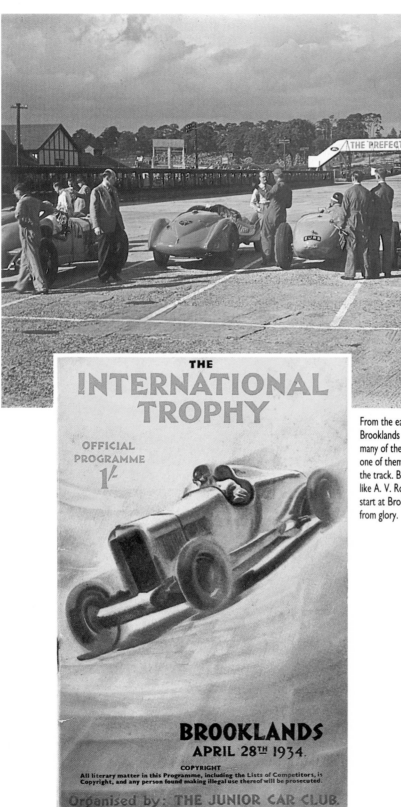

THE
INTERNATIONAL
TROPHY

OFFICIAL
PROGRAMME
1/-

BROOKLANDS
APRIL 28TH 1934.

COPYRIGHT
All literary matter in this Programme, including the Lists of Competitors, is
Copyright, and any person found making illegal use thereof will be prosecuted.

Organised by: THE JUNIOR CAR CLUB.

From the early years of the century, motor racing at Brooklands played an important part in the lives of many of the motor men. Hives of Rolls-Royce was one of them, amongst the first to exceed 100 mph on the track. Brooklands was also the home of early fliers like A. V. Roe and Sopwith. The top picture shows the start at Brooklands in 1939, after which it declined from glory.

going to be a big demand for a popularly priced car'. Some demand for such cars already existed, and was being met by very low-powered cars, cycle-cars and voiturettes. Taking these latter types in the total, the number of motor vehicles produced in England grew from about 11,000 in 1908 to 34,000 in 1913. However because most car-makers tried to design and build as much of the car as possible themselves, their prices tended to be comparatively high.

Both by inclination, and to some extent by the force of his personal circumstances, Morris chose the opposite course. He had managed to save £4000 by 1912 (equivalent of £200,000 today) from pre-tax profits of the garage and cycle business which averaged about £400 a year over the period 1904–9 and which increased to £1500, £2200 and £2600 in the next three years. In other words, Morris had managed to put away well over half of his pre-tax profits in the years 1906–12 inclusive. The rest of the money he used to buy the premises he had previously rented, as well as acquiring a new showroom for his car agencies. He now took the risk of going to suppliers – mostly in Coventry – and making arrangements to buy quantities of parts for a car which he would assemble on a large-scale basis. He decided to make virtually nothing in his own shops.

'To use the assembling method successfully' Morris wrote later, 'involves a detailed knowledge of scores of trades – a knowledge which is not readily available.' Morris had that knowledge – he had acquired it since he first began assembling bicycles of his own – and it centred on firms in the Midlands. In the areas of Birmingham and Coventry a large number of small component firms had sprung up, making parts for cycles, motorcycles and cars which were fed to a few central assembly points. He knew these people and their capacities, and as he began to put his new car together Morris would visit Coventry to find the components he wanted and negotiate prices. The most important firm was White and Poppe, set up in Coventry in 1899 by Peter Poppe (qv) a Norwegian engineer, and White, son of a director of Swifts, the big Coventry cycle-makers. By the time Morris came to them for his car components they had grown to be one of the largest British producers of proprietary engines; Morris knew Poppe well because he

had bought carburettors from him over the years.

He went to Poppe for the engine, the carburettor and the gear-box. He went to Wrigley of Birmingham for axles and other parts. The cylinder-blocks came from a firm in Rugby and the wheels from Sankey. The magnetos and sparking-plugs came from Bosch of Germany, presumably through their British agent. The coachbuilder who supplied the body was Raworth, an Oxford firm. He went to a small firm for the lights – they were called Lucas – and another small concern – Smiths – supplied the clock and instruments. Both were to become giant suppliers in the years ahead. Morris had to explain to all these suppliers that he was ordering components for a car which had not been sold to anyone, and was to be manufactured by a man who had not been in large-scale manufacturing before. He had in his own mind set a target output of some 1500 cars a year – some 10 per cent of the total UK market – but it says a good deal for Morris that suppliers were prepared to accept the risk of taking orders from a man who, while he was a figure of some substance in Oxford, had no large-scale manufacturing experience. He told them all to work on the basis of 50 units a week.

By 1912, his car was virtually ready and Morris booked space at the Olympia Motor Show. At the last minute, some key components were not delivered, and Morris had to go to the show stand with only blueprints to back up his sales pitch. To add to his difficulties, he was not, it seems, adept at reading blueprints although he was a brilliant mechanic. It is said that on the strength of the blueprints, Gordon Stewart the London dealer (later of Stewart and Ardern) ordered 400 cars and paid a deposit. This is not quite the whole story. After the show at Olympia was over, Stewart, who had premises off Bond Street, came down to Oxford where the prototype car was by now complete. Nuffield took him on a test drive towards London, but after only a short distance the universal joint snapped. When a new one was fitted, the car got as far as Dashwood Hill near High Wycombe before breaking down. It was the universal joint again. Stewart was however sufficiently impressed to confirm his order. Morris told him that he had asked Poppe to use phosphor-bronze for the joint but instead cast-iron had been chosen. Morris angrily telephoned Poppe, 'Are you all mad, you engineers at Coventry?' With its new universal joint, the Morris Oxford was born, and the first few hundred sold from the London showrooms of Stewart and Ardern. Morris's first car designs have been described as mongrels 'incorporating the best experience of other models' and it was like mongrels that they eventually sold – in their thousands. There were five versions of the Morris Oxford, in addition to the standard model. Two were called De Luxe and there was a commercial model – the cheapest by £2 – a delivery van and a sporting model. The chassis could be bought separately.

Setting up assembly on such a scale, Morris now needed more money and bigger premises. In 1912 he founded a new manufacturing business under his personal proprietorship. 'WRM Motors Ltd' and was the sole ordinary shareholder. Another £4000 in preference shares was subscribed by the Earl of Macclesfield. Morris's acquaintance with Lord Macclesfield had came about ten years earlier, when, as an undergraduate, he had collided with one of Morris's hire cars. He told Morris the other driver was responsible and threatened to prosecute. Morris said drily, 'I shouldn't if I were you. Do you know who the three passengers in that car were? The Chief Constables of Oxford, Buckinghamshire and Berkshire.' They remained on good terms after that and Macclesfield thought it was 'fun being in at the beginning' of a motor business.

Morris rented, and soon bought, a disused military training college at Temple Cowley which had been unoccupied for more than twenty years. By a coincidence, this had originally been the school where his father had been educated. Now it became his offices and assembly plant. It is not known exactly how much the first cars cost to build, but Morris's second car cost him £106 17s 5d in bought out parts, £5 10s 10d (i.e. 5 per cent) in labour and materials in the Morris works, and £1 10s overhead expenses – totalling £125 3s ex-works to the distributor, with about £11 gross profit to Morris. He had chosen Cowley, a straggling village near Oxford, for a base because labour in Oxford was cheap so he could aim to retail the Morris Oxford at £175. This compared with a basic price for the Model T Ford in England of £135. His car was not therefore the cheapest, but it was reliable and high-quality and easy to service.

Morris knew enough about the mechanical weaknesses of contemporary cars to be able to avoid building them into his own. He bought enclosed transmissions into which mud and water could not leak. He had the first steel wheels. His engine was easily accessible. The first Morris Oxford advertisements could proudly boast: 'Morris is the only light car which embodies the joint productions of the greatest British experts', by which he meant his suppliers. By the time war broke out, he had built 1300 cars and the demand for them was exceeding the capacity of some of his suppliers – particularly Poppe – to provide the hardware.

Another popular feature of the Oxford was that it was enclosed. At Whitsun 1914, Morris entered the only closed car in the London-Edinburgh trial, and emphasized the point by dressing himself and his passenger in lounge suits and straw hats in marked contrast to the padded clothing worn by other competitors. Although contemporaries said that Morris did not bother about his clothes, he seems to have had a salesman's sense of how to dress for the occasion and photographs of him in new model cars frequently show him wearing a bowler hat. He was a good-looking man who later developed a taste for wearing a blue blazer with brass buttons, and usually wore spats.

If Morris appears, on the whole, a rather dull dog, think what he did next. As his suppliers in Coventry were falling behind with deliveries, he decided that he would go for his components to the main source of high quality, low price goods – the United States. In April 1914, he set off across the Atlantic and within a few weeks had placed orders for engines with Continental Motor Manufacturing Company. The American firm needed more information, so Morris returned to England to see Poppe. While there he met an employee of Poppe's, the son of a Norwegian bishop, Hans Landstat, who was to work as a designer for Morris for the next 30 years. Together they went back to the States, Landstat travelling at his own expense, but doing drawings for Morris during the crossing. It has been said that the best-selling car of the 1920s, the Morris Cowley, was designed by Morris and Landstat on the SS *Mauritania* as they sailed to the United States.

Morris rented and then bought a disused military training college at Temple Cowley where he set up his first assembly works. This picture, taken in 1913, shows a line-up of cars in the road outside the building.

The Norwegian was an able designer, and the two men worked closely together with Morris taking a particular interest in what would now be called the styling of the bull-nosed Cowley. He said 'the radiator is the car's face; as soon as you see the radiator you know whether you are going to like the car or hate it.' Landstat provided Continental with the information they needed and also supplied Morris with drawings of the American components. After three weeks, Morris returned to England, but Landstat stayed on until the end of the year, paid by Continental, and also looking after Morris's interests. He joined Morris's firm in December 1914.

The first engines from America, which cost just under £18 each, were not delivered until September 1915, and the remainder of the 1500 which Morris had ordered followed slowly over the next four years, although some were lost at sea by enemy action. Slow as delivery was, these US-built parts enabled Morris not only to go on selling Oxfords, but also to develop a second car,

the Morris Cowley, which, had the war not intervened, would have been selling in 1915 at £165. Again, it would not have been the cheapest car on the market, but it was a reliable, highly quality model that offered great value for money. By 1914, Morris's sales totalled £182,000, but unlike his other British competitors, his capital requirements were extremely low. What is more he could already do something his competitors could not – turn out more than one car per man per year. Morris managed to continue to produce cars during the war, but in comparatively small numbers – 907 in 1914, 320 in 1915, 697 in 1916 and 126 in 1917. It is interesting to note that Morris's production in 1914 was nearly twice Austin's but Rover built 2000 cars and Ford UK well over 8000 model T's. In addition to the anticipated problems of wartime, Morris also hit an unexpected one – the imposition of the 33 per cent McKenna tariff on foreign cars to prevent the market being swamped with imports – specifically, Ford imports. This effectively wiped out all the cost advantages of his imported components from the States, and in 1915 he showed a loss of £1000 compared with a profit of £13,000 in 1914.

With car production edging down, Morris decided to try to enlist in the army, and when he was refused on the grounds that he would be more useful as a manufacturer, he decided to go into war production on a substantial scale. He obtained contracts to build a variety of munitions, including hand-grenades and bombs. He was introduced to Lloyd George, then Minister of Munitions, who gave him a contract for German-type mine-sinkers provided Morris would deliver the first in three weeks. Morris eventually employed 400 girls on this type of work and built, in addition to the bombs and grenades, some 50,000 of the mine-sinkers. Once more, he had found a magic circle of outside suppliers to provide the parts which he assembled at Cowley. The experience was invaluable. He later wrote, 'Before we could start making a simple mine-sinker, we had to prepare jigs to which the contracting firm could work.... We had to lay down standards, give jigs, drawings, and full particulars to each house; we had to test the raw materials supplied to these sub-contractors ... and we had to have an enormous central stock depot here [at Cowley] so that assembly could go ahead on a larger scale.' This experience was earned at government expense; the Ministry of Munitions paid Morris personally a salary of £1200 a year and the firm made substantial profits - £23,500 in 1916, £16,200 in 1917 and £18,900 in 1918. Of these sums, over £46,000 was re-invested in the firm - about £3,300,000 in today's money. Morris emerged from the war with a larger, better-equipped factory, a larger and better-trained workforce, sound finances, and a real grasp of the realities of mass-production assembly of bought-out parts. He also emerged with public recognition of his efforts - an OBE in 1917.

The strain of war production affected him, however, and in 1919 he had a bad nervous breakdown. The doctors sent him for six weeks to a German spa near Bonn and he made a complete recovery, although he was to remain something of a hypochondriac for the rest of his life.

Ford had gone ahead, during the war, to become the largest British producer - supplying two-thirds of the cars built in the country by 1920. If Morris had not been stopped by the war,

11.9 h.p. MORRIS-COWLEY SALOON

LUXURIOUS ECONOMY

THE fine, clean lines of the Morris-Cowley saloon command attention and respect wherever the car is seen. Its performance, too, leaves nothing to be desired. Yet its price insured for a year, is only £235. ★

Equipment, complete to the last detail, includes four wheel brakes, winding windows, adjustable seats, roof parcel net—in fact, everything that the practical motorist requires.

MORRIS

*buy British —
and be Proud of it.*

Morris   Motors   Ltd.,   Cowley,   Oxford.

The rather sophisticated advertisement in *The Autocar* in 1926 contrasts with the earlier crude wit of the cartoon.

he would have challenged Ford with his Oxford and Cowley models in 1915. As it was, he spent the war refining manufacture of the two cars in a small section of the factory, cushioned by the profits from his arms production. At the war's end he was still a small car producer, but he was getting ready to challenge Ford and by 1924 he would become Britain's biggest producer of cars. For the moment, limited by lack of components, he could only supply 198 cars in 1918 and 360 in 1919. By 1920 he had begun to get his suppliers on tap once more; output reached almost 2000 cars in 1920 and just over 3000 in 1921. This was in a period when British car production as a whole fell by a third. Morris had still not changed his works to Ford-type assembly methods, although he was developing in that direction. In 1913, his workspeople had moved along the line of laid-out parts and built up a chassis in batches. Now, the work-people stayed at one station on a line, and the chassis, as soon as it had wheels on, moved from station to station: Morris had evolved the basis of an assembly line.

In 1919 he also decided to cease production of the original small car and concentrate on the 11.9 hp Cowley and the more expensive Oxford. These 'Bullnose' models were destined to be the best-selling cars of the 1920s. His reputation for producing sound cars had grown, and customers liked to know that Morris cars were sold 'with all the necessary fitments' – unlike the majority of cars which were a basic body without tyres, tools, electrics, windscreen, lamps etc. Morris cars were admired by the middle-class who had begun to

'You have a winner there, Morris. All it needs is a distinctive shaped nose!'

feel that owning a reliable, quality and moderately priced car was the thing to do.

Morris settled down seriously to master the sub-contracting of parts and by 1923 he was employing over 200 suppliers. He wrote, 'Our method of using outside services is ... more thorough than is usual. To begin with, we buy our own raw material for the job; we fix up contracts possibly with four or five firms up and down the country, to maintain that supply of raw material for us. We personally inspect the raw material before it is delivered to contractors; we settle the method of machining; we supply guages and in many cases we design the actual fixtures.... The firms working for us simply undertake the machining .... [Their] financial liability is

limited.' Morris did much of this work himself and became a skilful 'buyer and chaser of supplies'. As a result many of the firms were run by Morris in all but name. In a few cases he did actually set up in business himself. For instance in 1919 he established a small iron foundry at Cowley to make cylinder-block castings. 'I only buy a concern,' he said, 'when they tell me they cannot produce enough of the article in question for our programme.' Continental had stopped making his engines after the war, so Morris took his drawings back and gave them to the Coventry-based branch of the French Hotchkiss firm. When they, in turn, could not keep up with his requirements, Morris bought them out for nearly £350,000 in 1923, changing the name to Morris Engines Ltd. He was soon producing 600 engines a week instead of the 300 the original owners had said was their maximum.

Morris also set about a financial reorganisation of his own firm. In 1919 he had put WRM Motors Ltd into liquidation and formed Morris Motors. This came about because he found that he had signed a document without reading it properly which gave distribution of his cars in England to a single dealer. The only way out of this was to close down WRM Motors and to pay compensation. Morris was then able to set up a balanced distribution system. Shortly afterwards, he fell out with Lord Macclesfield, his early backer. Their relations had deteriorated and when the Earl criticised Morris in front of his employees, Morris's pride was hurt and he retaliated by sending Macclesfield a cheque for the £25,000 he had invested. The two men never spoke again. In fact, Morris had been in considerable financial trouble in October 1920 when his enthusiasm for using outside suppliers led him to conclude a contract with Hotchkiss for 40,000 engines and, in the process, to run up liabilities of £137,000. He was saved from ruin by Arthur Gillett, a remarkable Oxford banker who had financed Morris until his bank had been taken over by Barclays. Gillett himself gave guarantees of £40,000 and a similar arrangement was made by Macclesfield. Morris's later attitude to the Earl did not perhaps reflect the debt he owed him for earlier generosity.

Morris's skill in buying components from outside suppliers has usually been described as the keystone to his success. That is only part of the story. True he pressed his suppliers mercilessly, in one case cutting the cost of a component by nearly half. 'People thought I was mean,' he said. 'I was always in the works cutting and saving expenses wherever it could be done.' But when the post-war slump hit all the manufacturers in 1921, Nuffield initially suffered just as badly as the competition. His overdraft rose to over £84,000 and Morris thought of abandoning the British market and setting up again in Australia. He was saved by his willingness to take risks. Because he knew he could cut costs, he alone in the industry decided to respond to the slump by cutting prices. He had re-introduced the Oxford and slashed the price of this and the Cowley by about £100. He believed that this might enable him to sell twice as many cars. Within three weeks, he had sold all his completed cars and was running out of supplies.

He seems to have found the savings above all by cutting the cost of the wooden car bodies, which the suppliers were originally making one by one. His own profit remained about £50 a car. Then, in October, sales fell again. Against the advice of his senior people, Morris decided to cut prices once more, before the Motor Show. His competitors failed to follow him and Morris sold many more cars. In 1922 he made 7000 cars, and although the prices were down, he was careful to insist that 'the new prices have not been obtained at the cost of quality'. He announced this in the press, adding that 'nothing but the finest material is used in the production of Morris cars'. Before 1922, stylistic changes and technical features had dictated demand, but, led by Morris, the popular makes now fought each other on price. Some makes lost market share rapidly. Rover, for example, priced their 12 hp car two or three times higher than the Morris equivalent and their sales were halved between 1922 and 1928. By contrast, Morris sales went from 20,000 in 1923 to 32,000 in 1924 and 55,000 in 1925 and reached a peak of 63,000 in 1929. In the 12–15 hp category Morris achieved a virtual monopoly. He knew that he could beat many of his competitors on price because they did not understand its importance. 'The one object in life of many makers seems to be to make the thing the public cannot buy,' he said. 'The one object of my life has been to make the thing they can buy.'

Now that he was selling so many cars, Mor-

Bull-nose Morris Cowleys were coming out of the factory in their hundreds when this picture of the paint shop was taken in 1925. Large scale advertising, an example of which is on the previous page, was employed under the direction of Miles Thomas who joined Morris from *The Motor* in 1923.

ris had to take a hand in building up his distributorship, just as he had been forced to take on the management of his suppliers. 'The problem of our sales side,' he wrote, 'is educating the retailer ... who has got into the habit of thinking of car sales in small numbers.' He changed all that. He also monitored every sale made by the distributors to find out if they were giving more than his recommended discount. 'When we have traced the dealer responsible, we insist on the payment of the difference between the price at which the car was sold and the list price.... Such a dealer gets squeezed out [and] there can be no wonder.' By such methods Morris made sure that his dealers realised the realities of pricing as he did.

One technique he employed was large scale advertising, taking on a promotional expert, Miles Thomas (qv) who joined the staff in 1923. This brought in the potential customers. To keep them happy once they had purchased the car, Morris came out with a unique idea for after-sales service. This was for all his dealers to charge a standard rate for repairs. Morris was one of the first manufacturers in the Midlands

to establish a service depot in London and one of the first to set up a nationwide repair service. He also pioneered hire purchase for his major period of expansion after 1923; three years later half his cars sold were by hire purchase.

Up to 1928, Morris's success had been built up on the two cars first developed about 15 years earlier. The Cowley was the bigger seller of the two. He tried to introduce other models but they were not a success. One was intended for Australia where Morris had great hopes of making big export sales. A similar attempt was made in the French market. Morris set up a company there and, when this failed to sell his cars, he bought an established motor firm; probably because he never really understood the character of the French customer, this too was a failure and he eventually pulled out of the market with losses of £150,000. He never forgave the French for his defeat and it is said that thereafter he would never shake hands with a Frenchman if he could help it. Overall, a very small proportion of his cars - well under ten per cent - were going for export in the later 1920s, keen as he was to ex-

pand in that direction.

Something must be said about Nuffield's attitude to his employees. Today it would certainly be called paternalistic. 'I remember he always gave us a chicken at Christmas,' said a female employee. In return they gave him of their best, increasing productivity year by year. The size of the Cowley workforce did not increase substantially between 1924 and 1934 yet car production nearly doubled and in 1935 was three times the 1924 output. Morris pioneered many employees' amenities such as holidays with pay, profit-sharing, sports clubs and medical centres. He also believed he should pay reasonable wages, claiming 'no factory can turn out a cheap car on low wages.... A low wage is the most expensive method of producing.' It is claimed that Morris was 'a hero to his men'. Even Miles Thomas, who was capable of being objective, said, 'We all worshipped the ground W. R. Morris walked on.' There were, however, no unions at Cowley before the war.

Morris claimed that the secret of high output was good management. He said bad management 'has the same effect as sand in the bearings of a machine. I have proved on many occasions that by removing someone from the top or the bottom the sand has been removed and production has gone up in consequence'. All the same, he did not seem to have much faith in his managers, always retaining the rights of the absolute monarch or, as he was described, the 'autocratic despot'. In his 1926 reorganisation he insisted on agreement that: 'Mr W. R. Morris has exclusive power so long as he is managing-director to appoint deputy managing-directors, general managers, sales managers ... etc, etc, or any other administrative or executive officer and to fix their remuneration.' This also gave him the right to terminate appointments, and Morris seems not to have had too many qualms about sackings. There is a story that when he decided to register his disapproval with Miles Thomas who had, against Morris's moral principles, married his secretary, he did so by removing all furniture from his office so that Thomas returned from the honeymoon to an empty space. Thomas does not mention this story in his autobiography so perhaps it is untrue. He does mention that, when he left Morris, his name was unscrewed from the door before he left the building. There was a very rapid turnover of the top people at Morris factories, particularly during the crisis of the early 1930s and in the immediate post-war years. All in all, Morris theories about good management does not seem to have had a great deal in common with his practice.

As the 1930s approached, it was clear that the market for the 10–15 hp cars in which Morris predominated was diminishing (it nearly halved in the last three years of the decade) and that the growth area was the 'baby' car segment in which Austin was so successful. Austins were now taking a third of the total market. Despite the fact that Morris himself thought that the bigger American-type cars would eventually take the lead in Britain, and were what the export markets wanted, he bowed to consumer demand, and produced an 8 hp Morris Minor. The story goes that Morris called in 'Pop' Landstat and ordered him to design a car costing £100, capable of a speed of 100 mph and able to achieve 100 mpg. Specially tuned and stripped down, the Morris Minor somehow achieved the required performance. But Morris had got the price wrong – people did not want their neighbours to know the price of their car, so it was put up to £125.

Morris was now the largest producer of cars not only in Britain but in Europe, and the question was, could he keep his lead? In 1926 he had gone public and his new shareholders had been delighted with his profitable growth, much of which went into reserves totalling several millions over the years. In addition, his bank in Oxford was generous with overdraft facilities. According to Miles Thomas, Morris also pressed his suppliers to give him credit and says in effect 'he was relying on the supplier's money to finance his business'. He appears, too, to have been adept in handling his tax arrangements in a way which reduced his supertax payments. In 1929, a case against him by the Inland Revenue was dropped because the Attorney-General thought that with the ingenuity Morris possessed 'he may be able to develop for this country a very important market which we should all like to see, and which will do, if it is developed, a great deal to assist in the terrible problem of unemployment'.

Morris now had the highest profits and the largest assets of any firm in the industry. He controlled ten separate businesses and two sub-

sidiaries and he employed 10,000 people. Nevertheless, as he himself wrote, it was the 'object all my life ... not to make money for myself, but, so far as I have been able to do so, to assist in the development of British manufacturers and industry'. On another occasion, he said, 'The main object of my life has been to manufacture a car which could be sold at a price at which the ordinary man in the street could buy it.' This apparent altruism sprung partly from his own simple tastes and partly from the fact that he was childless so had no-one to whom to leave his business. 'I have more money than any man can possibly want,' he is supposed to have said, 'and for what it is worth I have a title, but all that I have dies when I die. That is my personal tragedy.' Throughout the years he sought to find substitute 'sons' to succeed him.

In the early 1920s, when he had taken over the body-building business in Oxford, he had put Pratt, its owner, into the Morris business, calling him 'deputy governing director'. When Pratt died in 1924 at the early age of 44, Morris became so upset that he was taken ill (Miles Thomas said he 'suffered greatly'). He did not succeed in finding another 'substitute son' until Leonard Lord came into the business in the 1930s.

Up to this time, Morris had been dedicated to the expansion of his business and had led what some might call a narrow life. Now that he had reached a pinnacle of success he blossomed out into a man who both desired to be seen to be someone of power and influence and someone who could use that power to do good for others. Even the *Economist*, which did not like him very much, admitted that he was 'a power in the land' and Morris intended to use that power for good. In 1929 he was given a baronetcy for his work for the industry of which he had become a leading spokesman. In his own city, Oxford, the university made him an Hon D.C.L.

He had arrived. He had lived in the 'manor house' at Cowley until he moved to an even grander establishment at Nuffield. In 1927/8 he started taking a series of long sea cruises which he continued every year except during the war. These were 'luxury' cruises and he enjoyed them because he felt they gave him 'valued relief' from the pressures of business. He did not mind spending money on them, nor on other luxuries, although he actively promoted the myth that his basic living expenses seldom exceeded £40 a week. 'Can you use more than one toothbrush or eat more than one meal at a time?' he asked. For years he used to smoke the cheapest brand of cigarettes or roll his own, but this was because he could not be bothered to waste time finding a supplier of better ones (when he did so, he smoked expensive cigarettes thereafter). Thomas also says that he became a sporadic drinker. 'Sometimes he was on the water wagon or other times the gin and vermouth bottle were within easy reach of his office from anytime after eleven o'clock in the morning'. In the early 1920's he took up golf. He enquired through friends if he would be welcome as a member of the famous Huntercombe Club between Oxford and Henley, but the answer came back that 'motor agents were not regarded as suitable members'. By 1924 he had achieved sufficient emminence to become a member and in 1926 when the club was in hard times and put up for sale, he bought it. Nevertheless there was something a little cheerless about his life at home. For example he never slept a whole night long, and, because he was so frequently awake, found a solution in having two bedrooms. When he woke up in one of them he would read or write for a while and then move on to the second room. While he was snatching an hour's sleep there, an attendant would make the first bed again ready for his return. This swapping of beds went on all night.

His wife did not help to add quality to his life. Miles Thomas says she played a big part in their existence at this period. He claims she had been in business herself (most reports say she was a teacher) on the sales staff of a big Oxford draper's store. She kept in contact with the people in the works, where her brother was transport manager and reported back to Morris the name of any employee guilty of a social misdemeanor. 'Frugality was the keynote of her existence', making petty savings on food and on gifts to other. This matched Morris's own desire for economy. He was even mean about the use of soap in the washrooms at the factory saying, 'I can't understand people not using up soap to the last bit. It makes me mad.'

This desire to control expenditure in every aspect was related to his wish to retain direct personal control. 'All the directors are still under one hat,' he wrote, meaning his own head. He depended on personal contact for analysing information, apart from a weekly sheet of paper setting out the basic financial information on one side of it. Miles Thomas said, 'He was no conventional administrator. Not for him the chairman's seat at the top of the boardroom table, listening to arguments based on papers.... He was much better at explaining his thoughts and impressions face to face with one executive only.' Much of the decision making therefore took place at meetings at which he was not present. 'We had to sit without the boss around the management table,' according to Thomas, 'laying plans in the light of what we thought he was thinking.' Thomas also said that on the occasions when Morris was present he could only 'give vent to a considerable amount of negative thinking'.

His new-found role as industry spokesman pleased him greatly. He liked speaking at official functions both inside and outside the motor industry, particularly if the speeches were impromptu. He kept his talks brief-'capable of being put in a telegram without great expense' as he trenchantly put it. He also enjoyed, as most people do, meeting the mighty, when visiting politicians, prime ministers and even royalty came to Cowley to see how motor cars should be made.

Morris himself began to dabble in politics in the 1920s. He opposed the repeal of the McKenna Duties arrangements. These protected the industry against foreign car imports and the Labour Chancellor of the Exchequer accused Morris of waging a 'ramping, raging, lying campaign'. He was fervently pro-British and in 1927 was able to announce with pride that his cars no longer contained any American parts. The firm's slogan became 'Buy British and Be Proud of it'. According to Thomas he claimed that 'every penny spent on materials and labour ... helps to swell the volume of British trade and employment.... This is something on which we can reflect with a feeling of patriotic pride'. This may have been enlightened self-interest, but Morris put his money where his mouth was by becoming a founder of what became the League of Industry – a pressure group of which he was the first president. He also financed Oswald Mosley's New Party with £50,000 although he took no part in its activities. He did however observe, 'I could have stopped Hitler if only he had spoken

English.'

Morris's public pronouncements give the impression that his factories were humming away throughout the 1920s and 1930s in an unbroken rhythm of success. This was not entirely the case. For example in 1924, when the Labour government abolished the McKenna Act, he dismissed over 1300 men, a quarter of the Cowley workforce, and cut the working week from 54 hours to 44 hours, with a consequent reduction in their pay. Times were often hard for the Cowley employees, many of whom would cycle daily 12 miles or more from outlying areas to reach the factory by 8am. During one of these bad times at the factory, Morris was on one of his overseas cruises to Australia when hundreds of men had been stood off from work in his absence. Such was their faith in his ability to get the factory going again that they found out the time of his return and silently lined the route he would drive to his house. 'They didn't shout or anything; they just lined the road just before he got to his house.... Within three weeks those men were back at work.'

Whether it was because of his growing outside interests or merely the pressure of competition, the Morris empire did not expand in the 1930s as it had in the 20s. It grew, of course, but more slowly and less profitably. Instead of competing against a number of small manufacturers, Morris was in the thirties up against the other members of the Big Six. In 1928 he had over half their total production but by 1933 it was down to 27 per cent, and he had been overtaken by Austin. Both Ford UK and General Motors (Vauxhall) were providing him with significant competition and their type of cars were directly competitive with his models. The price 'lead' which Morris had established began to disappear as even he could not find it within his power to reduce prices indefinitely. Then again, the public began to demand a variety of models, whereas Morris's earlier policy had been to stick to two basic types. Now he blossomed out into a variety of cars and annual changes of model.

His decline was not, like the decline of empires, inevitable, but even with the benefit of hindsight it is not easy to pinpoint what Morris could have done to regain his former position. He had turned down a suggestion made in 1924 by Docker (qv) of Vickers that he should merge his firm with Austin and Wolseley, both of which were in financial trouble at the time. The proposal was that Morris would have been in virtual command of the enlarged empire. From his early experience, Morris was reluctant to become involved in partnerships of any kind, making the excuse that he had 'a firm aversion of being responsible for other people's money' and that he thought the merged organisation would be so big and difficult to control that 'it might strangle itself'. Whether an early merger would have saved Morris from his later decline must be a matter for conjecture. There are several reports that he turned down American offers to buy the business.

Two years later he bought Wolseley, partly to even up an old score. In 1908 he had gone to visit the big Wolseley firm, in his capacity as a garage owner in Oxford, to ask for their agency. The executive with whom he had an appointment refused to see him. Now Morris was bidding against Austin and the Americans for the firm. Austin's finance man asked him how far he was prepared to go. 'I am going just a bit further than you,' was his reply. This turned out to be £730,000, paid out of his own funds. He celebrated the event by giving a tea party in Coventry, saying, 'This is the most thrilling hour of my life.' Within two years he had recovered the whole of the purchase price.

Morris used the early 1930s as a breathing space to reorganise. Like many proprietors before and since, he saw the solution to his problems to be a management shake-up. He recruited Leonard Lord (qv) and moved some senior people like Miles Thomas to Wolseley and to the Morris Commercial company he had set up. Several other old hands left the company altogether after disagreements with Morris. Once the new management under Lord had been established, about 1935, Morris ended his close control of the day-to-day affairs of the firm. From now on, he spent more time in travel, various public activities, charity work and in the higher realms of policy – such as whether to enter the aircraft industry. By now, too, he was willing to recognise that his empire had outgrown the original conception of assembling other people's manufactures. He now made his own engines, bodies, radiators and carburettors.

He gave Lord £300,000 and instructed him to

Morris began to release his hold on the business in some senses in the
1930's when he felt he could leave much of the management to Leonard
Lord. But the two men fell out and Lord eventually went to Austin.

rationalise the business. All components of one kind were to be manufactured in one factory – all engines at Morris Engines, etc. Morris had already replaced his existing production methods by a full conveyor-belt and moving assembly-line *à la* Detroit. He did not, however, employ the term 'mass-production' (Morris called it mess production) because he thought it ran counter to a quality product. By 1934, Morris had the largest and technically most advanced factory not only in Britain but in Europe with a capacity of 100,000 units a year, greater than the total production in Germany and two-thirds of French output.

From 1935 Morris set about another financial reorganisation, and over the next 15 years he relinquished almost all his vast personal holdings in the company he had formed, mainly by issuing shares to the public. By the issue of shares in Morris Motors in 1936 he himself acquired something like £12m. His aim was to use his personal funds for charitable work. In all he gave away well over £25 million, much of it for medical work. It has been said that this was not entirely altruistic as Morris, despite constant good health, was a victim of fear of disease. Throughout all his working life he had protested that he was a sick man, although he was rarely absent from the office for that reason.

The re-organisation was a success. Under the direction of Leonard Lord, a new product policy was also devised. Morris once again began the climb back to leadership of the industry. His team designed a new car, the Morris 8, that was much superior to the ill-fated Minor, and instantly became popular. Within four years he had sold 200,000 and it became the best-selling car in the years up to 1940. He now produced a new range of cars from 8 hp to 25 hp (including MG and Wolseley and, from 1938, Riley) but many of the chassis and engines were standard and in reality the cars differed only in styling. They all incorporated the latest technical developments like hydraulic brakes and safety glass. Morris also set about expanding exports, making long tours abroad to stir up business. Exports had only accounted for 12 per cent of output in 1933 (only a little over 3000 cars) but between 1934 and 1939 he sold well over 100,000 cars abroad, or nearly one-third of the cars exported from the UK. By 1939 he had regained his position as leader of the industry and on 22nd May he rolled out his one millionth Morris car from Cowley.

In the previous year he had been granted his peerage and was now Viscount Nuffield of Nuffield in the County of Oxford. He celebrated by re-organising the firm once again under the name of Nuffield organisation.

An interesting insight into his way of working at this stage of his career is his attempt to get into aircraft. In the early thirties he had realised that if the war came there would be a shortage of aero-engines, just as there had been in the first war. The Air Ministry channelled its orders through four firms – Rolls, Napier, Bristol and Siddeley – who formed, in effect, a ring. Nuffield decided to join. With his own money (i.e. not with the firm's) he formed Wolseley Aero-Engines Ltd with a factory in Coventry. He 'head-hunted' one of the country's few leading designers and set about developing an engine. Having spent three years in the attempt, somewhat fruitlessly, Morris wrote to Lord Swinton at the Air Ministry asking for an interview. There was some months' delay before they actually met, and Morris believed he had been snubbed. At the meeting, which took place in November 1935, the Air Ministry declined to support his engine-building activities, and Morris, who was exceedingly touchy, is said to have left the room with the words, 'God help you in case of war.' Swinton's attitude was that there was no room for Morris if the Ministry was to support the four established firms. Morris made a fuss about what he considered to be a personal rejection and later, in the House of Lords, Swinton apologised 'if he had been unintentionally discourteous'. By 1935–6 a scheme had been formulated for the motor industry to build 'shadow' factories to produce Bristol aero-engines. The Air Ministry invited Morris to join. He did so in the belief that at last he would be asked to build aero-engines. Instead, an arrangement was made for each of the motor firms to build a part of an engine, and the seven sub-assemblies so built would be brought together for final assembly in one or two factories. Nuffield declined to build sub-assemblies. Later, Lord told the Air Ministry that the firm would after all join the other motor men in the 'shadow' scheme, but within two or three days Morris overruled him. This on-off process went on for some time, and the men at the Ministry called Morris's conduct 'disgraceful'.

In the middle of this muddle, Morris proposed to the Ministry that as he had already spent £100,000 trying to develop an engine at Wolseley, the Air Ministry should now subsidise its further development. They declined. He then proposed to build American Pratt & Whitney engines in England. Again, the Ministry declined. The latter in turn suggested that Morris might build an engine designed by the aircraft manufacturer, Richard Fairey, but nothing came of it. Possibly Morris's objection to the shadow scheme was aggravated by the fact that it was run by a committee of motor men, and Morris did not like committees, particularly as the chairman of this particular one was his old competitor, Lord Austin. Eventually, after Swinton left the Air Ministry, his successor, Kingsley Wood, made peace with Morris by inviting him to a meeting followed by lunch at 10 Downing Street. Morris was asked to build a new factory and became a producer of aero-engines, aircraft and tanks. The new aircraft factory, however, turned sour on Nuffield. He built it at Castle Bromwich, Birmingham, where it was intended to produce 70 per cent of all the Spitfires made. When Beaverbrook came into the new Ministry of Aircraft production in 1940 he discovered that only a handful of Spitfires had come out of the new factory. He at once phoned Nuffield direct, and attacked him. Nuffield said, 'If things are not going well, perhaps you'd like to get someone else to run my factory?' Beaverbrook's reply was, 'That's a mighty generous offer. I will.' The factory was handed over to Vickers. Morris's biographer says that 'the incident left a wound on his soul that never quite healed', and it must

The huge Castle Bromwich shadow factory full of Spitfires in 1940 was taken away from Morris's management by Lord Beaverbrook, a blow to the motor man's prestige which he never forgot. Vickers, the aviation firm, took it over.

have been ignominious to be left to build the little wooden Tiger Moth trainer instead of the glamorous Spitfire fighter.

By this time he was somewhat vague about what was happening in the business, and for the first time others noticed that he could no longer grasp detail. Because of his own lack of formal education, Morris had never recruited a professionally-trained management team, nor provided them with up-to-date research facilities. Even after the war, his research director complained, 'We had to do all our development thinking in pubs, at dinners and in washrooms.' Morris also drove his hard-pressed managers much too hard. For example in November 1939 when he joined the Air Ministry as Director-General of Repair Maintenance, responsible for repairing all damaged aircraft, he took with him, as deputy, Oliver Bowden, the original managing-director at Wolseley. Bowden took the full load, having already

been put in charge of the Castle Bromwich factory. Bowden died in March 1940, and someone at the funeral who saw that Morris was in tears said to him, 'Why cry? Why cry when you killed him. You worked the poor bugger to death.' Morris resigned from his Air Ministry job after Bowden's death and the row with Beaverbrook.

After the war, the Nuffield Organisation tried to adjust itself to the peacetime demand for cars. Morris was still the nominal head – Lord had left in a huff in 1936 – but in fact the leadership was taken over with increasing reluctance by Miles Thomas. Morris himself still thought in terms of pre-war car design, with the result that he was quickly overtaken by Austin. He blamed his managers and they blamed him. Thomas wrote afterwards, 'I should have been deaf as well as blind if I could not have seen that all was not well between the chairman and myself.' And inevitably Thomas left, like so many others.

Lord Nuffield, as he had then become, liked this picture showing him in a 'statesmanlike' role. He claimed he 'could have talked to Hitler'.

Peter August Poppe
1870–19

P oppe, a Norwegian, first met Alfed James White, son of one of the directors of the Singer cycle company, when the latter was visiting the Steyr Werke in Austria. The two men became friends, Poppe's engineering skills being complemented by White's financial and commerical acumen. The White family provided most of the money for the firm which the two men set up in Coventry in 1899.

Poppe was friendly with William Morris from the early days, and there is a story that when Morris was visiting his works early one morning the ɩmployees persuaded him to talk to Poppe about an engineering problem because they felt he could (handle) Poppe far better than they could. Poppe also introduced Morris to his employee Landstat who made one, and perhaps two, trans-Atlantic crossings with Morris during which they virtually designed the Cowley car.

White and Poppe concentrated on building light engines and, later, carburettors. They rapidly gained a reputation for the precision of Poppe's workmanship. The part they played in the standardisation of parts, with the consequent reduction in the cost of a petrol-driven engine, was significant for may car firms and particularly for Morris (qv). With the outbreak of war in 1914, Armstrong, Whitworths gave them an order for 10,000 fuse bodies and they switched over to arms production for the duration of the war. By its end they controlled not only their own factory, but a huge newly-constructed National Filling Factory in Holbrook Lane and a new detonator factory. In December 1919, White, who had financial control of the White and Poppe concern, sold out to the rapidly expanding Dennis Brothers. Poppe stayed on for two years, but then resigned and joined Rover as their chief engineer, acting also as consultant to Maudslay. His three sons were all connected with the motor industry and one, Olaf, became works manager and a director of Rover. In 1925, Poppe designed the 14/45 which proved a costly failure. Rover was not a happy firm and one of the many men brought in from outside to try to save it, Colonel Searle, gave Poppe the sack in 1930 and arranged for Olaf, the son, to be given six months' notice.

By 1947, the Nuffield Organisation's share was down to one-sixth of total British production – half the share they had held in 1939. Profitability fell far below the competition. People began to ask if there should not be a change at the top – was it not time for Morris to go? There were obvious inefficiencies – for example Morris was spending over £2 million a year transporting components round their group whereas Ford in highly integrated Dagenham spent virtually nothing. In the late forties there were major changes in management. Nine long-serving directors were sacked or resigned and Miles Thomas went off to become head of BOAC (now British Airways). Behind the scenes various proposals were made for a merger with Austin and Morris, and eventually William Morris agreed that negotiations could be held with Lord, now controller of Austin's. The merger took place in January 1952 and Morris retired for good to his estate at Nuffield in 1954. It was timely – some might say too late. As time went by, he had become more dogmatic and inflexible. Or had he just remained the same, and the world changed round him? His reign had lasted forty years. Miles Thomas wrote an apt epitaph – 'His imagination was fired with thoughts of greatness.'

Note: The name William Morris has been used throughout for simplicity. Morris was made a Baronet in 1929, a Baron in 1934 and a Viscount in 1938.

Miles (William) Thomas
1897-1980

Like Leonard Lord, Morris and a number of other senior Nuffield people, Miles Thomas had a powerful relationship with his mother which in his case contained 'a fierce possessive jealousy, that at times literally reached screaming point'. His father, a retired furniture dealer, died a year after he was born. The family money had been invested in property and Thomas's mother lived off the rents. Following a period at the local grammar school where he edited the school magazine, Thomas went to Bromsgrove which he describes as 'a redbrick Midlands public school'. He was given his first motorcycle in 1912 and at that time started writing articles for the technical motoring journals at a guinea a time. His mother wanted him to go into a 'respectable' profession but instead, encouraged by his headmaster, he took an apprenticeship in an engineering firm in Birmingham. Under age, in 1914, he joined the Motor Machine Gun Corps and was sent to East Africa. He learnt to fly in Egypt and was transferred to the Royal Flying Corps, becoming a stunt pilot and an instructor. Towards the end of the war he was posted to Mesopotomia where he saw active service.

After the war he was offered a job on the *Motor* magazine although he had no journalistic experience and only a general knowledge of cars. In the course of this journalistic career he came across William Morris, and impressed him with his commonsense. 'One dull afternoon in September 1923, he telephoned to enquire when I could join him,' wrote Thomas in his memoirs. His initial job was to control the Morris publicity and promotion machine although not, at first, the advertising. He married Hylda Church, Morris's personal secretary, and there is a story that this caused strained relations with his boss who, while the two newly-weds were on honeymoon, removed all the furniture from Thomas's office as a sign of his displeasure.

He rose to play a major role in the Morris hierarchy which suffered a temporary setback when Lord joined the firm. After Lord left, he regained his former glory and, in 1940 when Oliver Bowden died, Nuffield announced that he

The young Miles Thomas was a rising star in the Morris empire and some believe that if he had not fallen out with its leader, Thomas might have saved it from merger.

was to be vice-chairman and managing-director at £10,000 a year. 'Nuffield characteristically said that he was going to "leave it all" to me ... but that he "would like to know what was going on".' Thomas's technique was 'to see Nuffield every Tuesday morning between half past eleven and a quarter to one. The rest of the week I was travelling round factories or working from my own offices at Cowley or Birmingham.'

Thomas describes, no doubt in rather exaggerated terms, the relative parts played by himself and Nuffield in 1945/6 in the development of the famous Morris Minor. 'Will Oak, Alec Issigonis and a couple of all-round mechanics set about translating the sketches for our small saloon car into an actual prototype. ... The Morris Mosquito, as we first thought of calling it, had a terrific performance, particularly with the "export" engine. But it was obviously too narrow, so we decided to widen it by about five inches, simply cutting the prototype in half lengthwise with a hacksaw and welding in a gusset.' Later he describes how they concluded, 'What easier than to take the engine of the Morris 8, slightly increase its capacity, and fit it into the monocoque steel body-cum-chassis? We had a new model absolutely ready for the market and not requiring long periods of engine testing. What was more, the car had a delightfully balanced performance and I was all for putting it on the market as soon as the parts for the Morris 8 that we had on hand, and which had been coming through suppliers' pipelines when war broke out, had been absorbed. But Lord Nuffield was in no mood for change. His argument was that we had more orders for the Morris 8 than we could cope with, so what was the point of putting ... the Morris Minor on the market? ... I pleaded that the [prewar] Morris 8 was rapidly becoming out of date, the Morris Minor would give us a commanding lead. He was adamant. The frustration left a sour taste in my mouth.'

It was at this point that Payton of Austin invited Thomas to lunch at Longbridge and asked him to join him and Lord at Longbridge (Payton was about to leave the firm but if he knew this he did not tell Thomas). Despite Thomas's 'sour' feelings about Nuffield, he declined the offer. Early in 1946 Nuffield told him that, the war over, 'I'm going to step completely aside and leave the running of the whole business to you and the younger men. From now on the whole responsibility is yours.' Despite this assurance, there were rows, particularly when Thomas signed the Report and Accounts when Nuffield was away in South Africa. There was further friction when Thomas, who seems always to have been ambitious for public office, accepted a part-time appointment with the Colonial Development Corporation, which meant that he sometimes went abroad on their behalf. The 'unhappy atmosphere at the executive top permeated not only the board, but the staff.' As for Miles Thomas, he wrote in his autobiography, '... all was not well between the chairman and myself. At one of our regular meetings, in November 1947, I told him that I did not think we were getting on as well together in double-harness as we used to, and asked what was the matter? He crossed one knee over the other, waggled his foot – a sure sign of tension – and said, "I suppose you want your freedom?"' Thomas went on to become chairman of BOAC and, in the UK, of Monsanto Chemicals.

It has been said that had Thomas remained at Morris the fortunes of the company might have been very different following the merger with BMC which, in the absence of any strong personality such as his, became a virtual takeover by the Austin people.

Leonard Lord
1896–1967

'Perhaps the outstanding figure in the British motor industry by the 1930s' is how Lord is described, although his tough manner did not make him one of the most popular. He was born in Coventry and went to school there, obtaining a scholarship place at Coventry's old established public school, Bablake's (John Egan of Jaguar later did the same). On leaving school Lord went to Courtaulds as a draughtsman. He was inordinately ambitious and cheeky. One of the top men at Courtaulds asked him what he was going to do when he grew up. 'Sit in your chair,' he said. After working at Courtaulds, Lord was briefly apprenticed at Vickers at 4s. 6d. a week.

During World War I, Lord joined the Coventry Ordnance factory where one of the managers was Carl Englebach (qv), later to work for Austin. In the evenings he taught at the local technical college, it is said in order to have an extra income to buy little luxuries for his mother, to whom he was devoted. His temper was getting him into trouble even at that age, and he was severely criticised for throwing a wooden blackboard scrubber at a pupil who got on his nerves. Lord then moved to Daimler and finally, in 1920, to Hotchkiss, the Coventry subsidiary if the French engine builders, who were making engines for Morris. Lord did good work at Hotchkiss; when Morris bought the company in 1923 he came to his attention and both Morris and Frank Woollard (qv) kept an eye on the young man. Woollard was a pioneer of flow-production methods and machinery on the American style and Lord's *forté* was production. So Lord was moved from the drawing office to help in the reorganisation of Wolseley, acquired by Morris in 1929. Although Lord was still not 30 years old, his technical and managerial potential had now been recognised.

At Wolseley, Lord was partly responsible for the new engine developments which culminated in the engine for the Morris Minor. He did so well that Morris moved him to Cowley where he soon had differences of opinion with Oliver Bowden. Lord insisted on having full managerial control, and Bowden was moved to Wolseley and Morris

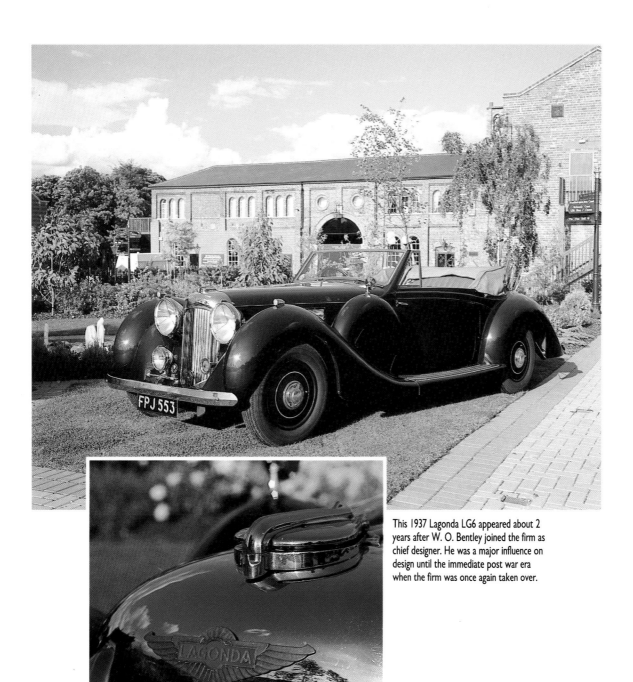

This 1937 Lagonda LG6 appeared about 2 years after W. O. Bentley joined the firm as chief designer. He was a major influence on design until the immediate post war era when the firm was once again taken over.

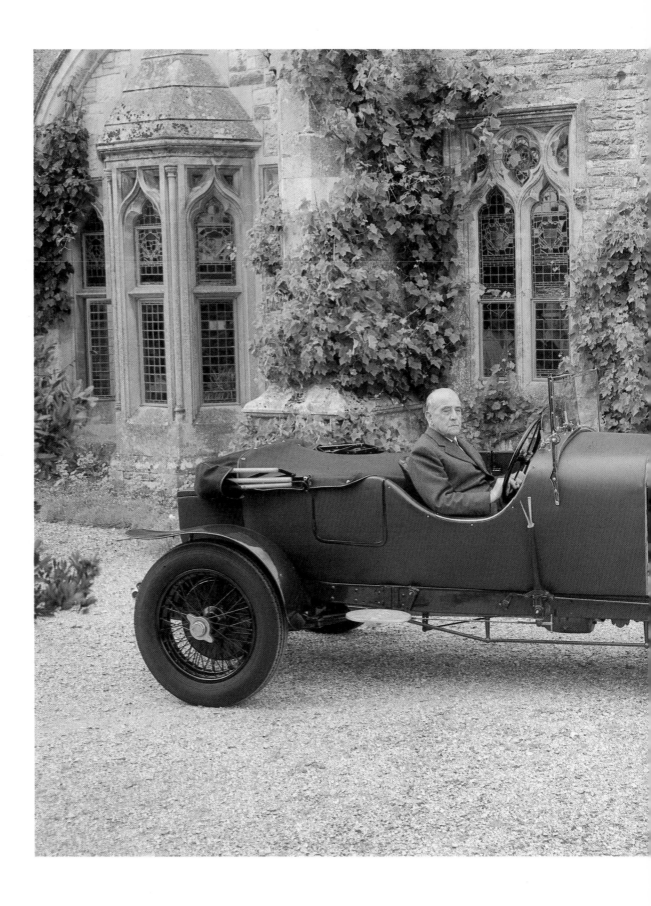

W. O. Bentley, seated here in his 1928 model, was to see his firm go insolvent in 1931. He hoped for a merger with Napier but instead Rolls Royce bought it, along with Bentley himself. He was not allowed to design cars and eventually left Rolls to join Lagonda. Later, when Lagonda wanted to use the Bentley name, Rolls Royce objected, wishing to continue to market the 'Bentley' cars themselves.

The Clyno was once a famous *marque*, which in its heyday was built at a rate of 11,000 cars a year. However the new model introduced in 1928, the Century shown here, was described as a 'miserable failure' and when Rootes the distributors cancelled their order, the firm was forced into liquidation the following year.

Lord worked for both giants of the motor industry, Morris and Austin, and eventually presided over their amalgamated empires.

Commercial. Miles Thomas, also at Cowley, was told by Lord that big as Cowley was 'it wasn't big enough for both of us'. Thomas, too, moved to Wolseley. Miles Thomas admitted that 'everyone admired Lord's methods if not his manners'.

He was a red-headed, bespectacled man whose appearance belied his roughness. He kept a lighted cigarette in the corner of his mouth, even when talking, and would blow the ash off it without taking it out of his lips. One of his typical remarks was, 'If the door isn't open then you kick it open.' In a short while he had opened many doors for Morris, particularly with the success of the Morris Minor – a kind of Ford with frills – and by 1938, nearly a quarter of a million had been built.

Lord's reign at Cowley coincided with a complete change of management at Morris. In addition to Boden and Thomas, Frank Woollard also left after a personal clash with Morris. Rowse, another long-serving director and manager, followed. Lord began a full-scale reconstruction of the company in 1934 but he was not to stay to see it through. Morris treated him like a son. With his talents as a production engineer, combined with a flair for business organisation, and a good eye for design, he seemed indispensible to Morris. Lord promised Morris that he would stay at Cowley until Morris regained market leadership of the motor industry and that he would only consider leaving after one year of peak output and profits. However each year, when Morris had to set Lord's salary, the latter would embarrass his boss by asking for whatever Morris thought he was worth, rather than stating an actual figure. Each time, he thought that the figure Morris settled on was an underestimate. The crisis came in 1936 when Morris wanted Lord to take over the entire Nuffield empire, including Wolseley, MG and Morris Commercial. This time Lord asked for a share in the business and Morris would not agree. There were also other disagreements, including Lord's desire that the firm enter the shadow aero-engine scheme. Lord's comment on the situation was, 'I was pig-headed and Nuffield had his opinions.... There wasn't enough room in the boardroom for two lords.'

Lord retired with his family to the Isle of Wight, and Morris's accountant Hobbs (with whom he used to travel on his long cruises, playing deck tennis) shuttled backwards and forwards trying to effect a reconciliation. They were unable to agree. Lord decided to resign, travel and recharge his mental batteries. Morris sent him off on his travels with a cheque for £50,000. He still remained on good terms with Morris, who much admired him and, after a year, enticed him back to run his £2 million Special Areas Trust (a charity for what today would be Regional Development) at a salary of £10,000 – considerably more than the one he had received as managing-director of Morris Motors. However his repulse by Nuffield hurt him deeply. According to Miles Thomas 'the stain and anger of the split hung heavily on him' and he threatened, 'Tommy, I'm going to take that business at Cowley apart brick by brick.'

Austin, who was now well over 70, was now looking round for a successor. It was not an easy task as 'one of his greatest failings was his anxiety to do everything himself and his unwillingness to allow his colleagues to undertake any responsibilities'. This made it very unlikely that he would find a successor inside the firm and, it was said, his temperament 'seems to have been entirely inappropriate for grooming the kind of successor eventually chosen' – the impetuous Leonard Lord. The latter had other qualities besides 'the priceless gift of youth' which was one reason given for choosing him. Lord was 41 in 1937–8 and as soon as Austin met him he was convinced that he was the man to replace first Carl Engelbach, and then, in due course, himself. Lord for his part said that as soon as Austin had taken him for a tour round the plant, he succumbed once again to the seductive smell of oil. Money must also have helped, as Austin insisted that if Lord was going to do his job, then they must be paid the same salary. No specific figure was mentioned, and Lord referred to the arrangement as 'Austin with the whole jackpot'. When he told Morris where he was going, the older man said, 'Go ahead. I don't see why we shouldn't have a lot of fun cutting each other's throats.'

In 1938 Lord replaced Engelbach as works director, becoming joint managing-director with Payton on Austin's death in 1941 and managing-director and chairman in 1945 when Payton retired. His arrival at Austin resembled in many ways his earlier move to Cowley. He would tour the Austin plant in a relaxed manner, hands in pockets and a cigarette dangling from his lips. Within months he had so gained the confidence of Lord Austin that he assumed a leading part in the introduction of two new cars, the Big Eight and the Ten, and promoted an Italian stylist recruited from Lancia in 1930 to have a free hand in body design. He also set about removing some of the older managers. At an ex-apprentices dinner at Longbridge in January 1939 he told Lord Austin, 'You'll need a couple of coaches to take them away before I've finished.' The staff became apprehensive and the graffiti on the washroom at Longbridge asked plaintively, 'Oh Lord, give us Engelbach.' The latter had been kindly and cultivated, neither of them qualities attaching to Lord. If his manner was rough, he soon galvanized Longbridge just as he had transformed the Morris plant in the mid-1930s.

It must have been in his mind during the years after the war to bring about some merger with Nuffield. On 10th Oct 1950, Lord, in an attempt to break the stalemate with Morris, phoned him to congratulate him on his 70th birthday. Lord and Nuffield subsequently met, but the Morris board turned down the idea of a merger. A year later, Nuffield made the running, and approached Lord without the knowledge of his board. The British Motor Corporation came into being in February 1952. This was, in effect, a takeover of Morris by Austin, with the headquarters at Longbridge and Lord in charge. He filled his threat to take the place apart, and did a great deal to 'humiliate the Morris directors freely criticising Morris Motors and all its works on public occasions' – according to Graham Turner, the BBC correspondent.

In 1961 Lord stepped down as chairman and became a theoretical vice-president, Nuffield still being the absent president. He was made Lord Lambury ('Lord Lord would sound bloody stupid,' he said) in 1962. Harriman (qv) who took over from Lord revered him so much that his office at Longbridge was left untouched and unoccupied until the day he died in 1967.

Alexander Arnold Constantine Issigonis
1906–1988

Issigonis was one of the most colourful car designers of modern times. Born in Smyrna, Turkey, in 1906, his father was a naturalised British subject of Greek descent who had married the daughter of a wealthy Bavarian brewer with a branch brewery in Smyrna. Alec's father ran a marine engineering business there with his brother, and the son soon developed a marked engineering talent. Like most well-off families in Smyrna he did not go to school and was taught at home by a series of tutors. At the end of World War I, the British community in Turkey (which had been on the side of Germany in the war) were evacuated by the Royal Navy for their own safety. Alec's father died in Malta *en route* and the family arrived in England almost penniless, in 1922. The boy was then 16. His mother wanted to send him to art school but he preferred engineering. He completed a three-year course at Battersea Polytechnic and in 1928 was working as draughtsman/salesman with an engineering consultant in Victoria Street, who was developing a type of semi-automatic transmission. He frequently visited the Midlands and was offered a job in the Humber drawing office at Coventry. During this time he lived in a house at Kenilworth with his mother.

After two years he met Robert Boyle, chief engineer of Morris, who offered him a job at Cowley, where he developed an independent front suspension. Issigonis concentrated on suspension experiments, saying, 'I found that cars ran much straighter and were more directionally stable if I put a couple of sandbags on the front bumper.' Miles Thomas takes some credit for the 'discovery' of Issigonis during the war. 'Working under the chief engineer, A. V. Oak, was a shy reserved young man named Alec Issigonis. In spare moments – sometimes during a night's fire watching session – the three of us would sit and exchange ideas. Alec always used to put his suggestions forward in a most tentative way. He had some very fundamental new ideas about motor car construction, and the first thing we decided in the make-up of this small saloon was that we would throw away the conventional chassis' and

put the engine 'outrageously far forward'.

The entire team consisted of Issigonis and two draughtsmen, who interpreted his freehand drawings. By 1942 he had completed a scale model for which Issigonis was responsible for every detail 'even the little knob that opens the glove box and the door handles'. He was going

Shown at the steering wheel in the top picture, Issigonis constructed this Lightweight Special in 1937 which embraced his basic design philosophy – stiff structure, independent suspension with rubber springs, inbuilt understeer, low weight and high torque.

through an American phase at the time and the design reflected the Packard Clipper of 1941. The car first ran in 1947 and when Nuffield saw his new Morris Minor for the first time, Issigonis reported 'he was furious. He called it a poached egg, and everything under the sun, and walked out. I wasn't there at the meeting, in fact I only met him twice in my life. The second time was eleven years later when we'd made a million Morris Minors. Then he had the grace to thank me.' Nuffield's attitude was not unique. In 1945, Sir Stafford Cripps had asked the car industry to provide a 'cheap, tough, good-looking car ... produced in sufficient quantities to get the benefits of mass production'. Examples of the Volkswagen Beetle were sent to every British car firm. Humber's response was typical: 'We do not consider that the design represents any special brilliance ... [and] is not to be regarded as an example of first-class modern design to be copied by the British industry.'

Issigonis went on to design the Mini. After the 1952 merger with Austin, Issigonis, who had 'always hated mergers' left Austin and joined Alvis, but the projected car he was to build was not put into production. Three prototypes were built but later burned.

In 1955 Issigonis returned to become technical director of BMC. There are many stories about his charm, his artistic approach to car design and his eloquent turn of phase. For example, he was quoted as saying, 'All creative people hate mathematics. It's the most uncreative subject you can study, unless you become an Einstein and study it in the abstract philosophical sense.'

George Harriman
1903–73

Born in Coventry, his father, also George, worked for Hotchkiss, later to become Morris Engines. A 'dynamic, fast-talking, fast-walking, bowler-hatted man', he became works manager, and in 1923, at the age of 15, the son joined the father at the Hotchkiss works at Gosforth Street. The young man completed his apprenticeship and Morris bought the firm. He

had started 'at 23s. a week ... and when I finished my time [as an apprentice] with 57s. a week, I felt like a millionaire.' The two became 'Old George' and 'Young George' to the workers. The factory was under the direction of Frank Woollard (qv) and Leonard Lord (qv) was in the drawing office. With such talented people, the Morris factory has been described as 'the centre

Harriman became a leading figure in the British motor industry but he was subserviant to the wishes of his mentor, Leonard Lord.

of the British adoption of American production technology'. Harriman became essentially a production man, perhaps the leading figure in the post-war development of BMC.

He was a keen rugby player and captain of both the Warwickshire and Coventry clubs, one year playing for England vs. the Rest. He was very reticent about his private life, but was married and had one daughter. He became friends with Leonard Lord and when Lord moved to Cowley, he arranged for Harriman to go with him. In 1938 he had risen to be assistant works superintendent and in 1940, Lord having moved to Austin, joined him there as machine shop superintendent.

By 1944 he was production manager and in 1945 was given a seat on the board, being very much Lord's right-hand man. In 1956 he became managing-director and 'wore an India rubber confidence as consciously as other men assume dignity'. He was undoubtedly charming, but he grew up in Lord's shadow and Lord was the stronger man. A former colleague said, 'George was one of the nicest men you could wish to meet but he did what he was told. That was why Len Lord liked him.'

On one occasion, Lord did not succeed in getting Harriman to obey him. This was in 1940 when a national drive to collect scrap for conversion into war material was in full swing. Lord seized on the opportunity to get rid permanently of the car designed by a man he had hated, Tom Murray Jamieson, who had died in 1938. Two of his Exquisite 1936 racing cars existed and Lord ordered Harriman to send their crankshafts, connecting rods, pistons and cylinder liners for scrap. Harriman sent off one set, but took the other home and hid the parts in his garage. After his death in 1973 they were discovered by his widow and returned to British Leyland, where the car was rebuilt and ran again for the first time 35 years after its début.

manufacture of front and rear axles and gearboxes to Wrigley.

When Morris acquired the old Hotchkiss plant in 1922, he persuaded Woollard to join him to organise it as the engine branch of Morris Motors Ltd. He made dramatic changes, but when the chief production engineer of Ford Motors of Detroit visited the plant in the mid-1920s he told Woollard he was 'twenty years too early' with the automatic transfer machines for engine block manufacture. His book on *Mass and Flow Production* is described as a 'rare insight' by an engineer who 'pioneered automation and its application to the British context.'

In 1932 Woollard fell out with Morris and left to become the managing-director of Rudge-Whitworth Ltd and, four years later, joined Birmingham Aluminium Casting Company. His motor industry days were over. 'His inability to find employment with one of the major motor vehicle producers is perhaps an indication of how little the British motor vehicle industry valued his pioneering achievements.'

Frank Griffith Woollard
1883-1957

Woollard has been described as 'probably the most gifted and creative of the engineers whom William Morris succeeded in attracting into his service.' He came of a humble family, his father being described on his birth certificate as 'a servant'. Nevertheless, he was educated at City of London School and at Goldsmiths and Birkbeck Colleges. Like many men of the age with engineering interests, he was apprenticed to the railway company, where he acquired some knowledge of flow production in building railway coaches. About 1905, he joined the drawing office of Weigel Motors Ltd who made racing cars and sold Cléments. In 1910 he was chief draughtsman of E. G. Wrigley & Co. of Birmingham, becoming progressively director and chief engineer and then assistant managing-director. During the war he was responsible for the large-scale production of tank gearboxes and made the acquaintance of William Morris (qv), who had sub-contracted the

John Harper Bean
1885-1963

The name Bean goes down in car history as that of a man who took on Morris and lost. Bean inherited a family company established in 1826 at Dudley, Worcs, making mainly hand-forged ironware. In 1900 the firm expanded to Smethwick, Staffs, and in 1907 changed its name to A. Harper Sons & Bean. It built up a considerable trade supplying stampings, forgings and castings to the motor trade. After the war, John Harper Bean, who was known as Jack, decided to go into the motor industry, with a planned output of 50,000 cars a year, and in May 1919 announced he had 'purchased the jigs, tools, drawings and spare parts pertaining to various models of cars produced by the Perry Motor Co Ltd.' The latter's car was put on the market as the 11.9hp Bean. They decided to make most of the components themselves and became part of a holding company called, confusingly, Harper Bean Ltd.

This acquired 75 per cent of the shares of

Vulcan Motor of Southport, who had been making cars since about 1902, 51 per cent of the ordinary share of Swift, originally a sewing machine firm which turned to bicycles and cars in 1899, half the issued capital of British Motor Trading Corp. Ltd, shares in Hadfields the steel firm and large interests in various other firms including ABC Motors (1920) Ltd. Bean himself was the managing-director, and the board included Robert Burns, director and general manager of Swift.

Bean's production got under way in January 1920, when 100 cars were produced and by March the firm was building 20 cars a day – only 10 per cent of their target of 50,000 cars a year. In October Bean cut their price by £100 so that it was only £20 dearer than the Morris Cowley which had recently gone up in price. They can thus be said to have pioneered the price-cutting policy which saved Morris but Bean's sales fell in 1921 when Morris cut his own prices, and Hadfields, the steel firm, had to step in with funds to support the family firm. The firm continued to be in trouble and John Harper Bean resigned to join the board of Guy Motors Ltd.

Hadfields took over the firm in 1926 when it was renamed Bean Cars with headquarters at Tipton, Staffs. But the unfortunately named Hadfield Bean car ceased production in 1929.

Beans Industries emerged as general engineers in 1933 from the ashes of the car business and Jack Bean subsequently became its chairman. In 1956 he negotiated its sale to Standard Triumph.

He also became, in 1938, chairman of Garringtons, the drop forging division of Guest, Kean and Nettlefolds. After the war he was responsible for building up Garringtons to be the largest producer of drop forgings in Europe.

Frank Smith

Clyno, like Bean, was a company famous in its day but now forgotten. Its founder, Frank Smith, was born at Thrapston, Northants where his family had owned a foundry since the 1850s. Smith found the atmosphere of

The Clyno, now almost forgotten as a marque, was famous in its day. Its founder, Frank Smith, was obsessed with what Morris was doing.

the market town too restricting and, in 1909, he and his cousin Alwyn started the Clyno Engineering Co. to make motorcycles. The first car, powered by a Coventry Climax engine, was introduced in 1922. By 1926, when he was selling over 11,000 units, Smith felt justified in leaving his restricted Coventry premises in Pelham Street and opening a new factory on a 70 acre site at Bushbury. 'As the years went by, the need to discover what Morris was doing and to undercut him became more and more of an obsession. It was a rivalry which Smith was fated to lose.' By 1928 he abandoned the Coventry Climax engine as an economy measure, but made no adequate arrangements to produce one of his own. His new model, the Century, was a miserable affair, and his main distributors, the Rootes brothers, terminated the agency and Clyno was forced into liquidation after 1929.

This interpretation of Clyno's failure as a psychological fixation of Smith's seems a more adequate explanation of their downfall than the story that Clyno had a contact at the same printers that produced Morris's catalogues and so acquired advance notice of the latter's price changes. William Morris was said to have found out how Clyno set their price levels and sent the printers a draft catalogue with ficticious prices which Clyno followed to their financial disadvantage.

It is believed that he went into the garage business, retiring in the early fifties to sail his boat on the River Dart in Devon.

Chapter Five

The Luxury End

In the early days of the industry, many British car makers, including some of the popular types like the Austin, were copies of French designs. It is not commonly known that the famous Rolls-Royce too started life as a copy (a much improved copy, true) of a French machine. The men who created that firm are described here. It may be interesting to compare Henry Royce with his rival Montague Napier, who appears in the first section. Another name immemorially linked with Rolls is that of Bentley, but the founder of that firm, W. O. Bentley, who had little to do with the Rolls connection, is described in detail in the Sports section.

Henry Royce
Charles Rolls
Claude Johnson
Ernest Hives
Arthur Sidgreaves
AE Claremont

Frederick Henry Royce
1863–1933

Henry Royce was born at Alwalton, near Peterborough, the son of an unsuccessful miller. It was a harsh environment and his success in life was a triumph of mental power over circumstances. He was the youngest child of a large family, but his father died in a London poorhouse when he had only just started at school and he had to leave after a year. He worked as a newspaper boy for W. H. Smith and, after another year at school, was again compelled to work, this time as a telegram boy for a London post office. He returned to Peterborough, where an aunt tried to help him by financing his apprenticeship at the Great Northern Railway works in the city. His interest in engineering developed and he was given extra tuition in the evenings at the home of one of the railway staff with whom he was lodging. Unfortunately, his aunt's money ran out and Royce had to leave the railway workshops to find a job where he could earn his keep. He was paid 11 shillings a week by a machine-tool firm. 'Part of this time,' he said, 'I had to work from 6 a.m. to 10 p.m. and all Friday night.' The boy decided that there were better opportunities in London, and he obtained employment with a newly-established electric light company – this form of power being considered, at the time, novel but unreliable.

He learnt a great deal about electricity, not only at the firm but also by attending night classes at Finsbury Polytechnic. He was promoted to be chief electrician of a branch of the London company, and sent to Liverpool, where he specialised mainly in theatrical lighting. Unfortunately, the firm went broke. By this time Royce had met and become friends with Ernest Claremont (qv). In 1884 (when Royce was 21) the two young men decided to set up their own business with a capital of £75. They made electrical appliances such as electrical bell sets, lampholders, switches, fuses and registering instruments in a small workshop in Manchester. Business prospered and Royce put his mind to more complex electrical items such as dynamos, switchboards and electric cranes.

The Royce dynamo quickly established a reputation in the Midlands where there was a growing demand in wool and cotton mills. By 1893 the two partners felt sufficiently settled to marry two sisters, who, incidentally, brought another £1500 into the business by way of dowry. In the following year the firm of F. H. Royce Ltd was founded and it is clear that Royce's engineering talents were the basis of its success. His cranes had a considerable reputation, and already 'his real genius lay in development work. There was nothing which he could not improve, and few mechanical devices which he did not want to improve or succeed in improving.'

Royce's problem was that he had trained himself to be a workaholic. He left himself no time for leisure, and even fitted up electric light bulbs in his garden so that he could work there when it was dark. He became ill from overwork and Claremont and his other colleagues at work persuaded him to buy one of the new French motor cars so that he could get out in the fresh air. By this time Royce (known as Fred to his close associates) was effectively running a medium-sized business which had been renamed Royce Ltd. The car was a Decauville and Royce felt sure he could improve on its design. He took it to the workshops and, with the help of two

Royce, known to intimates as 'Fred', was a more-or-less self-taught engineer whose idea of heaven was a garage full of cars, each one different from the others. He did however build a substantial number of basically-similar copies of the Silver Ghost, the most famous of his designs, (left) in production for a period of eighteen years from its design in 1906. Although Royce hardly visited the Derby works, he controlled designs from afar until his death in 1933. The portrait was taken in 1907.

prentice, describes the genesis of this first Royce car: 'After we got the sketches of the Decauville car, they were used by the draughtsmen, two experienced auto designers, Adams and Shipley, to design the Royce 2-cylinder car. But 'Old Man Royce' did the designing ... Every little detail. I personally traced, made blueprints, ran errands; small details all calculated out and each and every one with Royce's mechanical genius standing out all over it ... I helped assemble the first car and Royce worked right along with us in overalls at times. He wanted a leather washer or gasket one day – or rather night. Nothing in the stock room was suitable or at least I could not find anything. Impatiently he tore off one of the leather leggings he wore occasionally in those days and threw it at me to "make it out of that quickly". He sometimes came to the works with only one legging on or without a tie. Motor cars on his mind all the time. ...'

The first car ran in April 1904 and Royce decided to build three altogether, one for Claremont. The latter was friendly with Henry Edmunds, who was on the Committee of the Automobile Club as was the Hon. Charles Rolls (qv) and he also knew Johnson (qv) who had been the club's secretary. Edmunds told Rolls about the Royce car, and in May the two men met in Manchester and agreed that Rolls should sell the Royce car from his London showrooms at Fulham. It was agreed that Royce would design chassis for 10, 15, 20 and 30 horsepower cars. The names Rolls-Royce was first mentioned in one of Rolls's advertisements in the *Autocar* in December 1904 and a company was registered as Rolls-Royce Distributing Company Ltd. After the initial batch of cars, Henry Royce began work on what was to be his masterpiece, the 40/50 hp car later to be known as the Silver Ghost. It first appeared at the 1906 Motor Show and was to remain in production until 1925. 'The cars' smooth running and the undiluted refinement of its six-cylinder engine put it head and shoulders above its contemporaries. With every justification Rolls-Royce could claim to manufacture The Best Car in The World.

Rolls and Johnson pressed ahead with selling the cars, while Royce concentrated on development in his Manchester factory. When it was decided to move to Derby in 1907, Royce continued to run his Manchester electrical business –

workmen, stripped down the car and remade such components as he deemed were necessary – his view was that the Decauville was a 'brilliant achievement marred by careless workmanship'.

Ernest Wooller, Royce's first premium aphe 'had to return periodically ... to solve its problems and keep it going'. During the years 1906–1910, the production of cars expanded but, curiously, the part played by the two founders of the firm declined. Rolls gradually lost interest in cars as aviation took a hold on his imagination. Royce, in contrast, became more absorbed in cars, but left the sales and business side to Johnson, Rolls's partner. By 1907 the *Manchester Guardian* was able to say, 'In two years Mr Royce [has] obtained for his productions a foremost place in English industry, and a high reputation on the Continent.' The reputation was not matched by financial success and in the early years the firm relied on help from a bank overdraft. Rolls and Johnson had worked hard at competitions and publicity of all kinds and by 1908 Johnson managed to persuade the directors that 'no further purpose was to be served by entering cars for public trials and competitions ... the company had established its reputation.' Orders poured in, but production never caught up with them and deliveries were usually six months behind.

By 1908, Royce was seriously ill again and was unable to attend board meetings. He rarely visited the factory at Derby, which did not appeal to him, and in March 1909 Johnson was made chief executive. The following year Royce relinquished all executive duties in order to devote his attention to technical matters. His health was now a matter of serious concern to his fellow directors, because they realised that the future of the company depended on his technical direction. Although Royce had the appearance of a Victorian saint, he could be very difficult. It is said that 'in the factory he was somewhat autocratic, and his disapproval, either of an employee or of his work, occasionally resulted in the man's instant dismissal.' He is said to have been 'a glaring example of too much experimentalism. He was a poor production engineer, and manufacture did not flow in a shop where he was working. Where there was any possibility of design improvement, production was immediately sacrificed. Output did not concern him.... He would have been content ... with a workshop in the middle of a field.'

This, in effect, was what was provided for him. When he became seriously ill again in 1910, following Rolls's death, Royce was driven down to the south of France by Johnson who had acquired land at Le Canadel to build a villa. Royce liked the place so much that Johnson immediately put in hand the construction of three further buildings – Royce's own villa, Villa Mimosa, a drawing office known as Le Bureau, and a small staff villa for resident or visiting design staff from Derby, known as Le Rossignol. Le Canadel was to be Royce's winter headquarters from then on.

In fact, he had cancer of the intestine, and following an operation, the doctors told him that he had only a short time to live. His marriage had not been a success, and, from 1912 onwards, he was looked after by the devoted Nurse Aubyn, as well as, of course, by Johnson. It seems certain that this careful convalescence and his own will power were the major factors in keeping him alive for another 20 years.

When the war came, Rolls were quite unprepared, and the demand, initially, for their very expensive chassis for army use was negligible. Royce had declined to adapt his car engines for aeronautical use, despite the fact that there was a great shortage of aero-engines. The Admiralty rather than the army were the most forward-looking of the two services in aviation matters, and one of their officers, accompanied by another, the young W. O. Bentley (qv), took a Mercedes racing car to Derby at the outbreak of war and asked Royce to build an aero-engine to a similar design. This Royce succeeded in doing, although with his passion for perfection it only reached full scale use towards the end of the war.

During the war Royce, who had strong patriotic feelings, insisted on remaining in England. Johnson therefore found him a villa at West Wittering on the south coast, where he spent much of his time thenceforward. 'He was segregated as far as possible from all administrative and financial problems, often to his great annoyance.' Johnson ran the firm which, by the end of the year, had become one of the four major British aero-engine concerns, but not yet the biggest. Indeed Johnson and Royce were anxious to return to car building. They had plenty of 1914 orders on hand which they intended to fulfil, rather unsatisfactorily, at 1914 prices. Nevertheless the firm was on a sound economic basis because of war contracts. Royce was able to return to France to spend his winters at Le

Outside the villa la Canadol which Johnson built for him in the South of France, and where he lived continuously from 1910 to 1914, and periodically thereafter, Henry Royce stands besides his famous Phantom I car. This saintly appearance concealed some rather too-human characteristics, like a propensity for swearing hard in adversity.

Canadel and, on Claremont's death in 1921, Johnson was even more in charge of business policy.

Royce played no part in the attempt to set up production of Rolls-Royce cars in the United States, which was masterminded – unsuccessfully as it turned out – by Johnson. He was, however, partly responsible for the failure of the enterprise, as he refused to allow the Americans to build anything other than a Chinese copy of the Derby model – or to incorporate any of the technical improvements which American designers had brought to the automobile industry. Some of the British-supplied components were, to put it mildly, second best, and some American customers removed British items, like magnetos, and replaced them with their own. The mere idea of American mass production methods was horrifying to Henry Royce, but his car cost three or four times the price of the best American cars, which were not all that inferior. Royce nevertheless continued to refer to them as 'your cheap and

nasty American cars' and when, after Johnson's death, the American enterprise slowed down further, Royce took a pessimistic view of its future, saying that 'to make a profit is very difficult, and perhaps impossible, something like a single firm against a nation.'

The fact that the firm's management tried to keep Royce designing cars, rather than being involved in administrative or commercial matters, must not hide the fact that he 'possessed a shrewd insight into economic matters'. He expressed his views to the staff at Derby with great clarity. For example, when working on the 20/25 car in 1930, he wrote (his capitals):

MY GREAT MOTTO FOR BRITAIN AND OURSELVES IS MASS PRODUCTION WITH QUALITY. UNLESS WE DO THIS WE ARE FATED, SO LET US DO IT BEFORE IT IS TOO LATE, BECAUSE AT THE MOMENT ENGLAND CANNOT TRULY BOAST OF EITHER

By this time, he had somewhat reluctantly come round to devoting as much time to aero-engines as cars. Royce's philosophy about cars had been: 'A small output at Derby will not allow the Rolls-Royce company to exist. So ... our best field appears to be the smaller car market.' However, he concluded his memorandum on the subject, 'I would like it clearly understood that I should not for a moment recommend a smaller model if we could fill the Derby factory with the large.' He also wrote, 'With our small output, our only chance is that our production shall stand out by all round perfection, rather than price.' His partner Claremont once said of Royce that his heaven would be a place where he could produce one car at a time and in which no two cars need ever be exactly alike. The small car was a failure, but the firm was saved by the success of the aero-engines, which from this time onwards began to subsidise the cars.

Following the death of Johnson, the firm had been run first by Basil Johnson, Claude's brother, and from 1928, by Arthur Sidgreaves (qv), who had been trained at Napiers, the first and most serious rival to Rolls-Royce, in aero-engines as well as cars. Royce took charge of new aero-engine design from 1924 onwards and, rather against his first instincts, put a tremendous effort into engines for the Schneider Trophy races. It is outside the scope of this book to give details of his aviation work, although it is important to note that his attitude to the relative attention which should be paid to cars or aero-engines remained ambivalent. For example, he wrote in 1927, 'It looks as though there are too many of us in this aero business, and that we should do better by giving such talents as we have, and the capacity of our factory, to our automobile work, as it appears to be a job of sweated slavery to meet first one [Air Ministry] condition and then another, apparently putting off the reward until we are no longer in existence.' Fortunately for the nation, this view did not prevail.

In 1931, Captain J. K. Carruthers of Bentley Motors approached Sidgreaves about a merging of the two firms. Shortly afterwards the Bentley firm was declared insolvent. Napier intended to buy the firm but, in an astute move, Rolls-Royce stepped in and secretly paid a higher price, largely to block Napier. Sidgreaves, whose plan it was, also persuaded W. O. Bentley to join Rolls from Napiers, where he had gone after the

Henry Royce is rarely seen in photographs in a happy mood, and it is not believed that he smiled very often when in the company of his wife. Here, his faithful Nurse Aubyn is seen with him in a rare moment of enjoyment. She looked after him during more than 20 years when he suffered from cancer, a disease the doctor's told him would kill him in a few months. Although initially reluctant to design aero-engines, Royce turned increasingly to aviation, culminating in his R-series which powered the British Schneider Trophy race entries, like the SB6B of 1931.

failure of his own firm. Bentley tells the story of his rather frosty reception by Henry Royce. The latter said that he understood that Bentley was not a trained engineer, at which Bentley pointed out that he had served his apprenticeship in the railway works as had the master himself.

Although Royce was inherently conservative, he did not fail to be aware of the effects of this on the firm. In the late 1920s he wrote: 'I have long considered our present chassis out of date. The back axle, gearbox, frame and springs have not been seriously altered since 1912...I so fear disaster by being out of date, and having a

duction soon after midsummer 1929. I will take moral responsibility for the risk.' Despite this, Phantom demand continued to wane, and Royce, giving his comments on the 1930 Motor Show and the price of American cars, noted, 'We have to pay for our reputation as well as live up to it.'

By this time, Hives (qv) had established considerable influence on engineering development and was 'bluntly critical' of the position into which the firm had drifted in failing to offer the best technology that the car business could provide. Rolls-Royce could no longer claim technical superiority, and the changes which would be required were not within their financial or managerial ability before the outbreak of the Second World War. An historian observes, 'Royce had probably done more than most to develop a conservative attitude, but he cannot altogether be blamed for the failure of his successors to understand the consequences of changes in the structure of the industry which, as his minutes reveal, he himself understood remarkably well, even though he would not accept their implications.'

In 1931 Royce was offered and accepted a baronetcy, almost certainly because of his fame as a designer of the Schneider Trophy winning engines. An historian has summed up Royce's philosophy, the 'instinctive beliefs' which permeated the firm, as:

(1) there will always be a market for superlative quality
(2) quantity and quality were incompatible, but even if this were not so, the customer thought it was
(3) Selling a few hundred costly cars has always paid
(4) Derby was unfamiliar with quantity production.

This last point was as true for aero-engines as it was for cars, but Royce did not live to see the vast expansion at Derby, the move of cars to Crewe, or the final sale of the marque to the Vickers company following the bankruptcy of the 1970s.

Royce died in 1933 after he had completed the design of the V12 Phantom III, the last car he saw through from start to finish. The Phantom line had begun in 1925 in succession to the Silver Ghost. The smaller 20hp car, introduced in 1922, also bears his distinctive perfectionist stamp.

lot of old stock left, and by the sales falling off by secrets leaking out, that I must refuse all responsibility for a fatal position unless these improvements in our chassis are arranged to be shown next autumn, and to do this they must be in pro-

Charles Stewart Rolls
1870–1910

Rolls was born the third son of a baronet, later raised to the peerage when his son was 15 years old. His mother was the daughter of a Scottish baronet and the family were wealthy landowners in the Welsh border country. Educated at Eton, Rolls then went on to Cambridge, where he took up cycle racing and won his half-blue. Although cycling was not a socially inferior sport, there were few people of Rolls's calibre active in it. Edge (qv) who knew Rolls intimately from the time he was an undergraduate says, 'His enthusiasm for everything mechanical and electrical was without limit.' When only 15 he had set up a complete electrical installation in his father's house, although he did not like school (he only stuck Eton for three years) and his interest in engineering at Cambridge was desultory.

The turning point in his life came when, only 17, he went to France and 'discovered cars'. In his first year at Cambridge he imported a French car which was delivered by train to Victoria Station from where he drove it up to the University at an average speed of $4\frac{1}{2}$ mph. By the time he left Cambridge in 1898, Rolls was already heavily involved in automobile activities and was about to take up ballooning, encouraged, it is said, by his mistress. There was some talk of his taking a commission in the army, but instead he spent the next four years studying the practical aspects of engineering at the railway workshops at Crewe. He also obtained a third engineer's marine certificate which enabled him to act as third engineer on his father's yacht. Amongst the other rich young men he met at the time were Moore-Brabazon and the wine merchant, Frank Hedges Butler. The former says in his autobiography that Rolls and he also took an interest in aeroplanes and constructed small models of tissue paper and light wood, secured by sealing wax. Somehow they arranged entry into the Royal Albert Hall, where they tested the models by throwing them from the balcony.

Although there continued to be talk of his taking up a commission in the army, Rolls capitalised the allowance his father proposed to give him, and used the money to set up his car sales

Charles Rolls began his racing career with bicycles, but from his twenties he became more and more interested in cars, balloons and finally aeroplanes. The top picture shows Rolls at rear driving a French Bolleé made for two, with the passenger Louis Paul in front in 1897. Below he is driving the early Panhard which won the 1896 race from Paris to Marseilles and back. Rolls sold these French cars in his Fulham showrooms and it was only when he met sales resistance that he turned to Mr Royce's creations.

company, C. S. Rolls & Co. Ltd., with showrooms in the formerly well-known skating rink in Lillie Road in fashionable Fulham. He had already become a keen member of the Automobile Club (still not Royal) where he met Johnson (qv) whom he persuaded to join his firm. In addition to the £6500 put up for the Fulham premises, Rolls had an annual allowance of £500, but it is said his expenses amounted to ten times this figure. It was therefore essential for him to make money by selling his cars, but by 1902/3, despite the great publicity efforts of Johnson and the

racing expertise of Rolls, there was a lull in demand for the French models he imported – mainly Panhard and Lavassor. To boost income, he hired out cars and chauffeurs and sold accessories. He also wrote a book on carburettors. Things got so bad that he halved the price of the Panhards, but he still had half a dozen on his hands.

What sort of man was Rolls? Although described by Edge as an 'exceedingly nice fellow' he was very far from being a Champagne Charlie. On the surface he was a typical Edwardian gent, fashionably dressed, with a smartly uniformed chauffeur to hand (probably Hives (qv)) and his mechanic Smith not far away. He spent much of his time in the workshop he had built for himself at the family's London house in Kensington. There were ballooning weekends at the family estate, The Hendre, Monmouthshire, where his father gave silver trophies to the fastest balloonists between London and Monmouth. Beneath this smooth exterior, Rolls was a curious fellow, described by Sopwith as a 'loner'. There was his 'extreme closeness in financial matters' which is a polite way of saying he was downright mean.

He was never known to pay for anything which he could possibly get for nothing.

His parsimony was legendary, although in fact his abstinence from expensive food had a 'scientific' basis as he believed that by 'cutting off all food that is not actually required for the proper repair and sustenance of the body, his health would be improved.' He became treasurer of the National Food Reform Association. Those who did not know about his views were alarmed when they saw him taking his own sandwiches into luncheon at the Automobile Club, where he used the restaurant facilities only to supply him with a glass of water. When the club eventually started charging him for the use of the table, he was known to tip the waiter a penny or two. On the occasions when he went abroad with his rich friends, they would travel first class, but he went second or third, although allowing them to buy him dinner. He told Duncan (qv) 'I find when on a motor trip abroad, all that I require is a couple of flannel shirts, a pair of socks and a celluloid collar.'

It was ironic that such a mean man should establish the firm which would make the most expensive cars in the world for the most extravagant 'Owners' (the firm always spelt this word with a capital 'O' to indicate that they were a special breed).

Because of his difficulty in selling French cars, Rolls began to look around for an English design. He was told about Royce's car by a fellow member of the Automobile Club and, because Royce would not travel to London, went up to Manchester to meet him. He agreed to become Royce's agent and, so the story goes, rushed back to London to rouse Johnson from bed to tell him the good news. Together, Johnson's flair for publicity and Rolls's connections and racing ability ensured the success of the car which was soon known as the Rolls-Royce. Rolls even succeeded in giving Prince George (the future king) his first ride in a motor car. As for racing, Edge says Rolls had 'absolutely no sense of fear or danger.... He was an excellent racing driver, although inclined if anything to be rather too reckless and never sparing his car.' Rolls's sense of what would sell was immaculate, within the limitations imposed by the tastes of his aristocratic friends.

By 1906 he was on the technical committee

15 H.P. ROLLS-ROYCE CAR.

15 H.P. "R-R" LANDAULET.

THREE CYLINDERS.

95 inches behind dashboard.   Tyres, 32 × 3½ inches.

The Ideal lady's carriage for use in town and country.

THREE SPEEDS FORWARD AND REVERSE.
DIRECT DRIVE ON TOP SPEED.

Silent and Vibrationless.

PRICES:

With "Barker" Single Landaulet - - **£550**
With "Barker" Side Entrance Tonneau **£500**

10

20 H.P. ROLLS-ROYCE CAR.

20 H.P. "R-R" PHAETON DE LUXE.

FOUR CYLINDERS.

Length behind dashboard 100 inches.   Tyres, 34 × 3½ and 35 × 5 inches

THREE SPEEDS AND REVERSE.
DIRECT DRIVE ON TOP SPEED.

Fast.   Silent.   Easy to control.

With "Barker" side-entrance Tonneau, **£650.**
Phaeton de Luxe (as above) - - **£695.**
Extra for Brougham Top, with extension **£60.**

11

These pages are taken from the 1905 catalogue issued by Rolls in the early days of selling the new cars from his new premises in the West End.

of the Aero Club, having already ordered balloons from the Short Brothers which he flew with the likes of Moore-Brabazon and Warwick Wright. In 1908, when Wilbur Wright went to France with his aeroplane, Rolls visited him at his Paris hotel and tried to buy one of his Flyers. He was also the first Englishman to see Wright flying at Le Mans. By 1909 he was teaching himself to fly on a Short-built Wright aeroplane, having previously mastered a glider.

It was therefore no surprise to Royce and Claremont when, in July 1908, Rolls asked the board's permission to become consulting engineer to a company which proposed to manufacture airships. 'The permission was granted with the obvious resignation which accompanies a realisation of the inevitable.' Shortly afterwards Rolls annoyed Claremont by building, at the Fulham works, components for a War Office aeroplane and airship without formal permis-

Rolls was an intrepid racer of cars (the Isle of Man TT shown here) and then of aeroplanes. The portrait was taken at Dover after his cross-channel record.

sion. In December 1908, the Rolls board closed the Fulham works as an economy measure, which may have annoyed Rolls, although earlier he had borrowed a few thousand more from his father to finance the purchase of the Conduit Street showrooms, still open today in the West End. At any rate, when in February 1909 Rolls suggested to the board that they acquire the rights to manufacture the Wright aeroplane, this was turned down without further consideration. The reason for rejecting his proposal so unceremoniously was probably the shortage of working capital as well as the ever-present fear that Royce, still quite ill, might overtax himself. Early in 1910, Rolls relinquished all his routine work at the firm and resigned his post as technical managing-director with a major cut in income. Henceforth, he devoted himself to aviation. He had become something of a figurehead in the public eye, and was one of those greeting Blériot on his arrival at Dover. Afterwards, he took the Frenchman to the House of Commons to help propagandise flying and, in the same spirit, himself made a double flight across the Channel which made him a national hero.

In 1910 he was killed while flying in a competition at Bournemouth. The cause was a fault in the tail of his aeroplane, which he had recently modified to improve performance. In his notebook he had jotted a few days before, 'Sell Tail,' and the possibility therefore is that his parsimonious man knew that it was unsatisfactory but did not want to remove it from the aeroplane until he had found a buyer. Rolls comes across as an unusual man, a great supporter of his own enthusiasms but someone incapable of pursuing more than one interest at a time. Sopwith said he was a 'curiously unloveable person'.

Claude Goodman Johnson
1864–1926

Johnson 'the hyphen in Rolls-Royce' was born at Datchet, Bucks, the son of a man who spent most of his life as an official in the Science Museum. The son was brought up in a middle-class atmosphere where the virtues were energy and ambition. (The father also passed on to the son his love of music, especially Bach.) He attended St Paul's School where he became a foundation scholar and specialised in drawing. He went on to the Royal College of Art but decided his abilities were not as advanced as his tastes and, like his father, turned to administration. The director of the Science Museum gave him his first job in 1883 which was to organise a fisheries exhibition. Other exhibitions followed and when the Imperial Institute – as it was later called – was set up, Johnson became its first Chief Clerk, at a salary of £5 a week plus a bonus of 10 shillings for every new member. The job brought out Johnson's talent for publicity and his interest in motor cars and aeroplanes led him to organise exhibitions, trials and clubs, culminating in his becoming the first secretary of the Automobile Club and then the Aero Club. Under his leadership, the membership of the motoring club increased from 163 to 2000.

In 1891, while he was still in the museum business, Johnson eloped with the daughter of an army surgeon, Fanny Morrison. Despite the fact that they had eight children, including twins, only one child – a daughter – survived, and the marriage is said not to have been a happy one – 'the tragedy of losing seven children left its mark'. Not much is known of Fanny Johnson.

In 1903, Paris Singer launched his City and Suburban Electric Car Project, and Johnson

A portrait of Johnson, patron of the arts, by Ambrose McEvoy.

joined him, but within a few months he moved again to join someone he had met at both the RAC and Aero Clubs – the Hon. C. S. Rolls (qv). The story is well known that after his first meeting with Royce in Manchester in May 1904, Rolls went straight to Johnson's flat in London and woke him up to come to see the car made by 'the greatest engineer in the world'. Johnson's flair for publicity was essential to the growth of the Rolls-Royce firm. He organised shows, press receptions and TT races. More practically, he helped persuade Rolls's father, Lord Llangattock, to put up capital for the merger of the Rolls and Royce interests, the Rolls-Royce firm, of which Johnson became managing-director at £750 per annum and 4 per cent of the surplus profits. Royce's original partner, A. E. Claremont (qv), became chairman and after Rolls lost interest in cars in favour of aeroplanes, and Royce retired suffering from cancer to be, in effect, a consultant, Johnson 'proved to be the real architect of Rolls-Royce's development and success'.

He persuaded Royce to build the Silver Ghost and to concentrate on its production rather than to do what Royce would have preferred – build a variety of models each better than the last. Johnson was already well known as a rally organiser, rally driver and writer, and he became close friends with Alfred Harmsworth the newspaper proprietor who described himself as 'one of the Rolls-Royce salesmen' and gave Johnson plenty of advice about publicity. With this help, and his own skills, Johnson pressed ahead with a multiplicity of ideas, including a school for chauffeurs and painting of cars by top artists, one of whom, Charles Sykes, provided the *Spirit of Ecstasy* which became the Silver Lady mascot on the Rolls-Royce radiator. Johnson also helped the expansion of the firm with the move to the Derby factory and also fought a takeover by Max Aitken (later Lord Beaverbrook) who had acquired Rolls's shares. Harmsworth, incidentally, told Aitken that the Rolls-Royce business was 'a delicate orchid which owes its success entirely to Johnson'.

When, soon after, Royce was found to have cancer, Johnson lent him his own house in the south of France and later built a house in the grounds there where Royce could work with a small engineering team. When the war came, he also found Royce a house at West Wittering in Sussex. Johnson was slow to appreciate the impact the war would have on high-quality car production, and let many of the most skilled men leave the company. Rather against his instincts Johnson found himself and the firm pushed into aero-engine manufacture by the Admiralty. However, in due course he put all his energies behind this new activity as well as making armoured cars and shells. He even tried to set up an aero-engine plant in the USA, and spent many months there, fruitlessly as it turned out, as the Americans did not have the same view of the infallibility of Rolls-Royce as he. The government held him and the firm in high regard and he was offered a knighthood, but declined, suggesting it should go to Royce. It did not do so for many years.

Johnson did not believe that aero-engines had a postwar future to equal that of cars, for which many pre-war orders were still outstanding. Unlike Napier (qv) he did not grasp that the day of the big, luxury car was threatened by the social changes of the post-1918 world. He even believed there was an immense market for his cars in the USA and set off there for another

Johnson made his name in motoring first as secretary of the Royal Automobile Club and he probably designed its stationery with its telegraph pole and telephone motifs. Later he virtually ran Rolls-Royce.

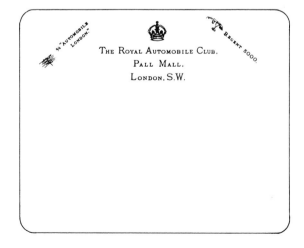

prolonged stay, which culminated in the formation of a factory. Largely through what must be described as the firm's arrogance this was 'Johnson's biggest commercial failure, but he did not live to know that the American company had failed'. Nor did he live to see Rolls re-enter the aero-engine field on a big scale and achieve considerable glory under the leadership of Ernest Hives (qv). Between 1907 and 1920, the net worth of the firm rose under Johnson's guidance from just over £100,000 to £1.2 million and net profits from £5390 to £202,833. Turnover in 1926, when he died, was over £5½ million.

Johnson did not, says the historian of Rolls-Royce Ian Lloyd, 'conform in any way to the modern stereotype of the industrial tycoon. He was a sensitive man who had a passion for music … relished the company of artists, entertained lavishly and generously in his home, Villa Vita on the Kent coast, which he loved so much. … [He] was not a man who lived for his work, but one whose work served his purpose and vision.' He became rich enough to spend plenty of time in France and to run two large motor-boats as well as his cars. He was married twice, and the second marriage is believed to have been a happy one. He died from an attack of pneumonia caught, probably, after attending the funeral of a friend.

Ernest Hives
1886–1965

Lord Hives, as he became, was probably the greatest man to have anything to do with the car industry in Britain – but his activities later moved away from cars as he became more involved with aero-engines. Hives was born in Berkshire, the son of a Reading schoolmaster. When only twelve, he began a three-year apprenticeship with an engineering firm which also dealt in cars. The boy worked long hours, and when the other apprentices had gone home, he would take instruction from the night shift. By the time he was 14 he was driving on the road and was soon teaching others how to drive. The story goes that he helped a passing motorist to repair his car. The driver turned out to be the Hon. C. S. Rolls. Hives became either his chauffeur or mechanic for a time. This was in 1903. He eventually became the chief motor salesman at Rolls's Fulham distributors, but for some reason moved to Owens and then to Napier, for whom he raced at the second Brooklands meeting.

In 1908 he applied for a job at Rolls-Royce, who were by this time established at Derby. He recalled that when he arrived at the Midland Road station there, 'It was raining so hard and seemed so drab that I span a coin to decide whether to go on to Rolls-Royce or catch the next train home.' Fortunately he stayed and was appointed an experimental tester before there was much experimental work to test. He was brilliant with engines and it is said 'he suited Royce' and 'he had a good ear for an engine'. Charles Rolls by this time had drifted away from the firm, and Hives became Royce's executive officer at Derby, corresponding to the design chief at Royce's French or English seaside base, who was A. G. Elliott. He continued racing and in 1911 drove the Silver Ghost at Brooklands at over 100 mph – he was said to be the first Briton to drive at this speed. He was head of the works team at that time.

By his strong personal characteristics and great commonsense, Hives established himself as a major figure at Rolls-Royce. In 1914/15 he had a prominent share in the work that led to the development of the Eagle aero-engine out of the Mercedes-Benz car engine. Two years later he was appointed head of the experimental department. He must have played a major part in the development of aero-engines during the war, but was probably a supporter of Johnson and Royce in wishing to return to car work thereafter.

Perhaps Hives's greatest contribution to the development of the Rolls business in the 1930s was the emphasis he placed on their costs. The firm itself was most inefficient in its cost-estimation, and major errors were made. Royce recognised the importance of Hives's dedication to the analysis of costs, but probably the other directors did not, as a form of self-deception continued for some years, with the board failing to recognise that the cars were now being subsidised by the aero-engines – that is, by the taxpayer.

In 1936, there were some major managerial changes. Lord Wargrave (Beaverbrook's nomi-

Ernest Hives (third from left) joined Rolls-Royce after an earlier employment as Charlie Rolls's chauffeur or mechanic. He tested their cars at Brooklands which is probably where this picture was taken.

nee), who had succeeded Royce's partner Clare-mont as chairman, died, and was succeeded by Lord Herbert Scott, a figure of some social prominence who had taken over the management of the London sales office in Rolls's day. Worm-wald, who had been the works manager at Derby, virtually throughout its existence, retired, and Hives took over. This was an immensely important change, as Hives alone had the courage and energy to see the firm through the war years. It is beyond the scope of this book to outline his major contribution to the development of aero-engines and particularly the jet engine.

His obituary says that 'having imbibed the Royce gospel of perfection, and proved that it could be approached without interminable delay by organising teams of young specialists and letting intensive testing sort out their ideas, he found a special, almost mischievous satisfaction in demanding, in the field of business, special terms for the privilege of using the services of his company.' Like most of the top Rolls-Royce people, Hives was arrogant, but this characteristic was matched by a deep commonsense of almost Churchillian proportions. Although Sidgreaves (qv) remained managing-director during this period, Hives was the key decision-making figure at Derby from 1936 onwards (ten years later he took over as managing-director) and like the other members of the board he opposed the aero-engine shadow factory scheme. When increased production of aero-engines at Derby became inevitable, Hives at first wanted to move car production to a factory at Burton but later agreed to a move to Crewe. He wrote that this might be 'the salvation of our motor car business. We can go in and start in a fresh atmosphere and not be tied to the traditions of thirty years at Derby'. In fact, Crewe was used first for aero-engines and the car business did not get going there for a further eight years. By the outbreak of war in 1939 car chassis sales were down to about half a million pounds a year, contrasted with aero-engine sales of over seven million.

Hives remained a keen driver, despite his rise to the top echelons of the firm. It was apparently hair-raising to be his passenger as he had little regard for speed limits. One of those who underwent the experience comments that Hives seemed to have a sixth sense which enabled him to know if another vehicle was approaching round the corner, so that he could anticipate with avoiding action and reduce speed. He had a keen humour, and the courage to argue with formidable opponents like Beaverbrook. He played a little golf and fished, but his favourite recreation was snooker, played at the Rolls-Royce guest house near Derby to a background of Ethel Merman on the gramophone.

Arthur F. Sidgreaves
1882–1948

Born in Singapore, the son of the chief justice in the colony, Sidgreaves came to England to be educated at Downside, the Roman Catholic public school. In 1902 he joined the commercial department of Napier, then headed by Montague Napier and Edge (qv). Claude Johnson's brother Basil also worked at Napier and thought highly of Sidgreaves. In 1914 he left to enlist in the RNAS and later the Royal Air Force and spent some time in the Ministry of Munitions which, led by Lloyd-George, was responsible for aero-engine production in collaboration with the department led by the [later] Lord Weir.

Sidgreaves returned briefly to Napiers but in 1920 he was installed as Rolls-Royce's export manager in their London office in Conduit Street, offered the job because of his connection with the Johnson brothers. When Claude died, his brother Basil Johnson took over as chief executive of Rolls for a time, but it was too much for him, he had a nervous breakdown, and his doctors told him to retire completely after only three years in the job. When Johnson retired, he recommended Sidgreaves as his successor and the latter almost immediately brought about the purchase of the Bentley company. He was also instrumental with Royce in making the decision to go ahead with the engine for the Supermarine Schneider Trophy entry, forerunner of the Spitfire, to which Rolls were not at first committed. He was one of those who refused to allow Rolls to enter the Shadow engine scheme, but when war came, he worked with Hives on the large-scale production of aero-engines. Like other Rolls people, he could not be persuaded that any firm outside Rolls could build their products – a major

One of the administrators who kept Rolls-Royce on an even keel in the difficult thirties when aero-engines began to subsidise motor car production.

cause of the failure of Rolls US car building venture in the 1920s.

Sidgreaves is described as 'a shrewd and able financier and aministrator. He was not an engineer by profession, but a life-long association with the industry had developed in him a considerable understanding between technical and economic problems.'

His first marriage, which produced two sons, was dissolved and in 1938 he married again. In 1945 he was knighted and in 1946 resigned from the firm at his own request. Two years later, he threw himself beneath a train at Green Park underground station 'his mind seemingly unbalanced by ill health', having convinced himself, erroneously, that he was suffering from cancer.

Ernest Claremont
1863?–1921

Claremont's claim to fame lies not so much in his own merit, though this must have been considerable, as in his having been F. H. Royce's first partner. The two men met when the young Royce migrated from Leeds to London to work for the Electric Light and Power Company, a pioneer in its field in the 1880s.

Claremont also worked for the firm and in 1884 the two young men decided to establish their own business to make electrical appliances, such as electric bell sets, lamp-holders, switches, fuses, etc, all then in their infancy. It is not clear what their respective roles were, except that Royce was the superior mechanic, and it is perhaps indicative that in 1894 when they set up a limited company, it was called F. H. Royce Ltd.

The previous year the two men had married sisters, the Misses Grace, and this brought a further £1500 of capital into the business, which was sorely needed, as twice the firm was on the edge of disaster. Gradually it prospered as Royce's abilities became more widely known. Unfortunately this coincided with a progressive deterioration in his health and Claremont may have been one of those who persuaded Royce to buy a car, a French Decauville, with a view to getting some recreation and fresh air. He redesigned this car, producing by early 1904 three examples of a 10 hp model, one of which was sold to Claremont and another to Henry Edmunds, also on the Royce board. The latter introduced Royce to Rolls in May 1904. The first result of this was a distribution company, and the first mention of a scheme to wind this up and establish a joint company on a firm basis appears in a letter from Ernest Claremont to his brother Albert, who became legal adviser to the new company, Rolls–Royce. Claremont became chairman.

Thereafter he appears to have played an active past in the affairs of the firm, although Claude Johnson (qv) became the real decision-maker amongst the top management, particular after the death of Rolls. There is a slight impression from the surviving correspondence that Claremont did not care greatly for Rolls, although he was immensely solicitous about the health of Royce. Indeed Claremont and Johnson seem to have seen their roles as being to lift cares from the shoulders of Royce, particularly after the move to Derby, when Royce virtually ended all visits to the factory. For example we find him writing in his 'quaint and somewhat stilted language' that he 'objected to spending on capital account one penny which could be avoided unless Mr Royce agreed to following his medical man's advice.' He was certainly, like Johnson, an exponent of the arrogance which typified the

Royce's first partner and contemporary, as well as his brother-in-law, Ernest Claremont.

management of the company in its formative years. Incidentally both Royce and Claremont continued to control the electrical business in Manchester until it was finally closed down in 1910.

Claremont led the opposition to Max Aitken (later Lord Beaverbrook) during the latter's abortive attempt to take over the company in 1911. During the war he was jealous in keeping, as far as he could, the firm's independence, and seemed to believe that great sacrifices had been made by concentrating on aero-engines at the expense of cars. He was one of those who believed that as soon as the war ended the firm should return to car manufacture. Despite this he was under no illusions about the difficulty of manufacturing cars to Royce's designs, being the author of the laconic comment that for Royce heaven would be a place where cars could be built one at a time, each different from the last. He died in 1921 and the firm's historian says that 'though he is an unobtrusive figure whose activities do not support a view of him as a colourful or robust personality, he must be judged as chairman by the success of the company over whose fortunes he had provided'.

Chapter Six

The French Connection

It was not only French cars that influenced some of the early British designs of the motor men. French designers also came to England and attempts were made to forge connections between French and British firms. The most famous of the French designers to come here was Louis Coatalen who worked for Humber and Hillman before making his mark with Sunbeam. The name Sunbeam was famous for touring cars of 'great refinement if not outstanding performance' which had first seen the light of day in about 1901 as the Sunbeam-Mably. When in 1920 the company merged with the French Darracq concern, the aim was to emulate the American General Motors' international operations with the STD combine (Sunbeam-Talbot-Darracq) as Darracq had already acquired Clement-Talbot. Unfortunately it was not a successful arrangement and by 1929 the rise of Sunbeam can be said to have been over.

Louis Coatalen

The Earl of Shrewsbury & Talbot

George Roesch

Thomas Pullinger

Louis Coatalen
1879–1962

Coatalen was born in the small Breton town of Concarneau, Cap Finisterre and was intellegent and hard-working enough to be selected for a three-year full-time course at the École des Arts et Métiers in Paris. When he graduated, he went to work in the drawing offices of the best automobiles factories in France, moving from Panhard to Clément and then to de Dion-Bouton.

At the end of his initiation he had become 'an aristocrat among technologists' but as the top positions in the national industry were full, he decided to come to England. His first position was as assistant to Charles Crowden at Leamington Spa. Crowden had been involved in the industry since before the turn of the century but when he abandoned attempts to go into manufacture on his own account, Coatalen moved to Coventry where he designed cars for Humber.

William Hillman (qv) wooed Coatalan away from Humber to his house in Folly Road, adjoining Humbers, where he had built a small works in the garden. Coatalen in turn wooed and married one of Hillman's six daughters – John Black (qv) married another. Before long Coatalen was enticed away from Hillman to join the Sunbeam company in Wolverhampton.

Sunbeam had been founded in 1859 by John Marston, a young man of 23, to make tinned plate and japanned goods in Wolverhampton. In 1887 he changed the name to Sunbeam Cycles, which had a reputation for turning out one of the best finished of bicycles. His works manager, Thomas Cureton, suggested to him that 'there is a good trade to be done with a good car. As a go-ahead firm, I think we should not let such a subject – so important – pass, without giving [the] same our serious attention.' However in 1906 Cureton left Sunbeam for Humber, and it was not until 1909 that the firm was transformed by the arrival of the eccentric Coatalen, who immediately set about designing and building cars.

From the first he insisted on an aggressive racing policy and by 1913 Sunbeams were competing in America. In 1914 Coatalan obtained a racing Peugeot which 'was driven to the drawing room of [his] residence, Waverley House, Goldthorn Hill stripped right down, and the pieces laid out on the floor. Two draughtsman, Hugh

A Frenchman, Coatalen came to England to work for Humber and then Hillman. He is seen here at the wheel of the first Hillman car produced in 1907. Later he joined Sunbeam.

Rose and Ted Hatlands, then set about making detailed drawings of the entire car.' This form of plagiarism was not uncommon at the time – other examples range from Henry Royce to Herbert Austin. Coatalen also set about reorganising production. 'He was not a man who muddled through doing everything in his head; he was all the time building up a team of reliable subordinates.' Coatalen's great skill was in the design of engines and the firm's aero-engines were popular during the first world war.

Coatalen had a driving ambition to build a winning Grand Prix racing car. In 1919 he resigned his directorship at Sunbeam and announced that he was about to set up a design centre in Paris. This did not happen but the Sunbeam-Talbot-Darracq arrangement provided him with a similar opportunity to fulfil his dreams. He shuttled between London, Wolverhampton and Paris, feverishly attempting to produce a winning car. He succeeded when, in 1922, Kenelm Guinness broke the world speed record in a Sunbeam and in 1923, Henry Seagrave drove his Sunbeam to victory in the French Grand Prix – the first British victory in a major race since 1902. Again, in 1925, Malcolm Campbell broke the 150 mph barrier in a Sunbeam and Seagrave eventually reached 203 mph in another.

But Sunbeam's fortunes continued to decline. So did Coatalen's. 'The boundless energy and enthusiasm which had brought this remarkable engineer international fame and rewards had burnt itself out, and he embarked upon a melancholy journey of personal decline which was soon to bring him to the verge of insanity.'

Always impetuous, Coatalen damaged his reputation by attempting to design a car to beat Seagrave's 1929 record with the Golden Arrow designed by Captain J. S. Irving. Coatalen's challenger, the Silver Bullet, was a failure. It was his first, but it was enough to cause him to terminate his association with England at the age of 46 on the grounds of ill-health. He sent for Roesch (qv) to return to London to take over. Unfortunately, Coatalen's ambitious racing plans had forced STD to raise £500,000 by 8 per cent redeemable notes. When these fell due in 1934, the firm could not pay and they were brought down.

In 1930, Coatalen returned to France to become chairman and managing-director of Lockheed Hydraulic Brakes, and after that a director of KLG Sparking Plugs (France) with which he was actively concerned at the time of his sudden death in May 1962.

20th Earl of Shrewsbury and Talbot
1860–1921

Shrewsbury was born in London in 1860, educated at Eton and settled down, after his father died in 1877, as the premier Earl of England. He was very fond of coaching and ran the Greyhound coach from Buxton to Alton Towers daily for several seasons. He was the first person to start up cabs fitted with 'noiseless tyres' in London and Paris.

Sales of Clément cars were handled in England by D. M. Weigel who was known to the Earl of Shrewsbury and Talbot. The two men decided

Ready to accomplish.

The 20th Earl (the first was created in 1442) gave his name Talbot to cars and it still survives as a marque nearly 70 years after his death.

to set up a firm to manufacture the Clément in Britain. The new company was formed in October 1902 and land for a factory purchased in Ladbroke Grove, North Kensington, in a rather grubby area not far from Wormwood Scrubs and Kensal Green cemetery. The first cars emerged in 1904. In 1908, Frank Shorland was appointed general manager, becoming managing-director in 1914. Shorland had been a famous turn-of-the-century cycle racer who had worked for Humber and Raleigh. The pre-war Talbot Invincible cars were designed by G. W. A. Brown who had previously been associated with Austin and who finally left Talbot in 1914.

In the war, the Earl's only son was killed on the Western Front and he lost some of his zest for developing the car firm. When Darracq made overtures for a takeover, Talbot put up only a token resistance. The principal shareholder of Talbot at the time was the restaurateur Oddenino, once a famous name in the West End. When Darracq had taken over, they proceeded to merge

with Sunbeam of Wolverhampton, so establishing the STD combine. The Earl died shortly afterwards but his name continued to be associated with cars through the firm's convoluted survival in France and was revived by Peugeot in 1980.

Georges Henry Roesch
1891–1969

Roesch was a Swiss who trained as an engineer. Just before the 1914 War, when he was visiting Paris, the young Roesch fell into casual conversation with an Englishman who was in France on business. He introduced himself as Henry Watts, Chief Engineer of the Coventry Chain Company. Roesch said he wanted to come to England and Watts promised to give him a start. When he stepped off the boat at Newhaven, he had only £10, but within a few days he was installed in the Daimler design department and the Watts family put him up in their home at Berkswell. In 1916, aged 25, after two rather difficult years as an alien with a German name, he saw an advertisement for a chief engineer for Clément Talbot Ltd who wanted to design a car to be ready for production as soon as the war ended. Roesch got the job but at first spent some time designing a radial aero-engine to meet a new Air Ministry specification for a 600 hp unit. He then turned to cars and by 1918 had completed the Talbot A12, which brought about a breach with the directors when they found that he had registered several relevant patents in his own name. After the war, and the Darracq takeover of Talbot followed by the liaison with Sunbeam, Roesch was afraid he would be submerged by the activities of Louis Coatalen who headed design in Wolverhampton.

STD, as the new arrangement was called, held up the launch of the Roesch car and Coatalen tore up not only Roesch's plans but also those of Owen Clegg (qv) who was in charge of design at Darracq. For a while Talbot survived by converting wartime ambulances into touring cars, but by 1921 the firm was in difficult straits. Roesch had by this time become something of a protégé of Coatalen's, and the latter sent him to

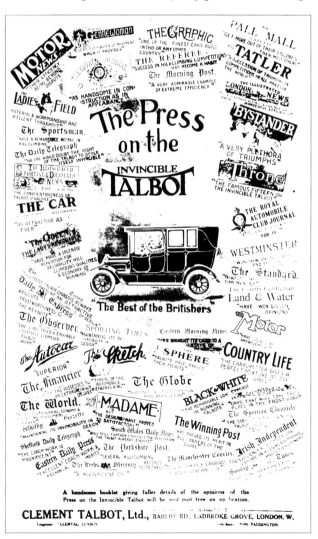

This advertisement, placed by the firm's London showrooms, appeared in the *Autocar* in 1912 when the Talbot was at its peak.

Wolverhampton. Before long, he was transferred to Paris to work with Clegg. Meanwhile at the Talbot works in London, production was falling off in the face of competition from Morris. Two Cowleys could be bought for the price of one Talbot and, by 1925, production at Talbot had virtually come to an end. Coatalen was now in a decline and he telegrammed to Roesch in Paris telling him to return to London.

If the firm was to be saved, Roesch had to produce a new model for the 1926 Motor Show. He decided to make an economical version of the Rolls-Royce Twenty. The result was the 14/45 which in open tourer form sold for £375. This one-model policy was a success for some years.

A new phase in Roesch's career opened in 1930 when he met Arthur Fox and Talbots began a successful racing career, ending in 1932 when the firm retired from competition and Fox turned to other cars. The factory was flourishing, selling a range of successful cars – including a special Talbot for Buckingham Palace in which the occupant could travel wearing his top hat. Talbots were in effect financing the whole of STD.

In 1934 Rootes took over and, in 1939, Roesch, who was 'the supreme egotist, incapable of making any concessions that threatened the integrity of his concepts', left to become chief engineer to the tractor division of David Brown. He was unhappy there but finally found solace, after the war, at the National Gas Turbine Establishment.

Thomas Pullinger
1867–1945

Like many others in the industry, Pullinger worked for several firms, and he is included in this section because of his interests in France and in Sunbeam. Thomas Pullinger was the son of a fleet paymaster in the Royal Navy, who retired to the Isle of Bute. He was educated in Kent, at Dartford Grammar School, and went on to serve as an apprentice with an engineering concern in the same town. Then he became a draughtsman at the Woolwich Arsenal. Like many other motor men, he was an eminent cyclist and won many prizes in 1889. The same year he set up a bicycle repair business in south-east London. In 1891 he was sent off to France by M. D. Rucker of Humber to set up a French branch of the Humber works, but this never materialised. He stayed on in France, motor racing and manufacturing bicycles and motorbicycles for French firms. In the late 1890s, still in France, he designed his first light car, called La Mouche (the flea), and for this he was awarded a medal at the Paris Exhibition in 1900. Back in England he joined the Sunbeam Company as works manager and it is said he turned a heavy loss into a profit in his first year. In 1905 TCP (as he was known) joined the Humber Company at Beeston where he was influential in lightening the frame of the car without reducing its strength. When the Beeston works closed, he moved to Coventry as works manager where he remained until 1909. He later left to go to Scotland as manager of Arrol-Johnston Ltd, and a year afterwards became its part-owner with William Beardmore (later Lord Invercairn) and also managing-director.

Pullinger set up a car plant at Dumfries, and took an interest in the Austro-Daimler aero-engines being built under licence. In 1914/15 the firm turned over to making the so-called Beardmore aero-engine of 120 hp and 160 hp, the latter designed by Major Halford with Pullinger's help. It was built in quantity not only by the firm but by Galloway Engineering, Siddeley-Deasy and others. Pullinger received the OBE in 1919 and the CBE in 1920. In 1926 his health gave out and he retired to Jersey. There he became a successful breeder of pigs and was the first to advise Edge (qv) that 'the animals for the British farmer to study are *Middle White* pigs.' Like other car pioneers who managed to deserve an entry in *Who's Who*, Pullinger did not include in his any mention of his connection with the motor industry.

He married a French woman in 1893 and they had four sons and six daughters.

Chapter Seven

Some Survivors

Few of the British motor men have left their own names to the industry they founded. In other cases, the motor men preferred to use an invented name for their marque or brand (as we should now call it) but again few of these have survived. One of the exceptions is Rover. Lack of space forbids dwelling on the failures, except perhaps to record some of their names. Before 1914, Straker-Squire had been a name to conjure with, and hundreds of others, like theirs, faded away. Bayliss-Thomas, Crouch, Rhode, Deemster, Calthorpe, Calcott, Gwynne, Albert, Horstmann (the first English car to fit a supercharger in 1923), Hampton, Palladium and Eric Campbell were all light cars of the 1920s. There was the Belsize Bradshaw, and the larger cars built by Arrol-Johnson, Angus Sanderson, Cubitt, Dawson and Ruston Hornsby. The HE (built by Herbert Engineering) emerged during the post-war boom, producing handsome, rakish cars that lasted to the end of the 1920s. The two most famous failures, Bean and Clyno, are dealt with in Chapter Five.

This section concentrates on the Rover men.

J. K. Starley
J. K. Starley Jnr.
J. Y. Sangster
Owen Clegg
Spencer Wilks

John Kemp Starley
1855–1901

Starley, one of the leading bicycle manufacturers of his day, was born in Walthamstow, the son of a gardener. In 1872, an uncle (James) who was an inventor, had been impressed by his drawings and invited him to join his office in Coventry. The uncle started a cycle business and Starley took charge of it until it was sold to another firm. He then set up on his own with a friend, who owned a small haberdashery shop in Coventry, providing the capital.

In 1885 Starley produced the Rover bicycle, which had small wheels unlike the then universal penny farthing – and he thus helped set the pattern for the modern safety bicycle. The name Rover had been adopted for a tricycle which was ideal for 'roving' round the countryside. Three years later he built an electric tricar, and another of his inventions was the Coventry chair (a bath chair propelled by a cycle at the rear). He formed a private company in 1889 to make bicycles, and he also attempted to acquire interests in tyre companies. By 1893 Starley was participating in the cycle boom which continued until 1897.

He had by this time become a prominent citizen of Coventry, partly because of his marriage in 1876 to the daughter of a city ribbon manufacturer and city councillor. They had ten children. In 1896, he went public and personally acquired £100,000 when J. K. Starley & Co. became the Rover Cycle Company. It was at this time that he built the largest cycle works in Coventry on a 2½-acre site, and started importing Peugeot motorcycles. He had been buoyant about the prospects for the motor trade, but when the cycle business declined again in 1897 Starley lost confidence. At the AGM in 1901 he was still counselling caution, and it was not until 1906 that a 6 hp car designed by Edmund Lewis (Daimler's chief engineer) was produced. Starley did not live to see it, as he died prematurely of gallstones in 1901, shortly after agreeing to serve another five years at £1200 per annum. The company secretary took over the running of the firm which started production of motor cycles in 1902. His son, J. K. Starley jnr (qv) later took over Rover.

J. K. Starley was a Liberal member of Coventry City Council, a supporter of the Salvation Army, president of the Coventry YMCA and a school board member. He had strong views on religion and was in regular charge of a Sunday school class. He even had printed special versions of the Bible, known as the *Starley Bible*, with the New Testament first, a copy of which he sent to Leo Tolstoy. He was so well-known in the city of Coventry as a philanthropist that some 20,000 people were said to have attended his funeral.

John Kemp Starley Jnr.
1887–1941

JK. Starley junior joined Rover before the first war and by 1916 had become general manager. He discussed with the managing-director, Harry Smith, the kind of car they should build after the war, and decided on a small 2/3 seater in addition to the 12 hp Rover or its replacement. Smith had been managing the firm since Starley senior died in 1901, when his son was only 14. A former employee described Smith as 'short, choleric, who could hardly say a dozen words without liberally sprinkling in what are known today as four-letter words. He was a dominating character, one that nobody crossed if they could help it.' In searching for people to staff this project, Smith and Starley met Victor Riley (qv) whose engine manufacturing business called Nero Engines was in Spon Street, Coventry. Riley offered to go into a joint venture with Rover, putting their own directors on his board. Immediately after the war, Rover also bought up the Components Munitions Co. Ltd. from Sangster (qv) to provide premises for the small car venture.

Losses built up as Rover did badly in the 1920s, and although Starley took over from Smith, things did not improve, and the company secretary Frank Ward was appointed general manager 'to assist in the control of the business'. This was the beginning of the end for Starley. By 1927 the loss was down to £78,000, following the appointment to the board of Sir Alfred Mays-Smith who had 'exceptional knowledge of the motor trade'.

In 1928 the chairman Colonel W. F. Wyley

These two pictures of J K Starley Junior show him, first, at the wheel of one of Rover's early cars, designed after his father's death by Edmund Lewis. This car was entered for the Isle of Man TT race in 1906. Note the multi-spoked wheel reminiscent of the bicycle which was the origin of the Rover company's fortunes.

Below an older Starley stands beside a specially-built Rover 16/50 which made several appearances at Brooklands in the late 1920's. Driven by Ehrling Poppe, a car of this type was able to lap at over 100mph. Soon after this picture was taken, Starley was deposed as managing director of Rover with a golden handshake.

resigned, having held the post since 1909. Starley went off to Australia, ostensibly to visit a Melbourne dealer, but in reality he was deposed, following a shareholders' revolt. He received a golden handshake of £4500 and was replaced by a Colonel Searle, a friend of Mays-Smith, who had no motor experience and was, in his turn, deposed following a visit to New Zealand.

John Young Sangster
1896–1977

Known as Jack, Sangster was born in King's Norton, the son of a mechanical engineer of Scottish origins. His father was director and general manager of a cycle firm from 1897 which acquired the Ariel firm which made motor tricycles, motorcycles and motor cars. Jack Sangster was educated at Hurstpierpoint public school and is said to have served an apprenticeship in French or German cycle and car factories before 1914. During the war he served in the army and when he returned to England in 1918 he decided to build a two-cylinder air cooled car in a factory at Tyseley. The Rover Company at Coventry became interested in it, and eventually the Rover 8 was developed. Rover then bought the factory at Tyseley and gave Sangster the job of organising production where he won a good name for himself. Rover spent £400,000 on tooling for this car.

By this time his father was managing-director of Components Ltd, and in 1922, Sangster left Rover to become assistant managing-director to his father. The firm was not doing well and Jack Sangster's venture into car production in 1924 with the Ariel Nine and Ten 'cannot have helped'. Poor financial results continued until the 1930s, when father and son were joint managing-directors. Despite the injection of new blood in the form of Edward Turner, Val Page and Bert Hopwood, Components Ltd went into receivership in 1932. Sangster was wealthy enough to buy the machinery and part of the premises and he began trading as Ariel Motors, being the chairman and major shareholder. His brother Charles died soon after the start up, and his other brother Harvey, who had been export manager in the 1920s, played only a minor role.

In 1935 he bought the Triumph motorcycle business, which was in receivership, for £50,000. Initially Siegfried Bettmann (qv) was chairman, but, from 1934, Sangster took over. In 1944 he sold Ariel to BSA, probably to reduce death duty liability, and henceforth he concentrated on Triumph. This was also sold to BSA in 1952 for £2.5 million, and Sangster became a director of BSA. He led the boardroom dispute which resulted in the departure from BSA of its chairman Sir Bernard Docker (qv). The BSA historian described Sangster as combining 'a clever head for business with a trained mechanical mind, attributes that enabled him to select the right men as his lieutenants'. Elsewhere he was described as 'needle-sharp' but he failed to see the obvious signs of change which brought about the decline of the British motorcycle industry. Although he was known as a 'shy millionaire', he married three times.

Owen Clegg
1877–

A Leeds-born engineer who trained, like so many other Victorians, in a railway workshop, Clegg joined Wolseley in 1904. There he was spotted by the Vickers management who transferred him to Glasgow to run one of their non-car companies. From there Clegg joined Rover in 1910 as works manager. Clegg was responsible for the 2.2 litre 4-cylinder, 12 hp car which was an instant success. Rover production increased from only 400 cars in 1911 to 1300 in 1912 and was still increasing when, regrettably, Clegg departed to take over the British-

owned Darracq factory in Paris. Clegg soon got the French firm running smoothly. He stayed with the company when it became part of the STD group (see previous chapter) and became managing-director of the French operations.

Spencer Bernau Wilks
1891–1971

Spencer Wilks not only helped bring Hillman to a significant market position in the 1920s, but built up Rover in the 1930s and assisted in the development of the jet aero-engine in the 1940s.

Born in Rickmansworth, Wilks came from a well-to-do family which sent him to Charterhouse and supported his training as a barrister from 1909–14. He served in the army throughout the war and became a captain. In 1919, for reasons not known, he joined Hillman Car Company, where he married one of the six daughters of William Hillman (qv) and became managing-director. When the brothers Rootes (qv) took over Hillman in 1928, Wilks resented this and left to join Rover, becoming works manager in 1929. Rover was then in serious trouble, losing £2–3000 a week and with a Lloyds Bank overdraft pegged at £235,000. The two main creditors, Lucas and Pressed Steel, put in H. Howe Graham as managing-director.

Boardroom wrangles continued, as they had in the days of Starley junior. The latter's successor, a former Tank Corps colonel, Frank Searle, had no previous experience, but he was a friend of Mays-Smith, a board director. Searle, like Starley, was sacked after a visit to the Empire, in his case New Zealand, but at least he had the opportunity to name a successor, Spencer Wilks, who was a relative. Before Searle left, he had complained that P. A. Poppe (qv) was not carrying out his duties satisfactorily, and Poppe too was sacked with a payment of £2000 compensation. His son was also given six months' notice. One of those who worked at Rover at the time says that the firm was not 'in the big time' and recalls that there were only nine people in the drawing office in 1931.

Meanwhile, the largest individual share-

The brothers Wilks revived the fortunes of Rover. Maurice (left) designed the famous Land Rover and Spencer (standing) headed the firm.

holder, one W. E. Sudbury, was suing Searle for having made 'slanderous' statements about him. There were further boardroom rows in 1932, when Howe Graham, the financial director, complained about the activities of certain directors. It was agreed that he and Wilks should henceforth control the firm. Later, Wilks was made managing-director and Graham reverted to being a consultant. By 1934 there was a 'wonderful improvement' and Graham came back on the board. By 1935/6 demand exceeded production. Wilks was by now receiving a commission, in addition to his salary, of over £10,000 a year, and the firm was building 6000 cars a year.

When the war broke out, Rover were building 11,000 cars a year and making profits of over £200,000. Car production had to be replaced with Cheetah aero-engine production, the target being 80 new engines a week. Later, other aero-engines were built. In 1940 the factory was bombed and Wilks rented part of his house at Street Ashton to the company. In 1941, Wilks waived £10,000 of the £15,000 commission to which he was entitled. He continued to run the company until his retirement in 1962, his greatest post-war achievement being the development of his brother Maurice's concept, the Land Rover.

Wilks was described as 'kind, courteous and considerate, almost to a fault.... Having had a legal training earlier in life, and possessed of a finely-honed analytic intellect, he never seemed to lose his impressive calm during any crisis.'

Wilks's brother, Maurice [1904–63], educated at Malvern College, had joined Rover at the same time as technical director. Earlier he had worked at General Motors and Hillman. In 1947 with his brother's assistance, he conceived the idea of a 'go-anywhere' vehicle which became the Land Rover. Before that, early in the war, Maurice's wife introduced her husband to Whittle of jet-engine fame. A short-lived and largely acrimonious relationship with Whittle developed, but it is probable that the Wilks brothers and the team at Rover contributed more to the development of the jet engine than they received credit for from the inventor in his books on the subject. Maurice eventually became managing-director of Rover.

The Wilks family, in the broad sense, were much involved in the car industry. William Martin-Hurst, Maurice's brother-in-law, was managing-director of Rover, and Peter Wilks, Maurice's nephew, was a director. Spencer Wilks's nephew, Spen King, played a prominent part in the development of the Rover turbine car.

Chapter Eight

Some Losers

Some of the greatest names in the motor industry did not survive. Daimler, the first of the names to achieve prominence in Britain (although Herr Daimler was German) still remains in use, even if vicariously. Others like Standard and Singer no longer exist. This section of the book describes the lives of those men who devoted themselves to the promotion of such names only to see them, for no particularly logical reason, fade away. Their names live now, if at all, only in the minds and hearts of the enthusiast.

Reginald Maudslay, Standard
Charles Friswell, Standard
John Black, Standard
Alick Dick, Standard
Siegfried Bettmann, Standard
Vivian Holbrook, Triumph
Lord Leigh, Triumph
George Singer, Singer
William Bullock, Singer
William Riley and sons, Riley
Roy Fedden, Straker-Squire
Edward Lisle, Star
Frederick Wolseley, Wolseley
Benjamin and William Jowett, Jowett

Reginald Walter Maudslay
1871–1934

Maudslay was described as a gentlemanly engineer of the old school and he had a rough ride when his firm came under the control of Friswell, known as 'Frizzy'.

Born in Kensington, London, Maudslay's great grandfather Henry had been a famous machine builder and marine engineer and his maternal grandfather had been the founder of a large firm of building contractors. After school at Marlborough, he followed the family tradition by becoming an apprentice and then employee of a firm of civil engineers. He left the firm in 1902 when his employer, Sir John Wolfe Barry, gave him the capital to start up on his own. Two other pupils, including Alexander Gibb, became shareholders in his new firm. His 'heart was always in motor cars' and in 1903 he set up in Coventry where his cousin, Cyril Maudslay, had become managing-director of the newly-formed Maudslay Motor Co. After a small-scale start, Maudslay acquired premises in Much Park Street, under the name Standard Motor Company.

Maudslay was a gentle soul and he soon fell under the control of Charles Friswell (qv) who first provided financial help and then took over financial management in 1907. Friswell found no detail too nit-picking for it not to be worthy of his attention. Friswell also baulked Maudslay's desire to introduce a small car which did not therefore come into production until after Maudslay again gained control of the firm. Maudslay must have had a miserable life, waiting for the visitations of Friswell, from which he escaped five years later when Friswell's own firm failed

to meet its obligations. In 1914 Standard went public, but only for the comparatively modest sum of £50,000. However, expansion was quite rapid in the pre-war period, reaching 750 vehicles annually, which put them in the top league.

During the war, Standard made aero-engines and air frames in a new factory at Canley, which Maudsley played a considerable part in developing from the 30-acre (later expanded to 300 acres) site he acquired from Lord Leigh .

In the post-war period it 'is difficult to assess' Maudslay's personal contribution to the development of the company, although he was a 'designer of considerable ability, reputedly developing the side entrance car body in place of the tonneau. . . . He relied heavily upon the engineering skills of John Budge,' who joined the firm in 1905 after working for the Triumph Cycle Co. and for Climax Motors. In 1924 they built 10,000 cars, on a par with Austin.

When Budge retired in 1929, John Black (qv) was recruited from Hillman as Maudslay's assistant and it was he who took over the direction of affairs. Maudslay had made a number of mistakes in the 1920s, several of which followed from his enthusiasm for export. In 1927 he allowed production to be largely devoted to an Australian order which left Standard in the doldrums when it collapsed. A new engineer, a graduate of Manchester University, Alfred Wilde, joined the firm from Morris Engines and helped to design the new cars which were to turn round the firm's fortunes in the 1930s. The board lost confidence in Maudslay and so did the bank. It is said that in 1929 the manager was about to withdraw its overdraft in face of losses of over £120,000, but that William Morris told the Barclays manager that if he did not continue to support Maudslay, he would withdraw his own account from the bank. Black appears as a director and general manager by 1930 and in 1933 Maudslay, still chairman and managing-director,

Standard

announced that Black was to be joint managing-director. Within a year, Maudslay was in a London nursing home recovering from a serious operation. He died suddenly a few weeks after the annual general meeting.

Maudslay is described as 'a gentlemanly engineer of the old school who found it difficult to adjust his ideas to the post-1918 industry'. He was married in 1908 and had three children.

The Maudslay Motor Co [1902-1923] was a branch of the well-known family engineering firm which had built marine engines for many years. It built cars in the period before World War I, but although an advanced twin overhead cam-shaft model was shown at Olympia in 1923 it never went into production, and the firm concentrated an commercial vehicle manufacture which had began in 1903. It had no connection with Reginald Maudslay, although the firm was founded by his cousins, Cyril, Charles and Walter Maudslay. Alex Craig designed for Maudslay, as well as for Singer and Lea-Francis (qv).

Charles Friswell
1871–1926

Friswell, the son of a well-to-do businessman, was educated privately. Like many other young men of the time, he developed an interest in cycles, and set up as an agent to sell them along with other business interests. He soon developed a parallel interest in cars, and in 1896 took part in the memorable 'emancipation'

drive. He established one of the first successful motor car agencies in London in 1894, with a capital of £40,000, specialising in imported Peugeot cars.

He was a tough and not very attractive character, and was appropriately chosen by the trade's Automobile Mutual Protection Association to spear-head the test case against Henry Lawson's (qv) British Motor Traction Co. which was trying to create a monopoly by demanding excessive sums for the patents it controlled in Britain. BMT claimed that Friswell was selling a car fitted with a type of carburettor which infringed a Maybach patent they controlled. Lawson's case was dismissed with costs.

Friswell's Automobile Palace Ltd, in Albany Street, London was a five-storey building where hundreds of Peugeots were stocked, as well as having repair shops and other facilities. After seeing the Standard exhibit at the Olympia Motor Show in November 1905 Friswell visited Coventry and was made sole distributor for Standard cars. This company had been founded by Reginald Maudslay (qv) in 1903, but two years later was already in a shaky financial

position. Friswell arranged for a guaranteed overdraft of £10,000 with Barclays Bank which enabled Standard to acquire additional premises in Coventry.

In 1907 Friswell grasped his chance and gained control of Standard, making Maudslay, although managing-director, a mere salaried employee with no share in the profits. He exercised strong personal control over Standard on his frequent visits to Coventry from London. Several different models were produced in small quantities, with frequent modifications and at relatively high prices, which were tailored to meet the demands of his agency which was selling the Standard exclusively. There was an inevitable clash between the demands of the manufacturer and the distributor which Friswell did nothing to resolve. Maudslay was able to make few decisions on his own, however trivial. In 1910, for instance, Friswell's visits averaged one a fortnight, despite several months spent trying to set up distribution in South Africa. Nothing was too minor for his attention – the rattling of the steering gear, the difficulty of replacing a broken valve spring, or the provision of a 'neatly bound guard book' for recording testimonials.

He was knighted in the birthday honours of 1909, probably for the prominent part he played in the entertainment of delegates to the Imperial Press Conference, which in fact was an opportunity to use Standard cars, driven by some hundreds of unemployed London cabmen paid for at his own expense. Perhaps as a result of this, he obtained a contract to supply 70 vehicles to the Indian Government for the Delhi Durbar of 1911 to celebrate the coronation of George V.

While he was in India in 1911 and 1912, a crisis developed in Coventry because of the failure of Friswells the distributors to fulfil their commitments to Standard as suppliers. Maudslay took the opportunity to give notice to Friswell to terminate the sole agreement. Standard was on the verge of liquidation, and many of the employees were on short time, and there was a confrontation with Charles Friswell on his return from India. Friswell spent most of the meeting regaling his fellow directors with a description of the Durbar but he did add that 'it would be advisable not to make any purchases which are not absolutely necessary'. Despite this, he pressed for a 60% dividend at the AGM, which was passed. It was clear that someone had to go. Friswell offered to buy Maudslay out but, with the help of friends and Barclays Bank, Maudslay made a successful counter-offer and Friswell was forced to leave. His motor agency went into voluntary liquidation in 1912 and was reconstructed as Friswells Ltd., but only lasted until shortly after the beginning of the war. Thereafter Friswell himself pursued other business interests, notably in South Africa, and in a silversmiths in Sheffield. He was married, but there were no children.

John Black
1895–1965

Although one of the most significant if least-loved figures of the motor industry for 30 years, little is known of Black's early life. Born in Kingston, Surrey, he studied law and it is believed he worked in a firm concerned with patent law where he was involved in patents for the Morgan car concern. In the 1914–18 war he joined the RNVR and saw service at Gallipoli and later transferred to the Tank Corps in France. He was demobilised in 1919 with the rank of captain. It is presumed that he joined Hillman soon afterwards.

Captain Black, as he was now called, married one of Hillman's daughters, but he was not popular in the firm. A former deputy of his said, 'No-one hit it off with him really, and this is nothing against him. He was an individualist. You either hated him or loved him ... and I alternated between the two fairly often.' In 1929 he joined Standard, becoming joing managing-director with Maudslay (qv). W. M. Heynes (qv) says that when he took over at Standard 'Black made a very good job of it and got the Standard car – which had been sluggish up to then – in a good state.' By December 1931, the whole of the assembly shop had been re-organised and mechanised for mass-production, with ten cars leaving the assembly line every hour.

In 1934, after Maudslay died, Black became virtual head of the firm. 'Many of his fellow directors were plainly terrified of his whims and the records show a process of men promoted, driven too hard and resigning, at times with their health broken.' His dictatorial ways were notorious and Alick Dick said, 'His word was all-powerful and he was feared.' Someone described his huge office at Banner Lane, Coventry, as 'Similar to Mussolini's in his heyday'.

A trade-union leader, who himself admired Black, admitted that 'he was rather conceited.' His managers used to stand up when he came into the room, and Black liked this, and was annoyed when the union men would not follow suit. In fact he was criticised by other employers in Coventry for being too soft with the unions. He had a chequered relationship with the other employers. During the war he joined their association, but when he tried to persuade them to reach advanced arrangements with the employees such as the closed shop and the 42½-hour working week, they fell out with Black and he left the association. He went ahead with his own form of industrial relations and was, in some ways, a far-sighted employer while, in others, tyrannical. His overall effect on labour relations was destructive, in the view of the hard-line management who succeeded him in the 1960s. This, they said, was because 'he paid them more, relaxed discipline and made the factory a nice place to work in.... The [Standard] assembly plant was the worst in that respect that I've seen in the world by a long way, far worse than anything at BMC. It was dreadful.' The quotation is from an interview with John Barber, a senior executive at British Leyland in a later generation.

After the war, John Black struck up a deal to build Harry Ferguson's tractors in the Coventry shadow factory at Baume Lane. There were inevitable rows between these two difficult men. The new Standard managing-director, Alick Dick, who was distantly related to Black by marriage through the Hillman sisters, had been his personal assistant for eight years, and had ambitions to take his place. When, in November 1953, Black was involved in an accident when travelling as a passenger in a Tritotype sports car, Dick and the other directors saw their chance. Black, nevertheless, claimed to be in good health and at Christmas took over the chairmanship and indulged in his usual entertainment at the firm's Christmas party of sacking some top men. On New Year's Day most of the board met at Alick Dick's house near Kenilworth and decided he must go. Dick's wife typed out the letter which they would force Black to sign. Dick and the directors then drove the few miles to Black's home at Bubbenhall. The butler announced them: 'The Board of Standard Triumph' – and they told Black they had come for his resignation on grounds of ill health. Black was ousted at the age of 58 and received £30,000, a Bentley, a Triumph Mayflower and the use of the company bungalow in Wales for five years at £50 a year. He lived, lonely and in some depression, in Wales where he described himself as a farmer. For about a year he was Deputy Chairman of Enfield Cables but his life can be said to have revolved around Standard and he never recovered from leaving it.

In 1943 Black married Alicia, daughter of the Right Rev. J. H. Linton, and there were three sons.

Black (right) chose the young Alick Dick to succeed him, but did not expect to be ousted quite so quickly. The two men were distantly related.

Alick Dick
1916–86

Alick Dick was born in Massingham, Norfolk, in 1916, son of a doctor, and educated at Chichester High School and Dean Close School Cheltenham. He joined the Standard Motor Co. as an apprentice in 1934 and after a wide experience of the factory he was soon promoted – spotted by John Black (qv) to become chief buyer for the shadow factories building Hercules aero-engines just before and throughout the war. During the war, Dick himself became production control engineer of both the Coventry factories which were building cars and aero-engines – yet he was only in his mid twenties. In 1945 he became Black's personal assistant, in 1947 he joined the board, and in 1954 he took over from Black as managing-director after three years as his deputy. He was then only 37. It seemed he would rise to the top as he 'quickly became a national figure, presenting a young, dynamic image, seldom out of the headlines'. Once he had got rid of Black (see above) it was assumed that his rise to stardom would continue unimpeded. However there was no place for him when the debt-ridden, loss-making Standard was sold to Leyland (a deal he personally masterminded) as he had little in common with Sir Henry Spurrier (qv). He is described as 'a deep thinker with an unconventional approach', revealed in his contribution to the Vanguard and the Triumph Herald.

He married in 1940 and had three sons. He was popularly supposed to have been Black's nephew, but was in fact only distantly related to Black through the Hillman sisters.

Siegfried Bettmann
1863-1951

Born in Germany in 1863, Bettmann was well educated by his Jewish father who was manager of an estate owned by a wealthy Bavarian. In 1884, aged 21, he came to London to seek his fortune, stopping in Paris *en route* for the conventional fling. 'I was engaged by Messrs. Kelly & Co. at a weekly wage of 25 shillings. My work was to compile out of foreign dictionaries a suitable collection of firms which would be listed in *Kelly's Directory*. The work was dull and after six months I had the luck to be engaged as a foreign correspondent by the White Sewing Machine Company of Cleveland, Ohio'. After a quarrel with his employer, he set up on his own. 'It was about that time that the bicycle began its successful career' and Bettmann soon became an exporter of bicycles which he had made for him by William Andrews of Birmingham. He gave them the name Triumph. He took on as partner a fellow German, Mauritz Schulte, who stayed with him until 1919. They looked for their own works in Coventry, 'at that time the metropolis of the cycle industry'. With a capital of only £500 from his parents and £150 from Schulte, the business grew slowly. Another German, Philip Schloss, invested his life savings of £100 in the business and was given a director-

ship. Other investments were made by their landlord, A. S. Thomson, Mayor of Coventry and the Bettmann's original White Sewing Machine employer, with whom he had remained friendly.

In 1895 Harvey du Cros (qv) invited Bettmann to Dublin and offered to invest in Triumph. In those days it was almost inevitable that bicycle makers would put engines on them, and Triumph was no exception. Bettmann talked to Humber about building the Humber-Beeston motorcycle and tricycle but nothing came of it, perhaps because Triumph slid into the red as the bicycle boom ceased. By 1905, Triumph had successfully developed their own vehicle. In 1906 some 533 units were produced; in 1907 double the number, double again in 1908, and 3000 in 1909. Bettmann also went into local politics, finally becoming Mayor of Coventry. He was a Labour Party supporter, becoming in the 1920s a close friend of the party leader, Ramsay MacDonald. Yet he was no republican having presented a pair of silver-plated bicycles to Queen Victoria on her birthday; alas, the *Autocar* reported, 'there is no record of Her Majesty ever having ridden one'. Triumph produced a tri-car in 1903 but did not enter the four-wheeler business until 1923 having acquired a factory in Coventry built by A. J. Dawson where, between 1921 and 1923, they built 65 cars.

In 1911 or 1912 Bettmann became chairman of the Standard Motor Company. This was presumably because he provided some of the cash by which the firm's managing-director, Reginald Maudslay, purchased control of the business. His relationship with Standard was short (although they were to join forces 34 years later). Soon after the 1914 war broke out, Bettmann, still Mayor of Coventry (a curious position for a German), was telephoned by a staff captain at the War Office who asked for 100 Triumph motorcycles to be sent to France. 'From our interviews sprang a lasting friendship. I was so impressed by his capabilities,' recalled Bettmann in 1949, 'that I later asked my co-directors to allow me to propose him to become the manager of the company.' This was Vivian Holbrook (qv). Walter Belgrove was, from 1934, chief stylist at Triumph at the time. Trained at Liverpool College of Art and then apprenticed at a coach builders, J. Blake and Co, Belgrove says that, when he joined Triumph in 1927, 'in addition to practical ability, orthographic projection, draughtsmanship, etc, I had a fair grounding in aesthetics.'

Relations between Bettmann and his former partner Schulte deteriorated so much by 1919 that the two were barely on speaking terms. Indeed, it was Bettmann who used his influence with the Triumph board to ask for Schulte's resignation, softening the blow with a golden handshake of £15,000. Holbrook took over his position.

Bettmann was still vice-chairman when, in 1936, Triumph decided to drop bikes for cars, and rather than see the cycles disappear, Bettmann persuaded John Y. Sangster (qv) who already owned Ariel, to take them over. Although he was now 73 years old, Bettmann became chairman of Triumph Engineering, retiring in 1939. The Triumph historian says 'one can't help wondering if his German background worked against him – he was then 75 and lived until 1951.'

Claude Vivian Holbrook
1886–1979

Son of the newspaper magnate, Sir Arthur Holbrook, Vivian Holbrook was a successful army officer in the First World War when he met Triumph's Bettmann (qv). The latter had fallen out with M. Schulte and, in 1919, Holbrook replaced him as their works manager. Holbrook was as keen on cars as Schulte had been, the latter having explored the market as early as 1903. A 2-litre experimental car was built in 1919 and in 1921 there was talk of a light car. A small car company, Dawson, was taken over, after Bettmann had talked to Hillman, whose manager was Dawson.

In 1927, when Triumph were trying to design a small car to rival the Austin 7, they recruited Stanley Edge (qv) who explains, 'I found that the staff was larger than the Austin Motor Company. A. Sykes, the chief draughtsman, had collected around him a man from practically every well-known motor car and motorcycle firm.' This team produced the Super Seven. One new member of the team was Walter Belgrove, Triumph's distinguished chief body designer. The Super Seven was a considerable success (selling

at from just under £150 to just under £200) and in 1930 Bettmann invited Lord Leigh, a local landowner, to become chairman of the company (he was 65 at the time) and Holbrook was promoted to assistant managing-director. He succeeded Bettmann as managing-director three years later. The firm now employed 3000 people.

Holbrook never really liked the successful Super Seven, and when he took over from Bettmann in 1933, he set about changing the kind of car Triumph made. The firm had made a steady living in Coventry when many other firms (perhaps as many as 40) had failed. In September

An army officer who helped Triumph in World War I, Holbrook went on to become Managing Director but gave up building their famous motor bikes.

1933 Holbrook hired the young but balding Donald Healey as technical chief.

The firm was in a bad way and ordinary shareholders had not had a dividend since 1930; there was a loss of £146,000 in 1932. Without Bettmann's knowledge, Holbrook arranged with

Lloyds, their bank in London, to investigate the company's affairs, with the result that Bettmann was forced to give up as managing-director of the company and to become vice-chairman. In 1932 Triumph briefly held merger talks with Rover, but Bettmann, Holbrook and Rover could not agree on who should be 'captain of the ship'. Talks with Riley also failed, but there was an influx of staff from the firm including Captain Charles Ridley (works manager) and his son. Bill Thornton (later Lea-Francis and S S Jaguar) also joined.

Holbrook was described as 'a pleasant businessman with a strong strain of the sportsman in him ... He has a merry twinkle in his eye and ... seemed very well-liked by everyone in the Triumph organisation.' In 1933 he led a team of cars and drivers to enter the Alpine Trials and the following year Healey himself entered Monte Carlo in which he finished third. By 1935 Triumph had stopped building 8 and 10s and were concentrating on Glorias, for which Holbrook bought a works in Coventry, originally built for White and Poppe (qv). The following year, Holbrook sold out the motorbike business to Ariel, a transaction encouraged by Bettmann, who was disgusted at the proposal that Triumph give up motorbikes. Bettmann went to the new Triumph Engineering as chairman. Holbrook himself was knighted in 1938, but by 1939 the firm was in the hands of the receiver. He served again in the Second World War, but thereafter played no active part in the car industry.

Lord Leigh
1885-1938

The Leigh's were one of the rather grand families in the Coventry area where they had been established since 1839 when the first baron was created. They lived in a baronial pile at Stoneleigh Abbey on the outskirts of the city. The third baron, who succeeded his father in 1905 when he was only 20, took an interest in cars and according to the share-register was a considerable investor in the Deasy (qv) company which, but for his intervention, might not have survived to the first world war, despite Siddeley's

considerable abilities. Later Siddeley showed his gratitude by naming one of his cars Stoneleigh.

Lord Leigh also put money into Herbert Austin's company in 1921/2 in the form of a personal loan of £200,000 on 10 per cent debentures, and this restored Austin's confidence at a time when

A local large landowner who helped more than one motor company financially, Lord Leigh had a car named after his family seat, Stoneleigh.

he was developing the Austin Seven. Lord Leigh was also a director and chairman of Standard Motor Co in the 1930s.

After he died, Lord Leigh's estates passed to his nephew and part were leased from him by Harry Ferguson the tractor maker. Harry Ferguson went on to design a revolutionary type of four wheel-drive car but this was after he had severed his connection with the tractor industry and with Stoneleigh.

George Singer
1847–1909

Born in Sussex, Singer worked for John Penn and Sons of Lewisham, a firm of marine engineers. He then went to Coventry to join Starley (qv) at the Coventry Sewing Machine Company, and in 1868 he became fore-

This picture of Singer was taken when he headed up one of the largest bicycle firms in the country. A distinguished Coventry citizen, Singer turned to cars in 1905.

man. The company diversified into bicycles and in 1875 Singer resigned to start his own bicycle business with his brother-in-law. He was the first builder to suggest making the front forks of the bicycle. The Singer Cycle Company became a prominent firm in the business and Singer himself became Mayor of Coventry 1891–3. In 1901, when the cycle boom was over, he began experimenting with cars and that year acquired the

rights to manufacture the Perks and Birch motor wheel. In the four years which followed, Singer built several forms of propelled vehicle with the help of a designer Alex Craig.

In 1905 he had acquired the licence to build the car designed by Lea and Francis (qv). After Singer died, the firm continued as one of the more active of the British manufacturers, under the leadership of Bullock (qv) until the latter resigned and the firm was reorganised in 1936. By this time Singer had 'come to the end of the road' but the war prolonged its existence until 1956.

William Edward Bullock
1877–1968

Born in Birmingham in 1877, the son of a smith, Bullock was educated at Smethwick Technical School. By the age of 14, he was a toolmaker's assistant at the Handsworth firm of Dennison & Wigley. He left to join an electrical firm but returned to his old employer. This became the Coventry Ordnance Works of which Bullock was appointed manager. In 1908 he moved down the road to become works manager at Singer at the age of 32. He was a small man in stature with a chin which was 'a caricaturist's delight', but his main characteristic was his energy and his dictatorial methods which were said to be 'in keeping with his name'. Bullock was always one of the first at the factory where he read everyone else's mail before they arrived. He was a strong advocate of advertising, and introduced novel sales features such as the sliding roof, safety glass, four brakes and rear-mounted petrol tanks. He was the first British car manufacturer to employ an artist with his own studio where car bodies were designed.

Singer was one of the basic Coventry cycle industry concerns. After the collapse of the cycle boom, the firm experimented with motorcycles and, in 1904/5, cars. These were unsuccessful and the firm was reconstructed in 1909, by which date it employed 600 workers in a plant in the centre of the city. It was making four models, and, by the 1912 Motor Show, the Singer Ten had been developed (by Bullock or by whom is not known). In 1913 it built 1350 cars. During the war the firm went into munitions and, by 1919, Bullock was managing-director. He adopted a policy of acquisition and by 1926 the firm was building 9000 cars a year. He prepared ambitious plans for growth and the capital was raised to £1 million and then to £1½ million, enabling Bullock to buy Daimler's wartime factory. By 1929 the firm was making 28,000 cars a year, 15 per cent of the total UK output, and with seven factories and 8000 employees was the country's third biggest car maker. Sales then began to fall in face of competition, and Bullock's leadership was increasingly questioned. At the 1936 AGM he was not re-elected to the board and he left soon afterwards. His weakness was his lack of skill in financial matters, and it is said that Singer was effectively finished in 1936.

He was married three times: in 1902 to the daughter of a moulder (she died in 1934), then in 1936, the day after he resigned from Singer, to a divorced daughter of a vet, and, after they were divorced, to the widow of his first wife's brother. His son William (b.1902) became director and general manager of Singer, leaving in the same year as his father to join Guy Motors.

After he left Singers, Bullock worked with Aron on the development of fire pumps. During the 1939–45 war he worked on the Warwickshire farm belonging to his daughter and her husband, and retired completely after his third marriage.

William Riley and Sons
1851–1963

Willaim Riley had a family weaving business in Coventry in the 1870s and when the industry began to decline he bought out a cycle manufacturer who was on hard times. Under his direction this flourished and in 1896 the Riley Cycle Company was formed. The firm's first vehicles were motor bicycles, tricycles and quadricycles, the latter being the first to be publicly exhibited at the Crystal Palace in 1899. Riley had five sons and in 1896 Percy Riley, the inventive genius of the family, left the Henry VIII Grammar School in Coventry and occupied

himself with the design of a car which he built in the cycle workshops. It was completed in 1898 and soon made a run from Coventry to Stratford-on-Avon non-stop, a journey of 18 miles. In 1900 a Royal Riley quadricycle was put on sale and in 1903 three of the brothers formed a Riley Engine Company to make their own engines. They are described as 'one of those magnificently practical Coventry families which could turn their minds and hands to producing anything which the market wanted'.

Percy took charge of their new factory and, by 1907, Riley tricars had reached the peak of their development, and the brothers had to move into larger premises. From 1905 they had been experimenting with four-wheelers and as cycle manufacture waned, car production took over. Their 12–18 hp cars were a considerable success and in 1913 the brothers set up the Riley Motor Manufacturing Company next door to their engine company. When the war broke out the

Designed and built by Percy Riley in 1896–8, this was not only their first car, but the first car fitted with an engine with mechanically-operated inlet and exhaust valves. Percy had the design brains in a family which could turn out anything mechanical.

four Riley brothers offered to enlist but were told to turn their works over to the Ministry of Munitions. By now a new Riley generation was arriving, with Percy's son working in the drawing office. Percy refused to take any profit on munitions contracts; his particular forte was still engine design and during the war he designed an aero-engine, which was not put into production. No more cars were built until 1919 when the name of the motor manufacturing company was changed to the Midland Motor Body Company.

Although Victor Riley was now in charge of the firm, it is said that it was Victor Wallsgrove, not Riley, who was responsible for turning the Riley Eleven of 1919 into a sports car. Wallsgrave was born in Warwick, worked in the motor industry as a young man, moving from firm to firm (perhaps as a result of his apparently brash, opinionated personality), then served in World War I before joining Riley as assistant works manager. Once there, he began competing in trials, using standard Rileys. In the summer of 1922 he took the body shell off the trial car he had been using and had a stark, new, two-seater aluminium body fitted. This was the Redwinger as the wings, chassis and wheel spokes were all painted red. Wallsgrove became official competitions manager and Riley's sports cars were put on sale – in all about 100 seem to have been made. Wallsgrove's further career is not recorded.

Meanwhile, Percy and his brother Stanley, in the Engine Company, had been working on the design of the famous Riley 9, launched in 1926. This was the smart Monaco fabric-bodied saloon, which introduced the concept of the boot to the British motor industry. Its lively twin camshaft/push rod engine endured, in essence, until 1957. Despite the fact that Percy was in charge of design, he was sometimes over-ruled by Victor, and when this happened in 1933, according to Vernon Barker, 'this led to Percy's virtual withdrawal from his heavy involvement in the design side at Rileys, almost for the rest of the company's independent existence.'

By 1937 Riley was heading for financial trouble and the brothers brought in from Humber the Canadian Lewis Ord as general manager. They paid him £500 a month to make economies but he failed to do so and when the firm made a substantial loss, Ord left after nine months. There was talk of a merger with Triumph but nothing materialised and a receiver was appointed in February 1938.

Victor Riley then went to see Nuffield, whom he had known since pre-war days, who agreed to buy the firm for £143,000, leaving Victor as managing-director. In 1947, in one of Nuffield's typ-

The head of the Riley family was William who started as a cycle manufacturer in Coventry in the 1890's, and let his sons take over.

ical purges, Victor Riley was sacked. The Riley marque continued until 1969.

William Riley, the father of the brothers, died in 1944 at Kenilworth aged 93. Percy died in 1940 at the age of 58, Stanley in 1952, Victor in 1958 aged 82, Cecil in 1961 aged 66, and Allan Riley, the last survivor, in 1963 at the age of 82.

Roy Fedden
1885–1973

Born into a prosperous, middle-class family in Bristol, Fedden went to Clifton College and, in 1903, was about to join the army when his father bought a car. This inspired the young man to take up engineering and his father paid £250 for him to become a premium apprentice at the Bristol Motor Company. By 1906 he was designing his own car. He was introduced to an Irishman called John P. Brazil who ran Brazil Straker, an engineering company in the city, and who agreed to build Fedden's car, called the Shamrock. The 21-year-old Fedden was put in charge of producing the car for the 1907 Olympia show. It was an instant success and in 1908/9 about 150 cars were built, though they were marketed under the Straker-Squire name. Fedden specialised in engines, and his cars were successful in racing. By 1914 he had built about 1,300 machines. When the war came, the works at Fishponds, Bristol, were turned over to staff cars, lorries and shells. The factory eventually employed 2000 workers under Fedden's control.

A sailing friend of Fedden's was in charge of engine development for the Admiralty air services and he gave Fedden's firm an order for the overhaul and, if possible, redesign of an American aero-engine supplied to the navy. Fedden made a success of it, as a result of which he was given a contract to build Rolls-Royce aero-engines and the French Renault aero-engines. Fedden went on to design an air-cooled engine which was in competition with the Rolls water-cooled type. After the war Brazil Straker was dispersed and its Bristol works became the Cosmos Engineering Company. Straker-Squire cars continued to be made in London until 1926. In 1920 Cosmos was bought by the Bristol Aeroplane Company to become their engine 'department'. Before that, in 1919, Fedden and his designer Butler produced the Cosmos, a small car with a three-cylinder air cooled radial engine which, when it was shown at Olympia, attracted 2000 orders. However, it never progressed beyond the prototype stage.

Although Fedden made a great success of the Bristol aero-engine business, he never got on with the owners of the firm, and in 1942 he was sacked. Within a few months he returned to Bristol for a meeting in the flat of Alex Moulton, also attended by the journalist Gordon Wilkins; the subject was what kind of car would be saleable after the war. Fedden had money to invest in such an enterprise (he was reputed to have been the highest paid engineer in Britain), and he also had considerable prestige – by this time he had been knighted. He moved into Moulton's flat, and the design of the car proceeded. Later they leased offices from the Dowty group in Cheltenham. By mid-1946 the design, with a rear-mounted sleeve valve power unit in the manner of Fedden's aero-engines, was complete, but Moulton left to complete his studies and then to join the family business. There were problems with the design and the car was finally abandoned.

Fedden had also worked for the government in the period 1943–5 and in the summer of 1945 while he was in Germany on an official tour, he returned to look over the Volkswagen factory which he had first visited in 1938. According to his biographer, Fedden commandeered a Volkswagen, brought it back to England in a Dakota, and called a conference of British motor industry leaders to study it. 'One and all were scathing' – Ford in particular saw not one good feature, and ridiculed the use of an air-cooled engine mounted in the rear. The only man who did not laugh was Rootes who said, out of pity, 'It's actually got some ingenious features. Indeed, I'm grateful to you, Roy, for bringing it over. But of course it's all a waste of time. Even if the Germans try to go on making it, it'll never sell.'

Other approaches were also made to British industry regarding the Volkswagen, but with similar lack of success.

Edward Lisle
1867–1922

Edward Lisle's father was a partner in the Sharratt and Lyle cycle company since 1883; and some time later he formed his own bicycle company, Star Cycle Co. The Star Motor Co, like the cycle company based in Wolverhampton, was an offshoot formed in 1898. Their first car was based on the Benz and other, longer cars of Panhard ancestry followed. Lisle's son, also called Edward Lisle, produced the Starling car at the cycle company and it seems that at one time both firms were building cars.

It was said that 'all Stars up to 1914 were extremely well-made, well-furnished, conventional, rather expensive cars, lacking in technical originality.' They sold well and were being turned out at about 1000 a year up to 1914, making Star one of the big six manufacturers. They went out of business in 1932.

Frederick York Wolseley
1837–1899

The Wolseley car was one of the leading products of the motor industry for many years, but its progenitor had little to do with cars. Frederick Wolseley, third of four sons, was born in County Dublin in 1837. His eldest brother became the outstanding Colonial soldier Field-Marshal, Viscount Wolseley. Frederick was the only one of the four brothers who remained a civilian and he went to Australia before he was 30 and became the manager of a sheep station in Victoria. As he had a natural flair for engineering, it was not long before he began to consider **mechanical methods of sheep-shearing. He took**

Wolseley himself never built cars, but he had the foresight to chose Herbert Austin to run his firm which later built cars.

a room in Melbourne where he made experiments, based on which he took out his first patents. In 1876 he purchased a large sheep station near Walgett to use his inventions in practice. The following year he established the Wolseley Sheep-Shearing Machine Company Ltd., with registered offices in Sydney, with the object of exploiting his 40-odd patents. In 1889 he established an English company and wound up the Australian. Unfortunately, the machinery he produced was unreliable. He recruited Herbert Austin (qv) to work in Australia and later in England and it was thus through his chance employment of Austin in the sheep-shearing business that the name of Wolseley's company came to be associated with cars. Wolseley resigned from the firm in 1894 and died in 1899.

Benjamin & William Jowett

The brothers established a small workshop in Bradford, Yorkshire at the turn of the century on £90 capital, one third from each of them and another from a sister. Their father was an expert on gas engines and the Jowetts graduated from cycle repairs to cycle building and then to motor-cycles and a little flat twin engine 'with a big pull'. They only experimented up to the 1914 war; in 1919 the company was recapitalised and they seriously set about car production, making one of the most practical of the light cars of the 1920s and 1930s.

After World War II, the Jowett name was attached to an utterly different type of car. This was a 'continental' design introduced by Gerald Palmer in 1947, with bodywork inspired by the Lincoln Zephyr from America, and named the Javelin. The old name died in 1954 after 30,000 Javelins had been built. The significant point was that the Jowett's little engine had continued in production for nearly fifty years.

Chapter Nine

Some Winners

Pioneers do not always win the race, particularly it might seem in British industry where the very characteristics that enable them to succeed in the early stages of growth – practical ability, courage, single-mindedness – may mitigate against them once the going is more sophisticated. Those interlopers who then take over the running are not always as loved as were the pioneers. Rootes for example are not as revered as Riley by the cognoscenti. To which the winners may well respond by laughing all the way to the bank. This section describes the careers of some of the winners – winners in the sense that their cars were still synonomous with quantity production in the postwar world.

William & Reginald Rootes, Rootes
William Lyons, Jaguar
W. M. Heynes, Jaguar
Donald Stokes, Leyland
Henry Spurrier, Leyland
Percival Perry, Ford
Rowland Smith, Ford
Patrick Hennessy, Ford
Laurence Pomeroy, Vauxhall
Charles Bartlett, Vauxhall

William Edward Rootes
1894-1964

Rootes was born in Hawkhurst, Kent, the elder son of a cycle and motor engineer. Educated at Cranbrook public school, where he was not a shining success, he became interested in motorcycle racing and took an apprenticeship with Singer Motors in Coventry, which he soon gave up. In 1915 he volunteered as a pupil engineer in the RNVR, and after becoming a lieutenant transferred in 1917 to the Royal Naval Air Service.

His father, Edward Rootes, had already established a modest engineering business at Hawkhurst and Billy (as his eldest son was known) had managed a branch at Maidstone which he opened in 1913. It was therefore natural that after the war he should suggest to his brother Reggie (qv), who worked at the Admiralty, that they should be joint managing-directors of Rootes Ltd, registered in 1917 to take over the car distribution business at Maidstone. It is said that they first set up shop in a shed at the end of the family garden. Their father gave them each £1200 to facilitate their progress, and they also brought into the firm a friend, John Chaldecott.

They are described at the time as 'a perfect pair in the business sense, Billy seeing the visions on the horizon and striding towards them in, so to speak, seven league boots; Reggie surveying the intervening ground with his keen and calculating eye and making sure that no loose ends in whatever project was afoot, were left untried.' Billy himself said, 'I am the engineer and Reginald is the steering and brakes.'

Rootes sold Singer, Austin, Humber, Hillman and Clyno cars, amongst others. By 1923, they were Austin distributors for London and the home counties and a year later had an interest in a Birmingham firm. Their offices in London expanded by 1926 into Devonshire House, opposite the Ritz Hotel, 'a move which staggered the motor distributing trade', of which they were by now the largest single component.

In 1924 they had tried to take over Standard and in 1927 to take over Clyno, but in both cases were rebuffed. Nevertheless, Rootes were determined to get into manufacture and persuaded Sir George May of the Prudential to finance them. They had already acquired an old established coachbuilders, Thrupp & Maberly, in 1925. Rootes had also taken on Humber's export distribution, so this company was the object of Billy's attentions. Slowly he built up his shareholding in Humber and by 1928 he had a controlling interest in the ordinary shares which enabled him to insist on a new scheme of finance and management. William became deputy chairman and Reginald managing-director. The same year they increased the capital of Humber to enable it to take over its neighbour Hillman. In 1934 they bought Karrier Motors, in 1935 Clement Talbot Ltd and Sunbeam Motor Car Co. Ltd. This came about because STD had defaulted on its 10-year notes and Hillman acquired Talbot. However, production of the Roesch-designed Talbots ceased in 1937 after Rootes had produced a prototype for Edward VIII with whom he was said to be on friendly terms.

By the end of the 1930s, Rootes had become one of the 'big six' with an output in 1938 of 43,000 cars or 10 per cent of the national output. William was now a pillar of the motor trade, a newcomer perhaps, but pushing enough to become vice-president of the SMMT in 1934-6 and president in 1939-1942. He never lived in Coventry, but he had a close interest in the city, particularly after the wartime air raids. He also was the main provider of funds for the new post-war University of Warwick. He was raised to the peerage in 1955.

Most of his life his main interest was farming and in the 1930s he moved to Stype Grange, near Hungerford, where he was well known as a breeder of pedigree livestock. He had married the daughter of a miller in 1916; they were divorced in 1951. Both the sons of this marriage were active in the business.

William was 'unquestioned head of the Rootes dynasty.... He provided the power unit for the firm while his brother supplied some of the checks and balances.' He was a superb salesman 'with the gift of persuading anyone he met that that was the person he had been waiting to see all day'.

By 1967 when the Rootes brothers could no longer control the organisation themselves, the business had been sold to the U.S. Chrysler concern and although a British board continued to

Advertising in the motoring press played a major part in promotion from the earliest days. This 1933 picture is captioned 'Yet Again Standard give the Public the Cars they Want' but many people, even at the time, felt that manufacturers were more inclined to try to foist on the public cars which the manufacturers preferred to build.

Rolls Royce pursued a 'one model' policy from the 40/50 h.p. Silver Ghost in 1906 until 1922 when the growing demand from owner-drivers for a smaller, less formal car from the now world-famous manufacturer resulted in the 'Twenty'. In 1929 the 'Twenty's' engine capacity was increased from 3,127 to 3,669 cc, and became the 20/25. Nearly 4,000 of these 20/25s were built, before they were replaced in 1936 by the 25/30 (4,257 cc).

The Riley firm did well in the early 1930's with cars like this 1934 Imp. But by 1937 they were making a substantial loss and the following year Victor Riley, who had known William Morris since before World War I, appealed to him to buy the firm, which he did.

The two Rootes brothers were complementary in character, with Billy (left) providing the sales drive and his brother Reginald the administrative backup. Here they are seen together on board ship returning from one of their many sales drives to America in 1946. Sir William, or Billy, was given a peerage in 1959 in recognition of the amazing post-war success of car exports from Britain.

exist under Gilbert Hunt, whom the Rootes family recruited from Massey-Ferguson because they thought he would be able to deal with the Americans, the British connection gradually dissolved.

effort, the firm building 60 per cent of all armoured cars, 30 per cent of scout cars, 14 per cent of all bombers and about 50,000 aero-engines. He was knighted in 1946.

Reginald Claude Rootes
1896–1977

Reginald's life is described in the notes on his dominant brother William. The only point at which he escaped that dominance was when his brother left the firm early in the war to head the Supply Council of the Ministry of Supply. Both brothers had been involved in the development of the shadow factory scheme by which the motor industry was brought in to manufacture large aero-engine, and later aircraft production, to assist the much smaller aircraft industry. Reginald played a major part in this

William Lyons
1901–85

Born in Blackpool, where his Irish-born father had married a local girl and founded a school of music, Lyons went to the grammar school and then to a private school, followed by reading engineering at Manchester Technical College. He worked briefly for Crossley and sold cars for a local firm. He then met William Walmsley, son of a prosperous coal merchant, who had started making Zeppelin-shaped motorcycle sidecars in his garage and front room where his wife did the upholstery. Together they set up the Swallow Sidecar Co in 1922 with a guaranteed overdraft of £1000, which was provided half and half by their respective fathers. Lyons said that the firm began with the proverbial three men and a boy. Their premises were two of the three stories of an old building. The sidecars were fitted to a chassis built by Montgomery's of Coventry. Finances were difficult and Lyons used to arrive at the bank late each Saturday morning with a cheque for the wages which usually exceeded the overdraft facility.

In 1924, soon after his marriage, Lyons bought an Austin Seven. 'The conception of this car had a strong appeal,' he said, 'except that the body was a very stark affair, albeit very practical. I believed it would appeal to a lot of people if it had a more luxurious and attractive body.' The result in May 1927 was the open Austin Swallow selling for £187. Lyons went to Henleys and obtained an order for 500. Walmsley told him 'he must be mad' as this meant building 20 a week – although they had by this time moved to larger premises and increased their staff. Lyons recalls that Frank Hough and Bertie Henley were the two partners at the distributor premises at 91 Great Portland Street. 'Hough was a dynamic man with a determination to do things quickly: Henley was the steadying influence and he was also the finest salesman I have ever met.' Henley played a significant part in the financial success of the Lyon's firm.

Lyons was determined to move to Coventry where there was an ample supply of labour, and he found premises in a disused shell-fitting factory five times the size of the Blackpool one. An employee says that in the new premises at Foleshill they were so busy that Swallow (the name of the firm) 'just didn't notice the Depression'. Lyons said, 'It was the most exciting time. We worked from 8 o'clock in the morning until 11 or 12 o'clock at night, for we aimed to raise production to 50 a week within three months.... Before Christmas we had achieved our 50 bodies a week. We were really in business.' By the summer of 1929 they acquired the adjoining factory and built up to something like 100 cars a week.

In the motoring press of October 1931 William Lyons announced his new product, the SSI, which was to be shown for the first time at Olympia that year. He had arranged for Standard Motors to supply a special chassis and this

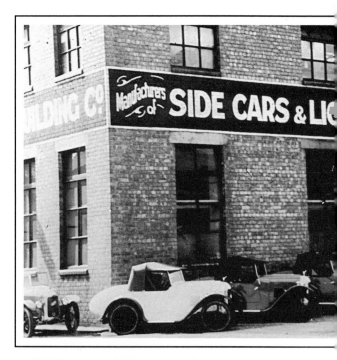

William Lyons started his manufacturing career by building sidecars for motorcycles similar to the one on which he was photographed (above) in 1920. Later he moved to Coventry and expanded production of his special version of the Austin Seven.

was the basis of the SS. It was intended, said the *Motor*, for 'discriminating purchasers, who wish to have in their possession what is something really exclusive in motor car design at a very moderate figure'. The first open model, the SSI tourer, was sold in 1933 and participated in that year's Alpine Trials. Two years later Lyons took on W. M. Heynes (qv) of Humber as chief engineer, who designed a new engine which was used in an entirely new range of cars named the SS Jaguar. The name Jaguar is said to have been chosen by Lyons from a zoological list drawn up for him by Ernest Rankin, the firm's publicity manager. By 1937 an accessory firm produced a Jaguar ornament but this displeased Lyons so Rankin, an amateur sculptor, produced another which was stylized by F. Gordon-Crosby. At first this was an optional accessory selling for 22 shillings.

It is said that Lyons did very little actual design drawing in these later stages of his career, preferring to direct a handful of trustworthy and sympathetic men working full scale in metal. W. M. Heynes says, 'He was no engineer – he just knew a good car when he saw one. English and continental cars would be brought in and driven for assessment and if there was anything good on them, we would copy it.'

When Lyons introduced the SS Jaguar saloon to his dealers at the Mayfair Hotel in 1935, he displayed the car on a stage and asked the seated audience to write their estimate of the selling price on a card which was handed to each of them. When the cards were gathered up, a calculation of the average estimate came out at £765 'so when I announced that the actual price was £385 it created quite a lot of excitement'. In 1935 Lyons's original partner wanted to retire and so Lyons arranged for a public issue for SS Cars Ltd. Walmsley took cash and Lyons bought up sufficient shares to ensure he had a majority. Walmsley went off to build horse trailers. During the war the firm made fuselages for Stirling bombers and centre sections for the Meteor, the first British operational jet fighter, as well as repairing Whitley bombers and making trailers. Six of the workshops were destoyed by bombing in 1940.

Heynes gives a few personal impressions of Lyons at this period. He did not have much of a light touch, and lacked a sense of humour. By temperament he was a hard taskmaster. For example, Heynes recalls how he told Lyons he would like to take a holiday in two or four weeks' time. Lyons responded sharply, 'Why? Are you ill?' Heynes replied, 'No, but I haven't had a holiday for two years.' Heynes also describes Lyons board meetings as 'really a joke. He just said

what he wanted to do, and everybody agreed with him – 'except,' Heynes says, 'me.' However Heynes admitted that Lyons could put himself out and be nice to people whom he knew he needed.

One of these was John Black (qv) with whom, in his earlier days, Lyons had worked closely, and who had personally bought one of the first SS sports models. Standard provide the chassis and Lyons had a hard job persuading

After his retirement, William Lyons came back to Jaguar on a number of occasions to meet the man who took over the company and led it to privatisation, John Egan.

Black to let him establish the SS marque as his own. Whether it stood for Standard Swallow or Swallow Special was 'never resolved' Lyons said. After the war, Black told Lyons he was going to concentrate all production on the Vanguard so would be unable to make their engine for Jaguar, as the firm was now called, and Lyons, worried that Black might sell the engine to another firm, even though the design belonged to SS, now saw the opportunity to become a self-contained manufacturing unit. He bought the engine tooling from Black, although later Black suggested a return to the previous arrangement. Lyons replied, 'No thank you John. I have now got the ball, and I would rather kick it myself.' Black later tried to compete with Jaguar by buying Triumph.

The change of name to Jaguar was made in 1945 in recognition of the fact that, as Lyons explained, 'The SS initials [had] acquired a tarnished image ... a reminder of the SS German

troops, a sector of the community which was not highly regarded.' During the war, Lyons had encouraged his team, William Heynes (qv), Walter Hassan and Claude Bailey to develop a new twin overhead camshaft XK engine and, in 1948, this was unveiled in the magnificent XK 120 sports car. The engine went on to power every Jaguar until 1975. Lyons had decided in the mid-1960s that he would have to merge with BMC, partly because Jaguar Cars' independence was threatened once the big combine had taken over Pressed Steel, which supplied his bodies. This happened in 1965 and Jaguar accordingly became part of British Leyland, created in 1968, although Lyons stayed on until 1972. Somehow or other, Jaguar retained its independence within the combine, even after nationalisation, and was returned to the private sector in 1984. A new rapport was forged between Lord Lyons, in retirement, and the new chairman of Jaguar, Sir John Egan.

William Munger Heynes
born 1903

Born in Leamington and educated at Warwick school, Heynes was a premium apprentice with Humber in 1922/5 and later worked in the drawing office. He then worked for the chief stess engineer at 30s. a week. Once the Rootes brothers took over in 1928, they put Lewis Ord in charge and he got on well with Heynes. Ord 'was quite a brilliant man who really stirred the company into life'. Prior to that 'Humber had allowed their car to get very old-fashioned and they were having a job to sell them. They were expensive and they weren't particularly good.' For example when Heynes tried to interest Cole (qv) in a new suspension, and explained its novelty, Cole's response was, 'Oh well, I think we're better to leave this to somebody else to try.' Heynes joined Lyons (qv) at SS (Jaguar) in 1935 where he held the position of chief engineer with some distinction, claiming that, unlike the other directors, he was not afraid to expresss his mind to his dictatorial boss. During the war, with Walter Hassan and Claude Baily, he developed the XK engine which powered the Mark VII.

Heynes retired to the countryside south of Coventry and is one of the few motor men who has left to posterity an illuminating tape recording of his experiences in the industry. This is kept in the Coventry City archives.

Donald Gresham Stokes
born 1914

Son of a transport manager in Plymouth, Stokes grew up with a passion for buses. Most of those in the city were Leyland and at the age of eleven Stokes had already decided he wanted to work for the firm. He went to Blundells public school but left in 1930 when he was 16 to be an apprentice at Leyland. His part-time technical education was obtained at the Harris Institute of Technology in Preston. During World War II he became a Lieut. Colonel in REME (Royal Electrical and Mechanical Engineers)

and while he was serving in Italy in 1945, the war over, Henry Spurrier (qv) asked him 'to write a brief on the way Leyland should organise its exports when the war was over'. Stokes's view was that 'it was the old Imperial markets, the Middle East and South America' on which Leyland should concentrate. In 1946 he rejoined Leyland as export manager and, in 1949, flushed with success, Spurrier made him general sales manager. Four years later he was on the board.

Although this book technically ends in 1945, mention must be made of Stokes's future connection with what became British Leyland. In 1963, when Spurrier was dying, Stokes replaced him as chairman of Standard-Triumph, acquired only

Donald Stokes became a figurehead of the car industry in the 1960's, but he started as an apprentice at Leyland, the truck firm in Lancashire.

two years earlier. He was by this time deputy chairman and managing-director of the new Leyland Motor Corporation. Himself 49, his seniors on the board were all in their seventies. In 1965 he was knighted and became chairman. In July 1965 Denis Healey, the Labour Minister of Defence, asked him to advise on arms exports. Stokes, then regarded as Britain's master salesman, recommended that the government should set up a special organisation for arms sales, similar to that operated by the Americans. He also became a founder member of the Industrial Reorganisation Corporation, formed by the Labour Government in 1966 to 'improve the competitiveness of British industry'. It was therefore inevitable that he should become, in due course, head of the BMC/Leyland merger. He admitted afterwards that Leyland 'were not exactly flooded with management skills' and some have suggested that Stokes's skills as a salesman were not the number one priority for BMC. He was raised to a life peerage in 1969 and handed over British Leyland to a new chairman after nationalisation in 1975.

Henry Spurrier
1898–1964

The family firm of Leylands, headed by the Spurriers, nearly went into motor car productions under Henry III, pictured here in his later years.

The Spurrier family's connections with Leyland Motors go back to 1896 when two brothers, George and Henry, persuaded their father, a retired businessman turned farmer, to finance the Lancashire Steam Motor Company to build steam-powered vans and lorries. The first petrol-driven vehicle appeared in 1905 and the first bus in 1906. The name Leyland, after a village six miles south of Preston, was adopted in 1907. The firm entered the car market briefly with a challenge to Rolls-Royce in 1920 with the Leyland Eight, but only eighteen models were built. The son Henry took over the firm in 1919 following which there were financial difficulties and bankruptcy was a possibility. In 1922 they produced another car (under the Trojan name) which continued in production in van form until 1956. By 1931 the firm was building its own diesel engines, buses and other large vehicles being its main output.

The managing-director, Henry, had a son also called Henry (or Henry III to differentiate him from his forebears). He went to Repton, then joined the family firm as an apprentice. During the latter part of the first war he flew as an RFC pilot in the Mesopotamian campaign where he contracted dysentery which plagued him for the rest of his life. Returning to the firm during the early post-war years of financial difficulty (his salary was cut from £500 to £400 per annum) Henry III set about motor car development.

With the chief engineer J. H. Parry-Thomas (qv) and his assistant Reid Railton (qv), Spurrier helped develop the 'straight eight' which was the most expensive car on the British market at the time. It was developed for racing by Parry-Thomas before he was killed in 1923. This was Spurrier's last pre-war incursion into cars, and he thereafter concentrated his attention on Leyland commercial vehicles.

In 1942, after his father's death, Henry became general manager, and in 1949, managing-director, when he appointed the 35-year-old Donald Stokes (qv) as general sales manager. In 1955, Spurrier was knighted. Five years later, Leyland made a bid for Standard-Triumph, not part of a master plan but because they were competing with the latter's commercial vehicles in export markets. The takeover was approved in 1961 and Spurrier took over from Lord Tedder as chairman. He had only a brief tenure, effectively handing over to his protegée, Donald Stokes, as he lay dying in 1963.

Percival Perry
1878–1956

Perry was born in Bristol but brought up in Birmingham where he won a scholarship to King Edward's School. He had set his heart on a legal career, but his parents did not have the money to finance him. One day he saw a newspaper advertisement for a £1 a week job with H. J. Lawson (qv) in Holborn, so he sold his stamp collection to pay for a rail ticket to London where he talked Lawson into giving him the job. In Queen Victoria's Jubilee Parade, his sales expertise was employed in using him as the driver of a Coventry Molette [a Bollée] labelled 'Even a fool can drive one'.

Eventually, he left Lawson to join his uncle's print business in Hull, but the call of London was too much, and when he returned there he met a young man who had obtained the Ford franchise for Europe for a payment of £500. Together they set up the Central Motor Car Company in London's Long Acre. In 1906, Perry sailed to Detroit, staying with Henry Ford at his Harper Avenue home. While in North America he visited Gordon McGregor in Toronto, one of the tyros of Canadian business, who had acquired the rights to sell Ford cars in Britain and the Empire. McGregor generously waived the British rights, saying that the Empire was big enough for him. Perry's firm now had the rights for the UK and Europe and this enabled him to reconstruct Central in 1907.

However Perry soon clashed with his partners and set up an agency selling another American car. By 1909, Henry Ford had decided to set up a permanent presence in Britain and Perry ran their London-based saleroom. When Ford opened its Trafford Park factory in Manchester in 1911 to mass-produce model T's, it put Perry in charge. He had paid only £2000 for a long lease on the 5½ acre site. By 1914 he had a network of 1000 dealers and the most effective car producing plant in the country – as well as a reputation as the most able business executive of his day. He had acquired the confidence of Henry Ford and his son Edsel and was constantly urging them to expand their facilities in the UK, although Ford preferred Ireland.

During the war, Perry was seconded for government service, for which he was knighted in 1917. After disagreements with Ford after the war, Perry decided to leave the company, and together with a group of business associates he founded the Slough Trading Estates in the Trafford Park model – a great business coup. Unexpectedly, in 1922 Perry withdrew from business, deciding to spend the rest of his life on Herm island, in the English Channel Islands, writing prose and poetry.

Meanwhile, Ford had fallen on hard times. An American executive visiting the Manchester

A strange picture of Edsel Ford, Henry Ford II and Percival Perry, the Briton whom the Ford family admired.

factory in 1923 found the British manager with his feet on the desk, reading the morning newspaper and drinking tea. This did not go down well. Soon the firm had fallen to fourth place in the market, behind Austin, Morris and Singer. When Henry Ford visited England in 1928 and asked Letts (qv) to suggest someone to take over his new operations at Dagenham, Letts proposed Herbert Austin. Instead, Ford decided to tackle Perry again. He accepted and recruited a new team, including Rowland Smith (qv). Dagenham became operational in the summer of 1932. Perry was instrumental in encouraging the introduction of the Model Y in that year, 'the best-selling small saloon of the 1930s' which by 1934 held over half the 8 hp market.

Ford, Dagenham, under Perry's direction, went from strength to strength. With Michigan USA and Ontario Canada, it became one of the three main centres for Ford production world-wide, producing vehicles for sale in Europe, Turkey, the Middle East and Africa north of Rhodesia (the rest of the British Empire was Canada's province, following the agreement made with McGregor). Forty per cent of the shares in Ford UK were offered to the British public. Yet like the rest of the British car industry, it remained curiously old-fashioned. John Barber, who joined the firm from the civil service in 1955, described it as 'a fairly old-fashioned company; the finance department was full of little men in green eyeshades. At the time we virtually had no graduates – there were about five or six in the company.'

Despite this, Ford's reputation was unparalleled in the industry and the credit was largely Perry's. Lord Brabazon described him as 'by far and away the most cultured, intelligent and attractive personality' of the car industry's founding fathers. It was sad that he should have worked for a foreign company. He retired in 1948 at the age of seventy.

Rowland Smith (left) and Patrick Hennessy (right) two of the Britons who built Ford UK up to its considerable eminence under the leadership of Perry. Centre is Stanford Cooper, vice-chairman of Ford of Britain

vehicles and controlling the two shadow factories in Manchester which made a major contribution to winning the war in the air by building Merlin engines for fighters and bombers. He insisted on using female labour there, an innovation which a sceptical Ministry of Aircraft Production resisted. He was knighted in 1944 and became chairman of Ford of Britain in 1950. He retired in 1956.

Rowland Smith
1888–1988

Born in Gillingham, Kent, and educated at the Mathematical School, Rochester, Smith started as an apprentice at Humbers at Coventry in 1904 and graduated as a jig and tool designer. He moved to Ford in 1924 after a spell as their distributor in the Far East, based in Calcutta. He had hoped to become assistant manager of the Manchester works, and when he was disappointed, left to join Standard as works manager. When Perry came back to Ford in 1928/9 to start up the Dagenham factory, he recruited Rowland Smith as his second-in-command and general manager. He became managing-director of the UK company in 1941 after Hennessy (qv) left to join Beaverbrook at the Ministry of Aircraft Production. He turned Dagenham over to war production, building nearly 350,000

Patrick Hennessy
1898–1981

Patrick Hennessy masterminded the rebuilding of Ford of Britain in the post-war period. He was born in County Cork in 1898 and from a rural Irish boyhood and an education in Cork, he joined Ford there immediately after the first world war, in which he served as an officer in the Royal Inniskillin Fusiliers. He rose to be production manager and in 1931 went to Ford Dagenham as purchasing manager. In 1939 he was made general manager. When Beaverbrook became Minister of Aircraft Production in 1940, he appointed Hennessy as his right-hand man, preferring his advice to that of the despised 'Air Marshals'. The following year Hennessy was knighted. After the war, he joined the board of Ford UK and became managing-director in 1948 and chairman 1956–1968. He married in 1923 and had three children.

Laurence H. Pomeroy
1883–1941

Pomeroy was one of the most distinguished and respected British designers. Like many other relatively well-off young men of his era, he served an apprenticeship with the North London Railway Co. Afterwards he went to work for Vauxhall, a firm which had acquired the name from the district where it was originally situated, near the Thames in London. By the time Pomeroy joined them they had built a factory at Luton. Pomeroy became their designer (this was many years before their take-over by General Motors) and already in 1908 when he was only 25 years old he had designed a car that 'put Vauxhall in the forefront of advanced thinking'. By 1910 he was 'coaxing 100 mph out of Vauxhall sports cars at Brooklands' and in 1912 he was appointed chief designer.

After the war Pomeroy decided to leave Vauxhall, much to their disadvantage as he was

described as 'a realist' who would have had a restraining influence on the kind of cars they decided to build for the post-war motorist. As soon as he heard Pomeroy was leaving Vauxhall, Lanchester wrote to Martin (qv) urging him to recruit the young man for Daimler. 'If I had shares in Vauxhall I would sell them quick,' wrote Lanchester. 'It was as nearly a one-man show as anything in the country!' Pomeroy in fact did not join Daimler and instead went to the United States where he built an all-aluminium car.

By 1925, Vauxhall had been bought by General Motors and at about the same time Pomeroy returned from America and joined Daimler. The early days of his ten-year stay there was characterised by frequent and resounding rows with Lanchester as Pomeroy was one of the few motor men of the time who was sufficiently well-versed in the technical aspects of automotive engineering to take on Lanchester. At first, under the amenable direction of Percy Martin all went well, and Pomeroy was made

Seen here at the wheel of a famous early Vauxhall, the Prince Henry C type, is the equally famous designer Pomeroy. He was about to take the car up the notorious Lynton hill climb.

managing-director in 1929. In 1931 the opportunity came to buy the Lanchester Motor Co. (run by brother George) and Pomeroy welcomed this as an opportunity to introduce his poppet-valve engine under their name which would, he hoped, lead to production of a more popular, middle-class Daimler car. It was not to be. Manville died in 1933, Percy Martin retired in 1935 and Pomeroy was pushed out in 1936 when he failed to achieve re-election to the board.

He decided to leave the car industry and went to de Havilland Aircraft as general manager of their engine division. This did not work out and he moved on to H. M. Hobson. Pomeroy's son, also named Laurence, became a distinguished journalist, joining the *Motor* as technical editor in 1938.

Charles Bartlett
1889–1955

The Vauxhall ironworks was founded in 1857 on the south side of the Thames and, like several general engineering companies, they experimented with cars in the early years of the century. Their first car was built in 1903, a 5 hp single-cylinder model with tiller-steering. In those days the firm was a relatively small one, and even after the move to Luton in 1905, Vauxhall sports cars, though much esteemed, were not built in large numbers. The managing-director in these early days was the Eton-educated Leslie Walton.

The post-war period was not successful, and by 1925 Vauxhall had built a mere 1400 cars since production began. General Motors of America, baulked in their attempt to buy Austin,

wanted to make a start in Britain and decided to purchase Vauxhall. Sloane said, 'It was in no sense a substitute for Austin. Indeed, I looked on it only as a kind of experiment in overseas manufacture.'

Their success in Britain was in no small part due to an Englishman, Charles Bartlett. Born in

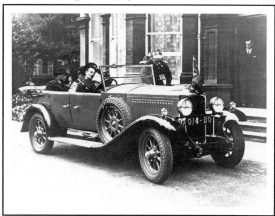

A 1930 Model T 20/60 Princeton Tourer built at Vauxhall after General Motors took over. The passenger in the back is the Prince of Wales.

Bibury, Gloucestershire, and educated at Bath Technical College, Bartlett had obtained a job as a clerk in a depot which General Motors opened up in Hendon to handle imported vehicles. He made such rapid progress that in 1926 he was appointed managing-director and in 1926 moved to the Vauxhall works at Luton, taken over by General Motors, as managing-director, staying there until he retired as chairman in 1954. Bartlett had a broad-based intellect and a colleague says he was 'a determined character [with] a strong, stocky physique and a sense of humour that leavened what could otherwise have been too paternal an outlook towards the Vauxhall workforce.'

Bartlett was knighted in 1944 for his contribution to wartime production.

Chapter Ten

The Sports

In horticultural terms, a sport is an offshoot from the true branch. In the motor industry, there were men who were not necessarily in the main line of the business but whose names are nonetheless revered wherever the motor men are in discussion because they gave a 'sporting' look to their products. The image of a car as some kind of latter-day four-legged charger has largely devolved from the products designed by these men.

Archie Frazer-Nash
Henry R Godfrey
Donald Healey
R. A. Railton
David Brown
Sydney Allard
Thomas G. John
Lionel Martin
A. C. Bertelli
Parry Thomas
The Jensens
W. O. Bentley
Cecil Kimber
Henry Morgan

Archibald Goddman Frazer-Nash
1899–1965

Archie Frazer-Nash and H. R. (Ron) Godfrey had been friends while engineering students at Finsbury technical college, and during their later apprenticeship at a Rugby steam-engine firm (later part of GEC) they worked together on what was to become the GN cycle car.

In 1910, Nash left Rugby to work for the infant British School of Motoring as an instructor and then for an engineering company where he concussed himself in an industrial accident. While convalescing, he designed a 'creepabout' the simplest form of four-wheel mechanical vehicle. This was publicised in the *Motor Cycle* magazine as a result of which many orders were placed. Called the GN, this simple vehicle went into production with the help of £1000 capital provided by an enthusiastic owner. Despite its

Most photographs in the press of Frazer-Nash describe him in such words as 'genial as ever'. He is at the wheel of 'Rikki-Tikki' a works racing car.

crudity, it had remarkable road-holding and steering. Godfrey designed the GN's engine based on the Clément cycle engine. Orders flowed in to such an extent that in 1913 the firm was able to move into specially-built premises at Hendon.

When the war broke out, Frazer-Nash joined up and was seconded to the War Office where he worked on the problem of firing machine guns through aircraft propellers, during the course of which he learned to fly. Post-war, the two men continued with the GN and an arrangement was made to build it in France. H. R. Morgan (qv) handled the publicity. At the end of 1924, they

decided to cut back production and go into the sports car market, but they had taken on other directors in order to obtain funds and the two men now only had a minority shareholding. The board insisted that they build cars of a type unpalatable to both Frazer-Nash and Godfrey. Both men left the firm, Godfrey to become the G in the later HRG Ltd and Frazer-Nash to open up

a business on his own in Kingston-upon-Thames. The first Frazer Nash car was built in 1924, which retained the GN's distinctive dog clutch gear change and chain drive.

In 1925, a year later, he amalgamated with William Thomas to form W. G. Thomas and Frazer Nash Ltd, with ten times the floor space but very little capital. Thomas then left the firm and wanted his money with the result that Frazer Nash was unable to expand. In 1927 he formed AFN Ltd, with Richard Plunkett-Greene, a schoolmaster from Aston Clinton, as the largest shareholder in the company with the title of sales director. Another investor was Eric Burt, a director of Mowlems the builders, whose wife went on the board too. In 1928 Archie Frazer-Nash became ill and went into hospital and during his absence the firm was taken over by H. J. Aldington, an active director who had left the previous year. Aldington was a businessman while Frazer-Nash was not. Frazer-Nash continued as a consulting engineer and his hydraulic gun turret for military aircraft proved highly successful during the Second World War. In 1938 he changed his name to Frazer-Nash, with a hyphen, though the cars were never so called. The last Frazer Nash car was built in 1957, with a BMW V8 engine, far removed from the original chain-drive sports car which had ceased production in 1938.

Aldington had some strange quirks. He would not use the hyphen which Frazer-Nash insisted was part of his name, and in 1931 he secretly bought Aston Martin but would not reveal the fact until years later. His ownership only lasted several months after which the failure to sell Aston Martin cars resulted in Aldington selling the business to Prideaux-Brune. Aldington later developed a relationship with BMW and, after the war, with Bristol Aeroplane Co.

Henry Ronald Godfrey
1887-1968

The son of an amateur engineer, 'Ron' Godfrey's interest in mechanics was encouraged by his father and at the age of 14 he was given a $1\frac{1}{3}$ hp Clément engine which he fitted on his pushbike. When he left school he took a job as an office boy with Werner motor cycles, but before long signed on at Finsbury Technical School where he met Frazer-Nash (qv). The two designed the first cycle-car and went into partnership with him as GN Ltd. Both he and Nash fell out with their later partners at GN and left the firm.

In the mid 1930s, when he had a general engineering business, he formed a new company with E. A. Halford and G. H. Robins to build the HRG car which has been described as 'a sophisticated Frazer Nash without that car's unique chain drive'. He stayed with the HRG firm until 1958 when he retired to live near Guildford.

Donald Mitchell Healey
1898-1988

Healey's father had been a car enthusiast and his son coupled this with a keen interest in aviation. He travelled over 300 miles to see Blériot after his cross-Channel flight and pestered his father to let him make flying his career. 'He eventually agreed and allowed me to leave school at a far too early age in order to become an articled pupil with Sopwith at

Kingston-upon-Thames. In spite of paying a large premium, it meant working ten hours a day for only six shillings a week.' This must have been 1912/13. He went to Brooklands and had many flights with his hero, Harry Hawker, who had a Gregoire racing car which he let the under-age Healey drive on the track. In 1915, still under-age, he joined the RFC, got his wings in 1916, was invalided out two years later and transferred to the Aeronautical Inspection Department which, he says, 'cured my craze for aeroplanes'.

Returning to his birthplace in Peranporth, Cornwall in 1919, he went in for racing and opened a garage on a piece of land his father bought next to his shop. From 1930–34 he was racing for Invicta, winning the Monte Carlo rally outright in 1931. Graham Robson says there is no doubt that if he had concentrated on a sporting career in the 1930s he might have become one of our most outstanding folk-heroes. Instead, he became immersed in automobile engineering. In 1933 he went to lodge at Barford near Warwick and joined the Riley experimental team. In 1935 he moved across Coventry to become experimental manager and the technical director of Triumph. From then until 1939, with only a short

Healey was a young pilot in the First World War. It is said that he saw no future for aeroplanes other than as weapons of war and therefore joined the motor industry.

break at Lucas as competition manager, he was in charge of design and development at Triumph. The latter collapsed in 1939, and after managing the Hobson aero-engine carburettor company for a short time, Healey joined Humber-Hillman to develop fighting vehicles.

Meanwhile he was working on his own design of car. He tried to sell the idea to the engineering group Thos. W. Ward who had taken over the remains of Triumph, but they were not interested. He therefore set up on his own with the help of friends including A. C. Sampietro and Ben Bowden. Also helping were Wally Allen, an ex-Triumph director who provided a small factory at The Cape, Warwick, and Peter Skelton who built the first bodies. Healey was now 47 years old, rather late in life to start up as a car manufacturer.

In 1939-45 he returned to the Royal Air Force, and after the war built Healey sports cars with Alvis and Riley engines until hitting the jackpot with the Austin-Healey of 1952. Produc-

A much older Healey sits in his Austin-Healey outside Longbridge in 1953, talking to Leonard Lord before setting off on a sales tour of America.

tion of the latter ceased when Leyland took over. Healey is described as an 'outstanding personality' who 'probably did more for the prestige of British sports cars than any other man'. He was an enthusiast and an extrovert with great charm.

Reid Antony Railton
1895–1977

Son of a Manchester stockbroker and educated at Rugby, Railton graduated in engineering at Manchester University and, in 1917, joined Leyland Motors where he became assist-

ant to Parry Thomas (qv). He left Leyland in 1922 to produce the Arab car but in 1927 he joined the famous Brooklands' firm of Thomson and Taylor and subsequently became its technical director. He was responsible for creating John Cobb's 1933 Napier-Railton which held the Brooklands Outer Circuit record at 143.44 mph— and also has the chassis of the ERA rally car to his credit. Railton designed Sir Malcolm Campbell's Bluebird land speed record cars of 1931/35 but his greatest achievement was the creation of John Cobb's Railton record car of 1938 which subsequently held the record at 394.7 mph in 1947, which stood until 1963.

Reid also gave his name to the Railton car of 1933/49 vintage for which he designed the chassis.

Railton emigrated to America in 1938 and died at his home in Berkeley, California, aged 82.

David Brown
born 1904

The first David Brown started the firm in Huddersfield in 1860 when 17 years old. He was a pattern-maker who later turned to making gears. By 1890 he had ten employees including his two sons. When David Brown died in 1903, the two sons took over as joint managing-directors.

In 1912 they turned the firm into a public company and, about this time, purchased the manufacturing rights of two types of car, the Dobson and the Valveless. These were not a success, and when war broke out they were put on one side. David Brown, son of Frank, one of the joint managing-directors, was born in 1894 and entered the firm in 1921 after an education at a grammar school followed by Rossall. His favourite subject was art. Quite early on he took an interest in cars and, while still an apprentice, set about designing his own. He tried to build it in the works, but his father stopped him from continuing. Later, he acquired parts from other firms from which he assembled his own car, which ran successfully. Quite soon he was put in charge of a subsidiary, which became profitable, and in 1929 he was on the board. Two years later, when his uncle died, he became joint managing-director. In 1934 he acquired the site for a new works, where a major item of production was transmission, rear axle and steering for the Harry Ferguson tractor. In the war he turned to gears for aero-engines but he had never forgotten his ambition to make cars and in 1947 he saw an advertisement offering a car manufacturer for sale. It was Aston-Martin, with which firm he became connected for some years.

He also bought Lagonda, it is said because he owned the last one built before the war. He eventually sold out to a firm called Company Development who 'fell under the spell' and continued to put money into the car, until they could no longer afford it. The company was bought by Ford in 1987. Brown went to live in Monte Carlo in 1978. He was knighted in 1968.

Sydney Allard
1910–1966

A llard was born on 9 June 1910, son of a successful building contractor in West London who lived in a large house in Leigham Court Road, a fashionable area of the suburb Streatham Hill. Allard learnt to ride on a motorbike when he was only 14 and joined a local club. He went to public school at Ardingly and, declining to join the family business, found a job with a garage and Daimler dealership, F. W. Lucas Ltd. He also acquired a Grand Prix Morgan three-wheeler which he entered in various competitions. In 1929 a garage in Putney came up for sale and his father bought it for development. He also put an experienced foreman into the firm, Alf Briscoe, and set his son up in business. Over the next few years, Allard specialised in sporting activities while, at the same time, developing the Putney garage and Ford distributorship. In 1937/8 he started building 'specials' but the outbreak of war prevented any more serious plans for production. During the war the firm concentrated on repairing army vehicles.

In February 1945 Allard formed the Allard

Motor Co with a capital of £100. The outcome was a famous car of the postwar years, the Allard sports car. Production of Allard sports cars, with distinctive two door bodywork, began at Clapham in 1946, still Ford V8 powered. However the make was popular in America by which time more potent Cadillac, Chrysler and Oldsmobile V8 engines were employed. Saloons were also produced in small numbers.

'One of the most popular figures in the racing and rally world'. This sketch of Sydney Allard shows the mature man after his Monte Carlo win.

In 1952 Sydney Allard won that year's Monte Carlo rally in one of his cars, giving the marque some much-needed publicity. Production was run down during the 1950s and the last Allard was built in 1960. A brief flirtation with dragsters followed.

Thomas George John
1880–1946

A Welshman, John was born in Argyll Street, Pembroke Dock and educated at the Royal College of Science and Royal Naval College, Greenwich. He was apprenticed as a marine engineer at HM Dockyard and won a considerable number of prizes in engineering subjects. At the early age of 31, he was appointed manager of Armstrong, Whitworth's shipbuilding department at Barrow-in-Furness. Early in the war he moved to Siddeley-Deasy as the works manager. By the end of the war, John had saved £3000 and decided to set up on his own. He acquired the business of Holley Bros & Co. at Hertford Street, Coventry, a firm of American origin which had been formed in mid-1917 to manufacture carburettors – there was a shortage of carburettors in England, particularly after the USA entered the war. The paid-up capital was £4240. In the first sales catalogue issued, John stated that he had acquired the manufacturing and selling rights of the Electra Stationary Engines from Hillman (qv) but at this period it seems John did not have a clear idea of how to get into motor manufacturing.

The firm built up a business making these engines, as well as motorcycle engines and castings. Determined to be independent of suppliers, John acquired a foundry in Lincoln Street, Coventry and recruited an old school friend and Pembroke Dock moulder, E. Morse. When he was working with Siddeley, John had met Geoffrey P. H. de Freville, whose company, Aluminium Alloy Pistons Ltd at Wandsworth, London, supplied them with pistons and castings. Towards the end of the war, de Freville began designing engines of his own, and within about six months had produced the final specifications and drawings for an engine suitable for a car. John realised that with such an engine he would be able to manufacture a motor car of his own, and he negotiated the purchase of the drawings from de Freville together with the name Alvis. The latter had been the registered trade mark used on the de Freville aluminium pistons. One explanation is AL (aluminium) plus VIS (latin for force, power or strength).

John's first car a 10/30 hp model, with 1.4 litre side valve engine, was introduced in 1920. It first appeared at the Scottish Motor Show that year. Production was initially only two a week, held back by design problems and a supplier's strike. The original bodies were made by Morgan of Long Acre, London. Production continued until 1922, by which time John had expanded by the acquisition of a machine shop in Holyhead Road and the original shop and the foundry had been disposed of. The firm of TG John went public in 1921 and the name was changed to the Alvis Car and Engineering Company. John became chairman and managing-director and continued to be a major shareholder. By the end of that year, about 150 cars had been built but the profit was only £3317. Finance was a problem, so John made an agreement with the Buckingham Engineering Co. to produce the Buckingham car which was cheaper than the Alvis. J. F. Buckingham had made his reputation with a cycle-car in 1912–14. The Buckingham venture was short-lived, particularly when the Austin Seven arrived.

John had also met, in his Siddeley-Deasy days, Captain G. T. Smith-Clarke who was officer in charge of aeronautical engine inspection for the AID in the Coventry area. The two men became friends and at the end of the war Smith-Clarke joined Daimler as assistant chief engineer. TJ (as John was known) asked Smith-Clarke's advice about the 10/30 car and was told by his friend, quite bluntly, that it was 'a bad car, badly built'. John replied that Smith-Clarke had better join the firm and put it right, which he did from July 1922, remaining there for 27 years. For his part, John concentrated on the business side of the company. As chief engineer Smith-Clarke introduced a new overhead-valve engine a year later, and this was fitted in the aluminium duckback-bodied version of the Alvis, redesigned as the 12/50. From 1923, Alvis became a significant name on the racing scene – although John had raced his cars from their earliest days. When an Alvis won the 1923 200 miles Brooklands race, Coventry crowds turned out to provide a torchlight procession through the streets as the car was returned to the works on a horse-drawn dray.

By this time, Alvis was employing some 300 people but the financial position had not improved and in 1924 the company went into

W. O. Bentley's great forte was engine design and during the 1914–18 war he produced the power for the Sopwith Pup fighter. After the war his 3-litre engined cars were highly successful like this 1924 model which won the Le Mans race that year.

The first SS car built by William Lyons came out of the Coventry factory in
1931. By 1935–6 he wanted a new name for his new models and Lyons
chose Jaguar which he said had 'an exciting sound'. This sports model, the
SS100, which made its debut in 1938 had a $3\frac{1}{2}$-litre engine.

A typical Dunlop poster from The Sphere, October 19, 1935, showing an
idyll of motoring before the war.

John at his desk in 1929 about ten years after he had started to build up the substantial firm which was later to go into aero-engine production as well as high-quality cars which are collectors' items today. He was a man of wide interests who never quite made the mark he intended.

receivership; within a year John had succeeded in retrieving the position and coming to an arrangement with his creditors, though he resigned as chairman and was replaced by Sir A. Lowes Dickinson. John is described as a man with considerable personal charm who exuded a confidence which enabled him to interest friends and relations in supporting the firm, despite the lack of accurate sales forecasts.

Like most of the industry, Alvis suffered in the mid 1920s, yet they succeeded in growing steadily in the years from 1925–9. The firm had also been working on a special front-wheel drive hill climb car which 'caused a sensation' when it appeared in 1925. There was also an advanced eight-cylinder Grand Prix derivative of 1926 but it achieved little success. Selling this FWD concept to the public proved difficult. Both Smith-Clarke and his colleague and chief designer, W. M. Dunn, tried to persuade John to redesign the car, particularly to reduce noise, but money could not be found and eventually the front-wheel-drive concept was abandoned after a production version had appeared in 1928/30.

Typical of John's approach to the business are the following extracts, written by him, from a 1929 catalogue: 'The making of Alvis cars has become very largely a labour of love on the part of all those employed, whilst thousands of Alvis owners esteem their cars in a personal way that, I really believe, does not exist in any other class of motorist or with any other make of car.' That very year, his profits dropped by £10,000 to £22,000 and by 1930 the profit was a mere £1600. His bank loan was £60,000 and he needed further funds. One solution was to abandon his factory-supported racing teams. At the Motor Show that year, John had the fortune to meet Charles Follett who ran a successful car showroom in the West End of London and also raced at Brooklands. They talked all night about the future of Alvis, and in the early morning made a fast drive to Coventry, arriving in time for breakfast. Follett contracted to take one-third of Alvis production and became the sole concessionaire for London and the Home Counties.

Meanwhile Smith-Clarke was ill, and in his absence W. M. Dunn designed the Ace, assisted by A. Kemp and A. F. Varney on engine and chassis respectively. 'When Smith-Clarke returned to work three months before the 1931 Motor Show he expressed disapproval of the Ace, and the project was abandoned.' Smith-Clarke pressed ahead with his own concept which was designed and built in 14 weeks to the drawings of A. F. Varney. This was the Speed Twenty, a touring car capable of 100 mph which was an immediate success. Smith-Clarke was rewarded with a directorship in 1932 and a net profit of £24,000 in that year saved the firm from further insolvency. One interesting sideline on John's character is that about this time he set off on a tour of Europe on horseback and later wrote a book about his experiences.

In his attempts to put the firm on a sound financial footing, John conceived the idea of building aero-engines which, by the mid-1930s, threatened to be a major shortage in the rearmament programme. Both he and Smith-Clarke had aeronautical experience, but the latter thought the project unrealistic. John persisted, certain that another war was coming, and in 1935, the issued capital was increased to £370,000 to enable the project to be started. His confidence was misplaced. His letter to the Air Minister informing him that Alvis had the capacity to build aero-engines was not even answered and there was no official encouragement for a firm which was outside the 'ring' of manufacturers. Eventually Alvis built components for Rolls-Royce and later John was given an order for a piston-engine for training aircraft, so the new factory capacity he built was eventually used. In the interim John had come to an arrangement with the French Gnôme et Rhône concern to build their engines under licence – a project abandoned in 1939.

John also entered into an arrangement with a Hungarian designer, Nicholas Straussler, who specialised in armoured cars and similar vehicles. A joint company was formed in 1936, and an Air Ministry order for armoured vehicles placed in 1939. These new developments put further financial strain on the company and, by 1938, with over £500,000 spent on aero-engines and no government contracts, the future looked bleak. There was a stormy Annual General Meeting and John and Straussler parted company.

Cars were still being built – 277 in the year ended July 31st 1938 and 337 in the next twelve months, with a 100 or so after that. Fortunately for John, his schemes for increased capacity for aero-engines and vehicles bought a new prosperity to the firm at the outbreak of war. The original factory was repeatedly bombed at low level in November 1940 but by the end of the year Alvis, in common with other armament firms, was operating more factories – eight sites rising eventually to twenty.

During the war, John suffered increasingly from illness and he retired in 1944, dying two years later at his home in Kenilworth. One of his employees says that shortly before he left the firm he called a meeting of the directors and explained 'that we should go back in the motor industry. He wasn't at all sure what part of the motor industry we should go into, whether it would be small cars, medium cars or big cars, and he asked all of us to submit a report (saying) what was the right thing to do.'

Ironically, Alvis car development after the war was a considerable disappointment as the main emphasis was placed on the successful launch of its piston aero-engine. In 1946, J. J. Parkes became managing-director after having been a test pilot and the senior manager at de Havillands, his main interest being aviation rather than cars. In 1951 Alec Issigonis briefly joined Alvis to work on a new car, but it failed to go into production, and in time cars were no longer a significant part of the Alvis story. In 1965, Rover bought the company and the last Alvis car left Holyhead Road in 1967.

Lionel Walker Birch Martin
1878–1945

One of the few leaders of the motor industry who went to Eton, Martin was born to parents living in comfortable circumstances in London whose wealth came from the English China Clay mines in Cornwall. They bought their son a bicycle at the height of the cycle craze and this became his passion when he went up to Oxford to study at a small private college of 20 or so students called Marcon's Hall. Just as Rolls represented Cambridge, so Martin cycled for Oxford. Incidentally, Morris, then building bicycles in Oxford, beat him by one foot at the end of a ten-mile race in 1900. After Oxford, he joined a London cycling club of which Montague Napier was a member. Ill with lumbago, he had to give up cycling and after 1905 he was more and more immersed in the motoring scene, as a rich young man who bought cars from his friend Napier, and visited him in France.

In 1912 Martin went into partnership with

Lional Martin looking at one of the very early forms of Aston Martin car
which derived its name from the hill climb. Despite the so-called 'cor-blimey'
cap in the photograph, Martin was an old Etonian, one of the few in the
motor industry top ranks.

Robert Bamford and before the outbreak of war
they had designed their prototype Aston-Martin
car which derived its name from the Aston Clinton hill climb. However there was no production
during World War I as the small premises they
had acquired in South Kensington was closed
down. (The firm began in even smaller works in
Callow Street off the Fulham Road.) The
machinery was sold to Sopwith and Martin himself went off to work for the Admiralty. In 1918
the old team re-formed, this time at Abingdon
Road, and when Martin married again (his first
wife had died in childbirth just before the war)
his second wife became intensely interested in
his motoring activities. In 1921 the first Aston-
Martin appeared, a solidly engineered small car
selling at about £800, but this coincided with the
departure of Robert Bamford, joint founder of the
company, who is said to have 'lost interest' in the
project. Martin bought out his share and put his

wife as director in his place. She was known to
many as 'Calamity Kate' while her husband was
accepted by everyone as in a different class – a
'dear old thing' someone called him, who in days
past would have been a 'dandy'.

The Aston-Martin car always had a reputation which 'far transcended its small-scale production'. The best year for sales was 1933 when
105 cars were delivered but by this time Martin
no longer had any connection with the firm or
the car that bore his name. He had re-formed the
company in 1922 with plans for quantity production but the company was wound up within a
year of the restructuring. The rich racing enthusiast Count Louis Zborowski then agreed to put
up £10,000 for two Grand Prix cars which were
entered in the 1922 French GP but with little
success.

Another young old-Etonian who had recently joined the company, John Benson, then

persuaded his mother, Lady Charnwood, to put up money. Benson went on the board. A year later, the company was in the hands of the receiver and on 13 November 1925 Martin left the works for the last time. He also sued Benson for damages for remarks he is alleged to have made. During the proceedings it came out that Martin had invested £31,000 of his own money in the company. Alas, Martin received only 1¾d damages – he should never have sued. This was the end of what was virtually a hobby for this well-off man.

In 1926 the Bamford & Martin firm was bought up by W. S. Renwick who with A. C. Bertelli (qv) designed a new car which began as the R & B Special and then became the Aston-Martin once more. The bodywork was designed by his brother Enrico (Harry) Bertelli. There was a brief link-up with Frazer-Nash (qv) in 1931 and in 1933 R. G. Sutherland took over and retained control until after World War II.

Amongst those with whom Martin talked with a view to raising funds were Vauxhall and the Bristol Aeroplane Co, presumably Roy Fedden (qv), but these were unsuccessful and Martin virtually retired from manufacturing in 1926-7, devoting himself to his mining interests. He continued thereafter to take an interest in racing as an RAC steward. He and his family moved to Kingston-on-Thames where they lived in some style. When the war came in 1939 Martin returned to his old love, cycling. He was knocked down at the traffic lights in Kingston when riding his tricycle in 1945 and died a week later. Had he lived, he would have seen the take-over of the name again in 1947 by David Brown (qv). Of the 11,500 Aston-Martin's built with the name, about 11,000 were built after Martin's death.

and attended technical evening classes at University College, becoming a devotee of rugger. He then went back to Italy, working at Fiat, and was taken on as riding mechanic to the leading professional driver, Nazarro. Just before the outbreak of war he returned to England and was working in the design office of Grahame-White at Hendon throughout 1914-18. Afterwards he worked in and around Birmingham, becoming General Manager of Enfield Allday and acting as a consultant to a number of Coventry firms such as Armstrong-Siddeley, Coventry-Simplex (now Climax) and Rover.

In 1926 he and William Renwick bought the Bamford & Martin firm over which Lionel Martin (qv) had lost control. His brother Enrico (Harry) designed the bodywork of the car they called the Aston Martin and which formed the basis of all subsequent models sold during the interwar years. However Renwick clashed with Benson and both left the firm, the former joining MG where he worked on the R-type.

Bertelli continued with Aston Martin during the depression, helped by finance from a number of sources. These included S. C. Whitehouse, the ex-Vauxhall managing-director Percy Kidner and H. J. Addington of Frazer Nash. In 1932 the company was bought outright by a Newcastle shipping tycoon for his son R. Gordon Sutherland, who became joint managing-director with Bertelli. The cars they produced competed regularly at Le Mans, Brooklands and the Ulster TT. Their Ulster Aston Martin is described as one of the truly great British sports cars of the 1930s.

By 1937 Bertelli and Sutherland had fallen out and Bertelli resigned, severing his connection with the motor industry and, like other prominent motor men, turning his attention to pig breeding.

Augustus Cesare Bertelli
1890?-19??

Son of an Italian socialist who for political reasons decided to emigrate to South Africa, Bertelli was brought up in South Wales which was as far as the family got on their journey, arriving there in 1894. After school, he was apprenticed at a Cardiff Iron and Steel works

John Godfrey Parry Thomas
1885-1927

Thomas's father was a country vicar in Wales and after education at Oswestry public school, Thomas attended the City and Guilds Engineering College in London. He subsequently worked for Siemens and for Clayton Shuttleworth prior to joining Leyland Motors in 1917. He became chief engineer at Leyland, designing for them Britain's first production straight-eight, which created a sensation at the Motor Show of 1920 and was, says Keith Richardson, 'Thomas's attempt to persuade the company to enter the quality car market'.

Failing to do so, Thomas resigned and moved south, intending to set up his own manufacturing company. In 1923 he based himself at

A motor car designer who became a famous driver and was killed while making record attempt, Thomas nearly succeeded in putting the Leyland company into large-scale car production. Instead he taught other famous drivers of the 1920's.

Brooklands, buying a bungalow called 'The Hermitage' inside the track and setting up what was to become a mecca of engineering for aspiring drivers. 'Soon to be numbered among the best drivers of the day, this quiet, donnish man, with a pleasant smile and love of children, is entitled to be considered a scientist in a way which does not apply to other record-breakers.' Amongst those who learned from him were John Cobb and Railton (qv). 'Parry Thomas may well have been sometimes difficult to approach, but John Cobb always got on well with him. The one thing they had in common, other than an absorbing love of speed, was a magnificent gift of silence.'

In 1926 Thomas held the world land speed record at 169.30 mph, but the following year was killed on Pendine Sands while making an attempt on the record with very little financial backing – in 'Babs', the car he had modified himself after buying it from the estate of Count Louis Zborowski. Georgano describes him as 'the greatest Brooklands driver of them all'.

Alan Jensen
born 1906

Richard Jensen
1909–1977

Born in Moseley, Birmingham, Alan was the elder of the two Jensen brothers, Richard being the younger. Their father was a food importer of Danish descent. Neither boy showed any academic interest at school, and Alan's only promising characteristic was skill as a draughtsman. Richard soon developed an interest in cars and he became a pupil apprentice with Wolseley Motors. Alan was apprenticed to Serck Radiators and rapidly progressed to the drawing office. Richard later left Wolseley to continue his industry apprenticeships at Joseph Lucas.

Both brothers always remembered the day in the 1920s when they had decided to build their own car. They had been playing tennis at a local club – they were both keen players – and were given a lift home in what Alan described as 'the most diabolical home-built car I had ever seen'. This fired them to do better themselves and the brothers persuaded their father to buy a 1923 Austin Chummy for £65. The car was delivered to their home at noon on Saturday and 'within an hour we had the body off, lunch was skipped, and by the evening the chassis was on its side and stripped down in the new garage we had just designed and built alongside our home'. This became a sleek two-seater with a pointed tail, Jensen Special Number One, and was soon showing its paces at a hill-climb meeting at Shelsey Walsh.

One evening when Alan was driving along the main road in Moseley, he found he was being followed by a car which kept flashing its lights and blowing the horn. The following driver turned out to be Alfred Wilde, then chief designer of Standard Motors, who was sufficiently enthusiastic about the Jensens' design to invite the brothers to visit the Standard works. This led to an invitation to buy a Standard Nine chassis for £168 and build Jensen Special Number Two on the same lines as the Austin. This Standard Special was written up in the press and Monty Tombs, then Midland Editor of the *Autocar*, took the trouble to introduce Alan Jensen to Avon Bodies, the specialist coach-builders in Warwick. Alan joined Avon to design a production model of the Standard, and this was the first of many specialist coachwork designs Jensen produced for Avon.

Meanwhile the brothers were looking for an opportunity to work together and this came about in 1930 when they were introduced to Albert Patrick, who had just set up his son Joseph (qv) in a garage business in Birmingham. Richard and Alan set vigorously about the reorganisation of the Patricks' garage, organising a coachbuilding section where they turned out special versions of the Austin and the Wolseley Hornet. However, by the end of 1931, they had fallen out with Joseph Patrick, and they then found, through an introduction by their next-door neighbours, some run-down premises at Carters Green owned by a firm called W. J. Smith and Sons. Alan Jensen recalled: 'Our first

Richard and Alan Jensen started, like so many others, in an amateur way, building their special Number One on an Austin Seven chassis which their father bought for them for a few pounds. They went on to go into production with their designs first at Patrick Motors and then under their own name.

day there was one of the most depressing in my life. The buildings were ramshackle, dark and dingy, the only heating coming from a coal fire in the middle of the workshop.' There was a small number of workmen who had been with the firm since the 1920s, and were to remain with the Jensens for several years. At the time, their average wage was 1s. 6d. an hour. The Jensens also enticed some of the coachbuilders away from Patrick Motors and set up operations with a team of about 60 people. Smith had contracts for designing and building timber bodies for commercial vehicles but in 1931 their turnover had been only £20,000. It is not clear how the Jensens managed to finance the revitalisation of this bus-

iness, because they cannot have done so merely from the cash they received from individual orders for 'specials'. Perhaps their father financed them. In any event in 1934 the firm's name was changed to Jensen Motors.

The first Jensen cars to leave Carters Green were sports conversions based on Wolseley Hornet, Singer, Standard and Morris Eight chassis. Richard recalled that 'the chassis cost £125 and we charged £40 for the body – £20 materials and £20 labour and profit. The whole car retailed at £225 and I remember that we charged an extra £2 for the tonneau cover.' This indicates an average gross margin of £60 for a job which took five weeks to complete – at one time the brothers were building ten cars per week, so the margin would have been £600 a week – not likely to leave much for profit. The Jensens also found that it was hard to compete with William Lyons's SS (qv) so they turned their attention to converting more expensive cars. They were also commissioned to build racing bodies for the MG Midget and Magnette designed by Ron Hornton.

A British car enthusiast in California who was associated with the film studios persuaded the film star Clark Gable to order a Jensen body on an American-built Ford V-8 chassis and when this was exhibited at the 1934 Ford Motor Show at the Albert Hall, before being shipped to the States, it caused a considerable interest. One of Richard Jensen's acquaintances, Lord Brabazon, the pioneer motorist, introduced Jensen to Edsel Ford, who agreed to supply more chassis, as a result of which some 20 Gable replicas were built, all sold by Bristol Street Motors, the Ford dealer in Birmingham.

By 1934, the Jensen brothers were designing and building their prototype car, a four-seater tourer called the White Lady whose open front wings, Alan Jensen recalled, 'threw mud in your face as well as everyone else's'. In fact, their first production car was a four-seater saloon which came on the market in 1935 and sales of this car encouraged them to put the White Lady on the market in 1936. These so-called S models remained in production until 1939. During this period from 1934–9, the Smith's traditional commercial vehicle body business also continued. During the war, the works concentrated on specialised military vehicles, ambulances and fire tenders and the Jensens also converted tanks for amphibious use for the D-day invasion of Europe.

In 1945 the Jensen brothers returned to their pre-war business by offering bodywork on Lea-Francis (qv) and Invicta chassis and introduced their own saloon in 1946. Later, the Jensen and Healey marques came together with a car aimed at the American sports car market, but alas by 1975 Jensen Motors went into liquidation, the Jensens themselves having already left the firm in the mid 1960s after a boardroom row.

The brothers were described as 'basically rather shy and retiring people; they were primarily designers with their own very individual ideas, and they were certainly not very good salesmen'. It has also been said that 'sub-contract work was the commercial foundation of their company, the intermittent success of which enabled it to indulge in car manufacture as a loss-leading luxury'.

Walter Owen Bentley
1888–1971

From his earliest boyhood Bentley wanted to be an engineer and his bedroom in the comfortable house in which he was brought up was filled with pictures and books about his favourite topic. He felt 'he had a calling, a vocation, and no one was going to stop him'. It was not however the car (which he thought was a 'disgraceful vehicle [that] splashed people with mud') but the locomotive which called him. He first went to public school at Clifton College like his five brothers, leaving at 16 to become a premium apprentice in the Great Northern Railway works at Doncaster. While there he became an enthusiastic motorcyclist, and after five years railway apprenticeship his passion for the internal combustion engine rather than steam power was such that he decided to dedicate his life to car engines. It has however been said that 'W. O. Bentley betrayed his locomotive-shed upbringing by a plethora of bolt-heads and bits and pieces'.

In 1912 he and his brother Henry took over an agency for three different makes of French car, housed in an old coach-house in New Street Mews off Baker Street, London. As early as 1913 W. O.

(as he was called) had become interested in aluminium pistons for engines (although he was not the originator of the idea) and in 1914 when war broke out, and he had enlisted in the Royal Navy Air Service, he joined a fellow RNAS officer, Commander Briggs, in its aero-engine development branch. At the time, there was a shortage of aero-engines in Britain and Bentley and Briggs took the engine of one of the Mercedes racing cars which had taken the first three places in the 1914 French Grand Prix to Rolls-Royce at Derby and persuaded the firm to copy its engine for use in naval aeroplanes. This became the Eagle. Bentley also designed a rotary engine of his own, the BRI, which was fitted to the famous Sopwith Camel, and, after a row with the authorities,

One of the most distinguished of British designers, WO as he was called, has left his name to describe a rather different type of car from those he personally built. Unfortunately after the early 1930's he had no more to do with so-called Bentleys.

Bentley spent part of the war in France helping the squadrons using it to get the best out of his engine. These and their successor, the BRZ, were said to be the most popular engines in service at a time when aero-engines were not, on the whole, popular with pilots.

After the war he returned to the small coachhouse which had very little in the way of equipment. 'We had a blacksmith's base pumped by hand,' said Walter Hassan, who had joined Bentley as a shop boy in September 1920, 'a big blow lamp, a large electric drill, and a few benches and vices.' Here, the first engine and chassis were built for the 3-litre Bentley car, first shown in London and numbered, from then onwards, as 'among the greatest of world sports cars'. The 3 litre was supplemented by a six cylinder 6/8 litre car in 1926 while a 4½ litre of 1927 reverted to the four-cylinder theme. A luxurious 8 litre appeared in 1931. But the Bentley marque is forever identified with the Le Mans 24 hour race which it won no less than five times in 1924 and from 1927 to 1930.

In the late 1920's, Bentley took on a part-time consultant, Harry Westlake, to improve engine performance. At the time Westlake was also working for Automotive Products on a retainer basis, although he later left the firm. Westlake did valuable work on engine development for Herbert Austin and for Lyons at SS cars before eventually setting up his own company and becoming a figure of considerable distinction in the aero, automotive and marine engine field.

From 1926, the chairman of the Bentley Company was the racing driver Captain Woolf Barnato, a millionaire and son of Barney Barnato, who had left the East End of London as a pauper and had risen to control the diamond fields of Kimberley, South Africa, alongside Cecil Rhodes. When the world slump of 1931 hit Britain, Barnato decided to withdraw his investment and this meant the end of Bentley Motors. While Bentley had been in charge of the business, some 3000 cars had been sold.

Now Bentley turned to Napier, who were keen to buy his firm. He had already set up a drawing office at Acton when he was surprised to learn that Rolls had beaten Napier to the purchase and gained control not only of Bentley Motors but of W. O. himself. Bentley describes the rather rough interview he had with the saintly-looking Henry Royce who observed that he had heard that Bentley was not a trained engineer. This was a gratuitous comment from a man whose firm was buying Bentleys in order to acquire superb competitive designs. Indeed, in some sense, the acquisition of Bentley Motors was essential to the future of the Rolls-Royce car business. Bentley retorted that he had been

trained as an engineer in a railway works just as Royce himself had been.

Bentley's tragedy at Rolls-Royce was that they would not let him design cars, and he was employed mainly on road testing. He came to feel that he was just 'part of the office furniture' and moved on to Lagonda where he became technical director and where, in 1935, he conceived the fabled V12 model, intended as a challenger to Rolls-Royce's Phantom 3.

The Lagonda Company had been founded by an American, Wilbur Gunn, who came to England from Springfield, Ohio about 1897. Starting with motorcycles, he turned to cars in 1905 and his first big tourer won the favour of the Tsar and many were imported to Russia before 1914. In 1925 Arthur Davidson designed the first Lagonda sports car but ten years later the firm was heading for absorbtion by Rolls-Royce. It was saved from this fate by a solicitor, Alan Good, who appointed W. O. Bentley as chief designer.

Bentley continued with Lagonda during the war, when he designed the 2½ litre all-independent suspension car, the engine of which was used by David Brown (qv) in the Aston Martin after he bought Lagonda. By 1947, Bentley had left to design a 3-litre engine for Armstrong-Siddeley which was not put into production.

Cecil Kimber
1888–1945

The name Kimber is synonymous with MG and with sports cars, but the marque has always been borne by more sedate vehicles as well; at first it had no true sporting connotations at all.

Born in Dulwich, London, Kimber's family had a somewhat scholarly background and the family firm, based in Manchester, made printing ink, but was in a financial decline when Kimber joined it as a salesman earning £1 a week. He had been educated at Stockport Grammar School and Manchester Technical School but left at the age of 16. A bad motorcycle accident left him permanently lame, and he used his £700 compensation to buy a Singer 10 car, refusing to put the rest into the family business.

Kimber stands on the left, quiet and restrained amid an enthusiastic crowd of motoring enthusiasts at Oxford in 1924. The following year he drove with the central character of this picture as passenger, Wilfrid Matthews, in a celebrated race to Land's End.

This estranged him from his father and, prevented by his injury from going into the army when the 1914 war broke out, he left the family business in 1915 to join Sheffield-Simplex, where he worked as a design engineer on airships and later as a buyer for AC Cars at Thames Ditton. He also worked for Martinsyde Aircraft. At the end of the war, he moved to Birmingham to join the staff of E. G. Wrigley, the car component suppliers, as an 'organisation expert'. (William Morris later bought up Wrigley, one of his suppliers.) In 1921 Kimber became sales manager of Morris Garages, Oxford. In 1922, following the suicide of their general manager, Edward Armstead, Kimber took over the post.

A. E. Keen had been making racing cars developed from standard Morris engines and chassis since 1922 and had been driving them at speeds approaching 100 mph. Kimber was enthusiastic about the sports car market and developed a special version of the Oxford which did over 100 mph. Morris Garages had already developed a sideline in special-bodied Oxford and Cowley cars, usually built by outside coach builders like Carbodies of Coventry. Kimber won a gold medal in one of these in the London-Land's End Trial of 1923.

Kimber was much helped in these early days by his wife Irene and by an engineer from Morris Motors, H. N. Charles, who worked for him in the evenings and at weekends. Hubert Charles was a graduate who had worked on fighter aircraft during the 1914-18 war and subsequently joined Zenith carburettors. He helped found Automotive Products Ltd and moved to Morris in 1924.

The first MGs were built in Oxford in 1924/5 and were merely modified Oxfords converted by Carbodies Ltd. The famous octagon shape was designed by the firm's accountant, Ted Lee, who had a flair for design. It immediately appealed to

Kimber, whose mother had been a competent artist, educated at the Slade. The octagonal device was developed by Kimber for side lamps, radiator caps, oil filters, instruments, gear-lever knobs and so on, to the point that cynics said it was surprising that Kimber did not fit octagonal pistons. But he did eat off octagonal plates. The success of the car meant that the existing premises were no longer big enough for production and in 1927 a new factory was built in Edmund Road, Oxford. In turn this was superseded by a move to Abingdon over the winter of 1929/30. It was to be MG's home for the next 51 years.

A Mr Cousins explains how things were done in the late twenties.

> Mr Kimber came to me one morning and asked me if I could draw. I told him that I had not done any other than that I had learnt at school. He said he had a blueprint with him of a suggested chassis frame for a new 6-cylinder model, and as this was the only one, and he did not like some of the details, would I trace it for him. I said (in the spirit in which we always carried on) that I would have a go. I succeeded in tracing this frame in a rough-and-ready manner, and when he came up the following morning, he said did I think that the Mark IV axles could be made to fit and also what sort of springs could we get in, so I commenced to draw in some axles from the blueprints we had obtained from Morris Motors. All this was done without any elaborate equipment and the drawing board was only a sheet of plywood. One part followed another and eventually with the aid of George King we succeeded in drawing all the main essentials of a motor car.... These drawings although not good enough for large production were sufficiently good for us to get patterns and castings made from them.

For several years the MG achieved much-publicised record-breaking and racing successes, such as Captain George Eyston's 103 mph in an experimental MG in 1931. Despite this, sales fell and did not recover until 1937. Financial pressures caused the company to withdraw from racing two years earlier, and the parent company to order more use to be made of Morris components. In 1939, MG car production ceased, to enable the

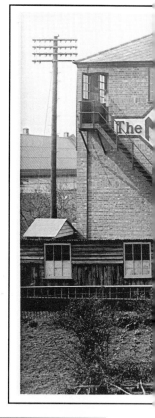

Rene Kimber played quite a part in the development of the MG cars built by her husband and (bottom left) she is shown with the all-aluminium Vee-front MG saloon of 1924. The main picture, taken in 1930, shows cars coming out of the MG factory at Abingdon where the famous octagonal badge was prominently displayed.

works to be turned over to war production, and Kimber, in his individualistic way, set out to find contracts. Miles Thomas says that:

> privately, Morris had never liked the idea of sponsoring a sports model ... but Kimber persisted. He was a brave man, and took periodic wiggings for lack of profit-making with impudent sang froid, confident that prestige gained in sporting events by the MG car one year would be recouped in sales the following. He was an originator; he designed [and] had everything possible made octago-

nal.... This kind of philosophy was all right during peacetime, but when Kimber wanted to maintain his acute individualism after the war had broken out ... it was clear that there must be a change. I therefore went to see him at Abingdon in November 1941 and told him that he had better look for another outlet for his energies.... He was thunderstruck, but accepted the situation with brave grace. ... I was sorry for Kimber. He was completely unorthodox, even in his domestic life, which did not endear him to Lord Nuffield nor, in particular, to Lady Nuffield.

It is not clear what Miles Thomas means by this last remark – Kimber's first wife, whom he married about the time of the outbreak of the first war, died in 1938 after a long illness which led to their separation. There were two daughters of this first marriage. After the death of his first wife, Kimber married again, the daughter of a musician. In his daughter's words, he was 'an adventurous idealist, brilliant as a designer, innovator, works organiser and, as a manager of men, a father figure to the MG concern'. A jour-

nalist said that 'in some ways he was quite ruthless and uncompromising, but in others there was a very kindly streak'.

Kimber had gone, after his departure from MG, first to Charlesworth Bodies, and then as works director to Specialloid Piston Rings. It was ironic that this man who had done so much high-speed driving should be killed as a passenger in a freak train crash while travelling on company business in 1945. His slogan had always been 'Safety Fast'.

Kimber would not have been amused to learn that at a party to celebrate the 50th anniversary of the Abingdon factory in 1979, which included exhibitions and demonstrations at the works and a visit by about 100 American dealers and their wives, Michael Edwardes, the ex-Chloride executive put in charge of British Leyland by the government, took the opportunity to announce the demise of the MG marque and the closure of Abingdon. His vice-chairman, who spoke to the assembled celebrators at the Connaught Rooms, said, 'It really was one of the worst things I've ever had to do, and I've had plenty, to stand up and tell them.' (Now, of course, the MG lives again).

Henry Morgan
1881–1959

H. F. S. Morgan was born in 1881 at Stoke Lacy, near Hereford, the son of a Prebendary in the Church of England whose father had also been a rector. The boy grew up in a small county village and was sent to school at Marlborough. He showed a technical bent and went on to the Crystal Palace Engineering School where he designed his own bicycle. Like many other boys with engineering talent he was apprenticed to the Great Western Railway works at Swindon where he stayed as a draughtsman until 1906.

In 1901 Morgan bought an 8 hp three-wheeler, having previously hired cars from a local garage in Hereford. In 1902 his godfather gave him £200 for his 21st birthday and he bought a Star four-wheeler. In 1906 he left the GWR to set up a garage in Malvern with his friend Leslie Bacon. He also spent more and more time with W. Stephenson-Peach, the engineering master at Malvern College, who was a descendent of the famous George Stephenson. His aim by this time was to design the smallest and lightest possible vehicle, something between a car and a motorcycle. With the help of the Malvern College workshops, a prototype was produced. This resulted in the three-wheel 'Runabout' and, with financial assistance from his father, Morgan put it into production. Two cars were shown at Olympia in 1910 but attracted few orders. However the following year, after trials with a new car, the Olympia exhibit attracted more interest, and in 1912 Harrods took on the agency. Production in 1913–14 was about 15 cars a week. Morgan continued to enter various competitions and trials. He also ran bus services from his garage, where he was agent for Wolseley and Darracq cars.

During the war, Morgan's production facilities, such as they were, turned over to munitions, but he also built a prototype four-seater. A factory had been built at Malvern Link, and in 1919 a new body and finishing shop was added. Capacity was now 2500 cars a year. By 1920, some thirty cars a week were being produced, and a version was being built in France. Racing success were achieved for both the three-wheeler and four-wheeler (introduced in 1935) much of the development expense was probably financed by Morgan's father, who was frequently to be seen at the wheel in the early days. The three-wheeler was basically unchanged in design until it went out of production in 1952. Morgan himself remained president of the Morgan Three-Wheeler Club until his death in 1959 at the age of 77.

In 1912, Morgan married Hilda Day, daughter of the vicar of Malvern Link.

Henry Morgan in 1913. The advertisement from a magazine front cover shows Morgan at the wheel of an early 4-4. The gentleman behind in the top hat is his father and financial supporter.

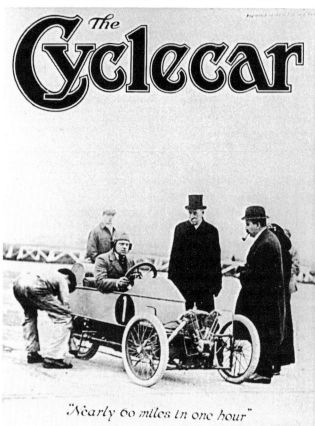

The **Cyclecar**

"Nearly 60 miles in one hour"

Chapter Eleven

Components

The survival of the motor industry in the Midlands area of England is largely the result of the growth of the component industry in that same area, which in part arose from the development of the cycle component business. If it had not been for firms like White and Poppe (qv), Nuffield would never have grown in the form it did. Thousands of small firms – and bigger ones – were the lifeblood of the motor men, as well as, on occasions, their financial support. Indeed one of the essential differences between the British and other national car industries was that it was, in essence, 'horizontal' and therefore dependent on the component sector for existence.

Alas space prohibits any full-scale treatment of the component industry so its existence is here symbolised, as it were, by the single firm of Lucas. Its founding family well symbolises the integration between the component men and the motor men which was so fundamental to the development of the car identity in Britain.

Joseph Lucas
Harry Lucas
Oliver Lucas
Peter Bennett
Kenneth Corley
Bernard Scott
Carl Breeden

Joseph Lucas
1834–1902

Joseph Lucas was born in Birmingham in 1834, the son of a plater. It is probable that he attended school only on Sundays and about the age of 14 was apprenticed to a firm of famous silversmiths in Birmingham. He became a manufacturer of utility articles in the 1870s and registered some designs of his own. By the age of 39 he had six children to support and was specialising in the sale of oil and lamps. He also sold oil from door to door in neighbouring streets. In 1875 he concentrated on one particular lamp and was granted his first patent. In 1878 he made his first cycle-lamp for the penny-farthing cycle. By 1888 he had 50 people on his payroll and the firm went ahead fast. Joseph was aided by his 17-year-old son, Harry, a capable administrator who was much irritated by his father's uneducated ways and lack of system.

The range of Lucas products increased as they began to supply the needs of the cycle assemblers who were springing up everywhere. In 1890 the works was greatly enlarged and in 1897 the firm went public with a capital of £225,000. Two of the five major shareholders were members of the Chamberlain family. The payroll rose to nearly 700. New factory premises, still today the headquarters of the firm, were built in Great King Street, Birmingham. Both Joseph and his son moved into larger houses, and Joseph pursued his passion for the temperance movement, sacking any workers who were seen drinking. The father died of typhoid fever in 1902 on a visit to Naples. Before he died he had already launched the Motoralities business which was to build horns, pumps, lamps and the other requirements of the motorist. Harry Lucas took over the firm at a time when profits were low, due to the heavy investment in Motoralities.

Harry Lucas
1855–1939

Harry was a much broader thinker than his father and he used the annual general reports and meetings to proselytise on such subjects as the evils of Free Trade and the need for tariff reform. Fortunately, he also continued with technical developments; cars – which had at first used cycle-lamps – were now fitted by Lucas with pairs of 'projecting' headlamps. The early Morris Oxfords did not have any Lucas components as standard but for the Cowley, produced in the war, Morris went to Lucas for dynamos and lamps. Harry Lucas was also keen to enter the battery business and to develop a magneto. Twice a day he would walk round the shops, regularly stopping to ask his employees 'Got anything for me today?' – on the lookout for new ideas. One of the problems of these factory tours was Harry's increasing deafness. He had the factory make him up an ear trumpet and later on a visit to Switzerland he found a battery-operated hearing aid.

The factory in the early days was lit by gas-lamps, and power for the lathes and other machines came by gas-engines fed from a gasometer of town gas situated on the premises. After 1906, an electricity supply was available. In 1910 the railways started to deliver and collect from the factories in horse-drawn vehicles and it was not until 1914 that Lucas bought his first Austin light van. Harry had bought several horseless carriages in the years between 1899 and 1906 when he was running a Lanchester with an open body. In 1909 he was using an Austin 118/24 hp for lamp testing. The contract to supply components to Morris in 1915 was a landmark – the quantity of 50 sets a week was considered to be enormous.

When the war came, Lucas turned to the vital job of developing a British magneto, because aero-engines depended virtually entirely on the magnetos supplied from Robert Bosch in Germany. Lucas bought up a small company in Birmingham which was making 25 magnetos a week at a cost of £9000. The acquisition of this firm – Thomson-Bennett – was to change the history of the Lucas company. The government was under the delusion that it could get supplies of magnetos from the German-controlled Bosch company in the USA. When, in 1915, their supplies ran out, the Admiralty set about acquiring British-built magnetos and took over the factories making them, including Thomson-Bennett. Later, in 1933, Lucas bought another magneto producer, Norths, at that time owned by Smiths.

The government was determined that Lucas should be in the aero-engine magneto business.

At the end of the war, there was a boardroom row in which one of the Chamberlains and Breeden (qv) took part and in 1919 Harry Lucas stood down as chairman though he remained one of the managing-directors – Peter Bennett (qv) being the other. In 1921 Oliver Lucas became a director. Carl Breeden had married one of Oliver's sisters.

Lucas did no electrical business with Austin at this time and it was said that Harry had fallen out with 'Pa' Austin. The arrangements with Morris were left in the hands of one man, Breeden, and there was 'consternation' in the boardroom in January 1922 when a quarrel involving the Lucas family caused Breeden to

An ardent cyclist, Harry Lucas took a header from this 'Ordinary' cycle while doing 12mph, quite a normal occurrance on what he called these 'tall, tricky machines'.

leave his brother-in-law's firm. Over half the output of the firm was supplied to Morris, although it had substantial contracts with other firms such as Rover and Standard. Although Harry resigned as managing-director in 1922, he remained as non-executive director until he was 83, coming in to his coal-fire heated office every day. After he retired he still remained a consultant, still coming regularly to the works. When he died in 1939, some 10,000 employees observed a two-minute silence in his memory on the day of the funeral.

Oliver Lucas
1891–1947

Born in 1891, son of Harry, and educated at King Edward's School Birmingham, Oliver went straight into the family business instead of going to university. He started in the experimental department with lamp design, and spent some time touring the motor firms such as Austin and Rover. Like his father he became an enthusiastic motorist. He became a director of Lucas in 1921, and from that year onwards spent part of every year visiting factories in America. He was appointed joint managing-director on his father's retirement in 1922. In 1925 Oliver Lucas negotiated the purchase of Rotax and CAV, thus acquiring a virtual monopoly in the supply of lighting, starting and initial equipment for cars which would last until the end of World War II.

It was said that the partnership between Lucas and Bennett (qv) was one of the most remarkable in the industry. They had no intellectual or social interests in common but worked well as a team. Oliver could be sarcastic to the point of rudeness, but was basically gentle. He really only liked talking to engineers, designers and men who made things, and while he had not much time for other people, he could explain technical details to non-technical people with great patience. Like Bennett, he was an autocrat, but he did not have Bennett's common touch. Yet although he had no technical training, he was a born engineer, and Bennett, ten years his senior, relied heavily on Lucas for technical as well as for commercial judgements. Sir William Lyons thought that 'Oliver Lucas held his own with Peter Bennett in all their decision-making discussions'. On the other hand, an American vice-president of Bendix thought 'Oliver has a wonderful brain but he doesn't know how to direct it'. He and Bennett were known to the staff as 'The Bing Boys' after a music hall act of the day. Oliver was not an amusing act – he was given to such aphorisms as 'the footprints in the sands of time were not made by sitting down' and he believed that employees should devote their lives – not just their working lives – to Lucas.

He was on close terms with all the head men of the motor firms such as John Black, Spencer

This piece of publicity material suggests that Joseph and Harry were ardent believers in teamwork and did not keep the limelight to themselves like some Victorian owners. Joseph and Harry are top left.

Wilks, Billie and Reggie Rootes, and Bill Lyons, all of whom would get him to drive their prototypes. He even got on good terms with Henry Ford, to whom he demonstrated Morris dancing, having previously found out that he had an interest in music. Yet he was passionately pro-British and savagely attacked Austen Chamberlain, MP for West Birmingham, when he bought an American Chrysler.

One day, when Oliver was talking to Herbert Austin, the latter said, 'Let me have a little motor – the smallest motor you make.' Austin took the resulting prototype away, mounted it on a model windscreen, and made up, with his own hands, a windscreen wiper. He gave it back to Lucas, asking, 'How much would you sell that for?'

In 1932 Oliver Lucas made an historic arrangement with the Bendix Aviation Corporation which secured their entry into the aviation business, which was to become one of their major enterprises. He also made a close association with Ford, and Patrick Hennessy said, 'One of the most enjoyable associations I had with anybody ... until he died, was with Oliver Lucas ... I always went round to see Oliver (when in Birmingham) and he always saved up something interesting to show me. I was not the technician he was, though I had a good working knowledge, and we had the most fascinating discussions about everything. He was outstanding.'

During the war, Lucas embarked on a wide range of military projects. For example, Spencer Wilks invited him to the Rover factory as early as the spring of 1940 to discuss development of the Whittle jet engine. He was also appointed controller of tank design and development at the Ministry of Supply, where he had a difficult time because, as another engineer said, 'His integrity was absolute. He would never go back on his word, even marginally.' On his return to Lucas, he found that the 20,000 employed in 1939 had doubled to about 40,000, spread over 33 factories by the war's end.

In the Standard Motor Company files held in Warwick University there is a signed Claridge's menu for 5 September 1945 noted, 'Dedicated to Oliver [Lucas] the parson who wed Harry [Ferguson] and John [Black].' So Lucas played a significant part in the formation of what eventually became the Massey-Ferguson company. In 1946 Lucas also supported Raymond Mays in the development of the BRM racing car.

The following year it was clear that his health was breaking down, and in 1948, on a beach in Nassau, Bahamas, where he was holidaying, he collapsed and died. He was 57.

Peter Bennett
1880–1957

Educated at King Edward's School, Bennett was a Band of Hope teetotaller and a religious man who in 1903 had worked for the Electrical Ignition Co. of Sparkbrook, a small company making sparking plugs. In 1907 Bennett decided to set up on his own, making similar items and magnetos, at a factory in Cheapside, London. Later he recalled that making magnetos was a heartbreaking business and 'time after time we faced the question whether it was worth going on'. Between them, the three companies that tried to break the Bosch monopoly before 1914 must have spent £100,000 in total.

When the Admiralty put the British into big-time magneto production after 1915, Bennett became chairman of the two trade associations running the new industry. In 1916, his factory was moved from Cheapside to the Lucas plant in Birmingham, and he became a director of Lucas, as did Carl Breeden (qv). The magneto business was run separately under Bennett. After the war there was a boardroom row, and Bennett became joint managing-director of Lucas with Harry.

Bennett's magnetos had been supplied to a number of motoring firms before the war, but it was the expansion of the Morris business, and eventually the acquisition of the Austin business after the takeover of CAV, that gave the firm a virtual monopoly.

The partnership of Bennett and Oliver Lucas after 1922 was remarkable. Both men were autocrats, but Bennett, deeply religious and a Sunday School teacher, was the one with a common touch. He could come out with a boisterous bonhomie and on tours of the factory would put an arm round a man's shoulders and ask after his family. He held his own with Lucas on most matters and the two men usually reached the same conclusion, even if considering it independently of each other. Despite his 'bonhomie' Bennett frequently lost his temper. Sir Kenneth Corley said, 'I've never known a man who could get into such a rage. He would fling his arms in the air and would roar and rage up and down the passage in the offices … until the windows shook and people outside would stop.' Despite this, he and Lucas had adjoining offices with a common door, often open, between.

Bennett was reluctant to give people titles, or observe them when given, and made it clear that he and Lucas ran the business. Staff were forbidden to put their names (let alone their titles) on their office doors. He was a considerable extrovert and was active in chambers of commerce, the SMMT, the FBI and political lobbying. In 1930, Bennett and Lucas made a deal with Bosch that the latter should have 49% interest in CAV, so further extending their monopoly and this put them into the windscreen-wiper business. Early in the war, when Lucas switched to military work, Bennett's contribution was recognised by a knighthood, and he was later raised to the peerage. Like several other motor industry leaders, Bennet entered politics, and in 1940 was elected a Birmingham MP in the seat vacated by the death of Neville Chamberlain.

Kenneth Corley
born 1908

Corley joined Lucas in 1927 at the age of 19 after being educated at St Bees School, Cumberland. At first he was 'a sort of office boy or runabout'. In 1933 he went on a tour of Morris distributors from whom he discovered that what was wrong with the Morris cars was the back axle, not the Lucas electrics. At that year's Motor Show, he was bold enough, in front of Oliver Lucas, to make this point to Miles Thomas, then managing-director of Morris. To his surprise Thomas replied, 'Young man, you are absolutely right' – and Corley went up

greatly in the estimation of Oliver Lucas who shortly made him his personal assistant.

Corley went on to become chairman of Lucas in 1969. He was knighted in 1972.

Bernard Scott
1914-1987

Educated at a London grammar school and Epsom College, Bernard Scott failed to matriculate from school so he could not follow his chosen medical career. In any case, his father was in financial difficulties in the 1931 slump, and his mother suggested he should try to 'join a decent Birmingham firm like Joseph Lucas'. When he was interviewed by the courteous company secretary, the 16-year-old boy was asked if he would 'like to give the company a trial for, say, three weeks'. He stayed and, after being ticked off for taking out patents on a couple of ideas, was promoted in 1936 to become Oliver Lucas's PA when Corley moved on to higher things. He became chairman in 1974 on Corley's retirement. He was knighted in 1980.

Carl Breeden
1891-1951

Breeden worked as Oliver Lucas's (qv) assistant before 1914 and married one of the Lucas daughters. He assumed considerable prominence in the firm and took part in the boardroom row after which Harry Lucas stood down as chairman. Breeden controlled the Morris business there and caused some consternation when he left in 1922. Later he started a motor component business with a Birmingham hardware manufacturer, Wilmot, and this firm, Wilmot Breeden became a considerable supplier in the motor component industry.

Chapter Twelve

Special Bodies

In the early days of the motor industry, the bodywork was often the prerogative of the specialist coach builders, some of whom had literally, up to that time, made their living building coaches. Rolls-Royce continued to use such firms for many years. The Thrupp family of Thrupp and Maberley had been making coaches in London since 1760. G. H. Thrupp, Junior, a founder member of the Automobile Club, fitted his vehicles with electric motors as early as 1896. Other well-known coachbuilders were Vincents of Reading, Cockshoots of Manchester, Egertons of Ipswich, and Mulliners, originally from Northampton (all four built Daimler and Rolls-Royce bodies to the requirements of individual customers), Joseph Cockshoot of Manchester, James Young of Bromley, Angus Sanderson of Newcastle, and J. K. Hunter (taken over by Young), Hamshaw of Leicester, Barkers and Windovers. Vanden Plas (a Belgian firm) opened a London works in 1913 and Park Ward started up shortly after the war ended in 1919. Windover's list of patrons for the years before 1914 include Esterhazy, Rothschild, S. B. Joel, and 350 names of royalty, rich industrialists and financiers.

Later, specialist body builders complemented the work of the coach builders. The more sporty designs of body designed by William Lyons (qv) and Kimberley (qv) were just the tip of the iceberg – there was an immense public demand for car bodies which were more stylish than the normal staid, solid touring cars of the major manufacturers. Patrick Motors of Birmingham were typical of many such firms, producing mildly tuned-up versions of standard chassis, fitted with dashing bodywork, for the man who could afford to pay a little extra for something more sporting.

Joseph Patrick
1911–1982

In 1889 Joseph Patrick senior moved from Hull to Birmingham where he continued to work for the Britannic Assurance Company, a firm of which he was eventually to become chairman. His son, Albert Patrick, followed an active business career in Birmingham which included property dealings. His son, also called Joseph, was educated at Warwick School after which he decided to start a career in stockbroking. At the age of 18 he had just embarked on his first job when a shadow was cast on the future of financial institutions by the great depression of 1930. His father immediately became worried about his son's prospects, and knowing that Joseph was interested in cars, suggested that he should give up his stockbroking aspirations, at any rate for a time, and enter the car business which was less affected by the slump than other industries. In 1929, Joseph's father bought a prime garage site on the Bristol Road, Selly Oak, known as Edgbaston Garages. Initially, Joseph worked alongside his brother-in-law William Shakespeare, who had married Joseph's sister, but within a year or so the young Joseph was in effective control. About 1930 Patrick senior met the Jensen brothers (qv) through a mutual friend Arthur Clackett. Richard and Alan Jensen were at one of the most creative phases in their career having already designed bodies for the Austin Seven and the Standard Nine. They quickly had Patrick's permission to set up a coachbuilding section in his garage where they produced Wolseley Hornet Specials and the four-seater Pendine Hornet.

Somewhat against Joseph Patrick's wishes, the Jensen brothers talked themselves onto the board of Patrick Motors and the company was soon renamed Patrick Jensen Motors. The historian of the Jensen brothers explains how this nomenclature had 'drastic repercussions ... One day Joe Patrick overheard a couple of his most favoured customers talking. One asked the other whether he knew either of these two young Jensen fellows. 'Oh yes,' replied the first man, 'I know one of them well enough to call him Pat.' Understandably, Joe Patrick was enraged. Not only had the Jensens re-organised his business,

The special body shop at Patrick Motors in the early 1930's and (below) Joe Patrick at the wheel of his Wolseley Hornet special in the first MCC London – Scarborough rally of 1932, where he obtained the Premier award.

but now his own surname was being taken to be nothing more than the Christian name of one of his new partners.' He called a board meeting for the following morning and, following a rather stormy discussion, the two brothers left that afternoon. By the end of 1931, the Jensens had started up again under their own steam.

This was the end of the Jensen connection but it was not the end of the body-building business at Patrick's. Joseph obtained the services of a freelance designer who used to come to the works two or three days a week. The Austin 7 design was followed by an Austin 10 – Patrick's were Austin's dealers – and the Wolseley was continued. Before long he had built up a team of about 70 skilled men and apprentices to handle the work. Meanwhile, Joseph had taken up competition trials where his performance in his Wolseleys attracted much attention. In 1934 he was selected for the Singer team and drove the first $1\frac{1}{2}$ litre Le Mans. The technical press were enthusiastic about his performance, one journalist noting that he 'deserves special mention in connection with his gear changing, as his use of the two lower ratios of his four-speed gear-box was a sheer joy'.

Patrick made considerable progress with the 'Specials' which were built in quite large numbers and advertised in the motoring press – he had reached the point where a 'Special' was no longer necessarily a 'one-off' but could be put into quantity production. For example his Hornet Sportsman's Coupé was described as having 'charm', part of which resulted from 'the clever way in which the spare wheel was concealed in the rear panel (boot) the lid of which, when down, forms a useful luggage grid'. A similar arrangement on the Austin was taken up by the parent firm as standard across their range. In 1932 Patrick produced a special body for the original Triumph Southern Cross and built 70 before handing over manufacture to Triumph. At the same time individual commissions for exclusive owners continued to be produced, including special designs for Rover and Daimler cars. In all, some 1000 Patrick 'Specials' were built.

By the mid 1930s the demand for special bodies had dried up as the motor firms themselves offered a greater range of models and features, some copied from the 'Specialist' firms like Patrick. When Citroën announced their new model in 1934 amongst many new features it included 'fully integral body-cum-chassis.' Joseph Patrick realised that other manufacturers would soon follow which meant that it was time to move away from body building on small chassis. Joseph Patrick therefore decided to run down the coachbuilding side of the business, concentrate on distributorships and develop other specialist aspects of car manufacture. One of these was a form of draught-excluder for car windows which eventually led to the formation of Draftex Limited, now part of the Laird Group. Another was specialist work in aluminium bronze which during the 1939–45 war was devoted to Sten-gun manufacture in the firm's specialist foundries.

In recent years, Patrick Motors' connection with specialist body design has been commemorated in the Patrick Collection Motor Museum, developed in his father's memory by Joseph's son, Alexander Patrick, who joined the company in 1962.

General Index
and Bibliography

Bibliography

Published Sources

Allen, Sir P & Robson, G.
  Transport Pioneers of the Twentieth Century,
  London, 1981.
Andrews, P. W. S. & Brunner, E.
  The Life of Lord Nuffield.
  Blackwell, 1959.
Bardou, J. P. & others.
  The Automobile Revolution.
  University of North Carolina, 1982.

Barker, R. & Harding, A.
  Automobile Design; Great Designers.
  David & Charles, 1970.
Bird, A.
  The Motor Car 1765–1914.
  Batsford, 1960.
Bird, A. & Hutton-Scott, F.
  The Lanchester Motor Car.
  Cassell, 1965.

Brown, D.
  Desmond Donnelly.
  The Company, 1960.
Brunner, E.
  see Andrews, P. W. S.
Castle, H. G.
  Britain's Motor Industry.
  London, 1951.

Caunter, C. F.
History and Development of Light Cars.
HMSO, 1957.
Caunter, C. F.
The Light Car
HMSO, 2nd ed., 1970
Caunter, C. F.
The Light Car – a Technical History.
London 1979.
Church, R.
Herbert Austin: The British Motor Industry to 1941.
Europa, 1979.
Church, R.
Family Firms and Managerial Capitalism.
Business History, April 1986.
Church, R.
Growth of Joseph Lucas Ltd.
Business History Review Vol. LII (1978).
Church, R.
Markets and Marketing in the British Motor Industry before 1914.
Jnl of Transport History. Vol. 3 (1982)
Clew, J.
Lucky all my life.
Yeovil, 1979.
Clutton, C.
The Vintage Motor Car.
London 1954.
Critchley, J. S.
British Motor Vehicles.
London 1912.
Culshaw, D.
The Complete Catalogue of British Cars.
Macmillan. 1974.
Davenport-Hines, R. P. T.
Dudley Docker.
Cambridge University Press 1984.
Davy, J. R.
The Standard Car 1903–63.
Coventry, 1964.
Day, K.
Alvis.
Gentry, London, 1981.
Donnelly, T.
see Thomas, D.
Du Cros, Sir A.
Wheels of Fortune.
London 1938.
Duncan, H. O.
The World on Wheels.
Paris, 1926.
Edge, S. F.
My Motoring Reminiscences.
London 1934
Ensor, J.
The Motor Industry.
Longman, 1971.
Foreman-Peck, J.
The Rover Company in the Inter-War Years.
Business History Vol. XIII (1981)
Georgano, G. N.
The Complete Encyclopaedia of Motorcars 1885–1968.
Ebury, 1968.
Gunston, B.
By Jupiter! The Life of Sir Roy Fedden.
London 1978.
Harding, A.
see Barker, R.
Hutton-Scott, F.
see Bird, A.
Jackson, R.
The Nuffield Story.
London, 1964.
Jarrott, C.
Ten Years of Motors & Motor Racing.
London 1906
Jeffries, J. B.
The Story of the Engineers 1800–1945.
Lawrence & Wishart, 1946.

Kingsford, P. W.
F. W. Lanchester.
London, 1960.
Lambert, Z. E. & Wyatt, R. S.
Lord Austin the Man.
London 1968.
Langworth, R. & Robson, G.
Triumph Cars.
Motor Racing Publications, 1979.
Light, B.
Alvis – A Short History.
Alvis, 1966.
Lloyd, I.
Rolls-Royce. Growth of a Firm.
London 1978 (and two subsequent volumes)
Maxcy, & Silberston,
The Motor Industry.
London 1959.
McComb, F. W.
MG.
London 1978.
Minter, A.
The Midlands – the Motor Industry.
Coventry, 1974.
Montague, Lord.
Lost Causes of Motoring.
London, 1969/71.
Nicholson, T. R.
A Study of the Origins of the Motor Car in Britain to 1896.
London 1978.
Nicholson, T. R.
The Age of Motoring Adventure 1897–1939.
Cassell, 1972.
Nicholson, T. R.
The Vintage Car 1919–30.
London 1966.
Nixon, St. J. C.,
The Simms Story.
London 1952.
Nixon, St. J. C.,
Wolseley.
1949.
Nockolds, H.
Lucas. The First Hundred Years.
David & Charles, 1976.
Oliver, G. A.
A History of Coach Building.
London 1962.
Oliver, G. A.
The Rover.
London 1971.
Overy, R. J.
William Morris, Viscount Nuffield.
Europa, 1976.
Price, B.
The Lea Francis Story.
Batsford, 1978.
Reeves, E. H.
The Evening and the Morning.
Austin Siddeley Motors, 1965.
Reeves, E. H.
The Riley Romance.
The company, 1930.
Rhys, G.
The Motor Industry.
Butterworth, 1970.
Ricardo, Sir H.
Memories and Machines.
London 1968.
Richardson, K.
The British Motor Industry 1896–1939.
Macmillan, 1977.
Robson, G.
see also Allen, Sir P., Langworth, R.
Robson, G.
The Rover Story.
Stephens, Cambridge, 1981.

Rolt, L. C. T.
A Picture History of Motoring.
London, 1956
Rolt, L. C. T.
Great Engineers.
London, 1962.
Saul, S. B.
The Motor Industry in Britain to 1914.
Business History Vol. V (1962)
Scott Moncrieff, D.
The Thoroughbred Motor Car 1930–40.
London 1983.
Sedgwick, M.
Cars of the 1930's
London 1970.
Sedgwick, M.
Passenger Cars.
London 1975.
Sedgwick, M.
Vauxhall.
Beaulieu, 1981.
Setright, L. J. K.
The Designers.
London, 1976.
Silberston, *see* Maxcy
Thomas, D. & Donnelly, T.
The Motor Car Industry in Coventry.
London, 1985.
Thomas, Sir M.
Out on a Wing.
London 1964.
Trebilcock, G.
The Vickers Brothers.
Europa, 1977.
Turner, G.
Business in Britain.
London 1969.
Turner, G.
The Car Makers.
London 1963.
Turner, G.
The Leyland Papers.
London 1971.
Ware, M. E.
The Making of the Motor Car 1895–1930.
Moorland, 1976.
Whiting, A.
The View from Cowley.
Clarendon Press, 1983.
Whyte, A.
Jaguar.
The Company, 1980.
Williamson, G.
Wheels within Wheels.
London 1966.
Wood, J.
Wheels of Misfortune.
London 1988.
Wyatt, R. J.
The Motor for the Millions.
London 1968.
Wyatt, R. S.
see Lambert, Z. E.

Reference
Directory of Business Biography
London, 1984–6

Unpublished Sources
University of London Library
  F. R. Sims papers
Modern Records Centre,
  Warwick University
British Motor Industry
  Heritage Trust, Studley
Coventry City Record Office
National Motor Museum, Beaulieu
Royal Automobile Club
The Museum of British Road Transport, Coventry

D'Arcy Baker (Fiat)   W R Morris   Hamilton Hobson   S F Edge   S Shorland   C

S M Lanchester   Sir W M Letts   Sir H Austin   H T Vane

C Johnson